Country Parsons, Country Poets

George Herbert and Gerard Manley Hopkins
As Spiritual Autobiographers

Country Parsons, Country Poets

George Herbert and Gerard Manley Hopkins As Spiritual Autobiographers

Mary Theresa Kyne, S.C., Ph.D.

With Introductory Notes by:
Samuel J. Hazo
and
Albert C. Labriola

Illustrations by:
Scott McGrath
and
Mary Seton Wacker, S.C.

In Honor of the 400th Birthday of George Herbert

Mary Theresa Kyne, S.C.

EADMER PRESS
Humanities Series 5

©Eadmer Press, 1992

Eadmer Press
614 Ridgeway Avenue, Greensburg, PA 15601 (USA)

Library of Congress Cataloging-in-Publication Data
Kyne, Mary Theresa, S.C., Ph.D.

Introductory Notes by:
Samuel J. Hazo
Albert C. Labriola

Illustrations by:
Scott McGrath
Mary Seton Wacker, S.C.

Country Parsons, Country Poets
George Herbert and Gerard Manley Hopkins as
Spiritual Autobiographers

Humanities Series V

Herbert, George (1593-1633)—Criticism and interpretation. Hopkins, Gerard Manley
(1844-1899)—Criticism and interpretation. Christian Poetry, English—History and criticism.
Poets, English—Biography—History and criticism. Spiritual life in literature. Clergy in
literature. Self in literature. Autobiography. PR3508.K96 1992.

ISBN: 0-929914-12-0

LC 92-54450

Printed in the United States

First Edition

Dedication

For two of Ireland's children,
Edward and Mary Kyne:

Father and mother dear...
Kind love both give and get.

Enrich my heart, mouth, hands in me,
With faith, with hope, with charity;
That I may run, rise, rest with thee.
—George Herbert, "Trinity Sunday"

For I greet him the days I meet him,
and bless when I understand.
—Gerard Manley Hopkins,
The Wreck of the Deutschland

George Herbert—From An Original Woodcut

Table of Contents

Gerard Manley Hopkins

Introductory Note

THIS STUDY BY DR. MARY THERESA KYNE, S.C. of George Herbert and Gerard Manley Hopkins meets a double need. First, it re-focuses our attention on two poets whose sensibilities are comparable, despite the decades that separate them. Secondly, it shows us how the work of Hopkins was in various ways influenced by Herbert, not only thematically but in terms of prosody as well. The centrality of Christ to the work of both poets is beyond dispute. This is understandable, as Dr. Kyne explains, not only because both men were clerics and should have been expected to personify such a belief, but because it had its roots in something beyond their vocational calling—in their very personalities. The poems that resulted, therefore, were not merely religious but truly spiritual.

Comparative literary criticism is undoubtedly the hardest criticism to write. There are always the many variables, the cultural differences, the linguistic changes and so forth. Sister Mary Theresa somehow manages to write comparatively of these two poets in a way that permits her comments on one to elucidate what she says about the other. This is no small achievement. Because Herbert and Hopkins are not minor figures in the literary universe, Sister Mary Theresa's definitive treatment of their work should be required reading not only for those interested in Herbert and Hopkins, but in the Christological tradition in English literature itself.

—**Samuel J. Hazo**

Foreword

IN A RECENT ISSUE OF *HARPER'S* (January 1992) appears an essay by Frank Lentricchia, a foremost critical theorist at Duke University. Despite his reputation for being *au courant*, Lentricchia writes an installment of what presumably will become a full-scale spiritual autobiography, a very traditional genre. The occasion for the piece is his visit to Mepkin Abbey, maintained by the Trappists in South Carolina. Lentricchia writes that "something had been happening" to him over the past two or three years, a change whose significance was not fully evident to him and others. Although his visit to Mepkin Abbey seems to bring into focus his self-perception, Lentricchia comes to realize that his *account* of the experience at the abbey is what clarifies the change that has been taking place in him. Spiritual autobiography, though a traditional form, can be accommodated to individual experience.

While spiritual autobiography originated with St. Augustine's fourth-century *Confessions*, St. Paul's conversion in Acts of the Apostles is the basis for the genre. St. Augustine, in effect, appropriated the biblical account of St. Paul's experience of personal change and adjusted it to his quest for self-understanding. Whether written by St. Augustine, Thomas Merton, or even Frank Lentricchia, the language of change and conversion intrinsic to spiritual autobiography not only records but also effectuates the breakthrough from oneself to the "other."

More incisively than most studies of spiritual autobiography, Sr. Mary Theresa Kyne's book on George Herbert and Gerard Manley Hopkins analyzes the language of the genre. By reference to the prose and poetry of these two authors, Sr. Mary Theresa Kyne highlights the language of destabilization, disintegration, and reintegration crucial to spiritual autobiography. The "other" to whom both Herbert and Hopkins reinscribe themselves is Christ. In short, the "I" or personal pronoun that inscribes the self gives way to the "I" or iota, the initial letter of Jesus's name in Greek. Having been destabilized and disintegrated, one is thereafter reintegrated or reinscribed in the Christogram. The runic significance of the "I"—at first separating the self from "thou," then integrating the one with the "other"—is merely an example of the linguistic paradoxes analyzed by Sr. Mary Theresa Kyne.

By its extraordinary sensitivity to the sounds and syllables of spiritual autobiography, this book charts the dynamic processes associated with self-discovery. Imbued with spirituality and mysticism, spiritual autobiography, whether composed by Herbert or Hopkins, is a genre of introspection and meditation, though the confessional aspects also make it a public mode of address. Both the journey and journal of a soul, spiritual autobiography has vast implications for the study of related genres—for example, autobiographical lyrics and narratives, partially fictionalized but still personally revealing. Prime examples include works by disparate authors such as Dante, James Joyce, and Dylan Thomas. The *Divina Commedia* charts the self-disclosure and self-understanding of its author despite the array of topicalities involving Florentine history. James Joyce's *A Portrait of the Artist as a Young Man*, while renouncing religious belief, is ironically framed as a personal narrative whose elements at times parody spiritual autobiography. Dylan Thomas's sonnets are better understood when examined in light of, say, Hopkins's so-called nature sonnets.

The consummate success of Sr. Mary Theresa Kyne's book is the breadth of vision with which she encompasses both Herbert and Hopkins and the depth of insight that she brings to the language of their works. Moreover, while treating these two authors, she also constructs a framework of understanding and analysis applicable to any and all spiritual autobiographers. More than any other expert in spiritual autobiography, Sr. Mary Theresa Kyne explores the puzzles and epiphanies of the genre. She cites how the experiences and language of an author are mediated by culture and history, but she highlights the transcendent quality of spiritual autobiography—in sum, its timelessness. Coming as it does on the eve of the 400th anniversary of Herbert's birth (1593), Sr. Mary Theresa Kyne's book is a timely summons to renewed attention to a genre in which the "I" of the self stands large, but the "I" of Christ's presence emerges even larger.

—Albert C. Labriola

Preface

THIS COMPARATIVE APPROACH to the English devotional writers George Herbert and Gerard Manley Hopkins represents the converging of several interests sparked by my teaching and study of these authors. My study attempts a twofold method: to establish a critical approach based on the genre of spiritual autobiography, and to apply that method to certain verse and prose by Herbert and Hopkins.

The primary texts used in this study include: *George Herbert: The Country Parson, The Temple* (1981), edited by John N. Wall, Jr., with occasional references to *The Works of George Herbert* (rpt. 1964), edited by F.E. Hutchinson, and *The English Poems of George Herbert* (rpt. 1986), edited by C.A. Patrides. Wall's volume is based on the earliest printed versions and includes Herbert's major writings. It also modernizes the spelling and punctuation, thus facilitating the reading of Herbert's seventeenth-century verse and prose.

Gerard Manley Hopkins (1986), edited by Catherine Phillips, is the main source used for Hopkins's primary works—including his poems and "terrible" sonnets, *Journal*, letters, *Sermons* and *Devotional Writings*, and Retreat Notes and Meditations. Phillips's selection of prose complements and elucidates the poetry while it conveys Hopkins's personality and the breadth of his interests. Occasional reference is made also to *The Poems of Gerard Manley Hopkins* (rpt. 1980), edited by W.H. Gardner and N.M. MacKenzie.

The Spiritual Exercises of St. Ignatius (1952), translated and edited by Louis J. Puhl, S.J., provides a clear and readable text for a study of the *Exercises*.

In addition to the sources listed in the Bibliography, particular recognition and gratitude are accorded scholars—Dr. Samuel J. Hazo, Peter Milward, S.J., James Olney, and Dr. Albert C. Labriola—as well as writers of dissertations and theses—Sister Rita Marie Yeasted, C.D.P., Ronald G. Shafer, William Stallings Smith, Varghese Mathai, and Nancy Allen-Stainton—whose incisive interest in Herbert and Hopkins rendered their studies particularly beneficial.

Dr. Samuel J. Hazo is acknowledged for his extensive work on Hopkins in his Master's thesis from Duquesne University, titled "An Analysis of 'Inscape' in the Poetry of Gerard Manley Hopkins." My attendance at Hazo's reading of Hopkins's poems at the 1989 International Poetry Forum commemorating the centenary of Hopkins's death stimulated my impulse for further Hopkinsian study.

Attending lectures by Peter Milward, S.J., titled "The Spirituality of William Shakespeare and Gerard Manley Hopkins" on December 5, 1988, and sponsored by the Duquesne University Institute of Formative Spirituality, advanced my interest in the works of Hopkins as studies in mystagogy. Additional articles and texts written by Milward treat the responsibility of the reader in imparting meaning and voice to the works of Herbert and Hopkins, thus prompting my study of their works as spiritual autobiography.

The dissertation from Duquesne University of Sister Rita Marie Yeasted, C.D.P., titled *George Herbert's Poetry and the "Schola Cordis" Tradition*, proved helpful in situating Herbert within an historical and religious framework, and in providing a variety of sources from which to view both the author and the "school of the heart" tradition. The multiple and diverse perspectives from which Yeasted views the emblem of the heart in relation to the poetry of Herbert persuaded me that studies of Herbert are far from exhausted.

Ronald G. Shafer's dissertation from Duquesne University, titled *The Study of George Herbert and the Epistles of St. Paul: A Study in Thematic and Imagistic Similarities*, demonstrates the influence of Pauline teachings and the biblical tradition in the works of Herbert. This interrelated study of the letters of St. Paul and the writings of George Herbert advanced my theory that Herbert lends himself to comparative treatment.

The dissertation of William Stallings Smith from Duquesne University, titled *The Poetry of Gerard Manley Hopkins: A Continuity of the Romantic Tradition*, examines Hopkins within the Romantic and Victorian framework of such writers as Wordsworth and Tennyson, and Hopkins's poems as embodiments and extensions of Wordsworth's *The Prelude*. While I challenge the premise on which this study is based—that Hopkins's works present a unified and tranquil vision of existence—a critical reading of Smith's dissertation confirms the crucial significance and contribution of Hopkins to studies of the self and the soul.

The Master's thesis from Duquesne University of Nancy Allen-Stainton, titled "Spiritual Autobiography in the Poetry of George Herbert and Gerard Manley Hopkins," proved valuable in reading their poems as spiritual autobiography, thereby providing me with the challenge of adding the prose works of Herbert and Hopkins to this framework. Allen-Stainton's Bibliography, particularly on the topic of Auto-biography, was of great assistance.

In his works on the topic of Autobiography, James Olney cites his 1963 dissertation from Columbia University, titled *George Herbert and Gerard Manley Hopkins: A Comparative Study in Two Religious Poets*. I found this work advantageous for the parallels it draws between the lives and works of Herbert and Hopkins. Although I disagree with Olney's premises that Herbert and Hopkins represent oppositions in poetry and thought, and that both authors sought secure definitions of an ideal philosophical system rather than an articulation of the inherent paradoxes and ambiguities of human existence, this seminal study furnished me with many ideas.

For his ambitious undertaking of a 325-page dissertation from Baylor University on *The Evolution of the Inner Man as Seen in the Writings of Gerard Manley Hopkins and George Herbert*, Varghese Mathai merits acknowledgement and commendation. I maintain as my position what Mathai avers in his Introduction: that the inner man in Hopkins and Herbert "is synonymous with the authors as confessed by them." Since Mathai approaches Herbert by "using Hopkins as the springboard" of his study, I remained free to advance and interrelate the sequential study of the poetry and prose of Herbert and Hopkins.

My gratitude is also extended to Dr. Joseph J. Keenan, Jr., and the faculty of the English Department of Duquesne University for their support—both academic and financial—of my doctoral degree, and their encouragement in the writing of this text.

For their assistance and resourcefulness in obtaining books and dissertations for me, I am most grateful to the staffs of the Duquesne University Library and Saint Vincent College Library.

Since the day I met Shakespeare, the Metaphysical poets, and Milton in his classroom, Dr. Albert C. Labriola, my mentor and friend, has provided me with many academic and professional opportunities. The expert skill and scholarly attention by which he directed the dissertation out of which this book emerged is matched only by his generous encouragement and mutual interest in Herbert and Hopkins. Any advancements which this book might make to the study of Herbert and Hopkins reflect Dr. Labriola's gentle and disciplined guidance and genuine regard for "the beloved Herbert and Hopkins." Moreover, two of Dr. Labriola's articles published in the *George Herbert Journal* provide clear explications of the stylistics of the poetry. "Herbert, Crashaw, and the *Schola Cordis* Tradition" and "The Rock and the

Hard Place: Biblical Typology and Herbert's 'The Altar'" treat the
experience of *agon* or the soul's reckoning as a prelude to sancti-
fication.

   A debt of gratitude is also rendered to Mary Ann Winters, S.C.,
Major Superior of the Sisters of Charity of Seton Hill, the Community
Board of Directors, and my religious congregation, for their continued
spiritual and financial support that facilitated the completion of my
studies and this book.

   To my mother, family, and friends, I offer my extreme apprecia-
tion for your constant affection, encouragement, patience, and prayers.
Hopkins's eloquent rendering expresses the gift which you have provid-
ed me:

> Grace that day grace was wanted.
> Each be other's comfort kind.

It is my sorrow that my father's birth to new life preceded my com-
pletion of this degree. I pray that his humility, enduring love, generosi-
ty, and good works may

> Bear Him to heaven on easeful wings.

I am deeply appreciative of Rev. V. Donald Hall, priest of the
Greensburg diocese, who introduced me to the complexities and re-
wards of word processing, and whose patience, encouragement, and
friendship sustain me in my writing and scholarship. Fr. Hopkins
anticipates the spirit of Fr. Hall when he writes:

> I say more: the just man justices;
> Keeps grace: that keeps all his goings graces;
> Acts in God's eye what in God's eye he is—
> Christ.

For their diligent and perceptive reading of this manuscript and artistic
depictions of the story of the self contained herein, I am indebted to
artist Scott McGrath, and Mary Seton Wacker, S.C., who conceptual-
ized the illustrations. Their sketches enhance and complement the text
by casting the poetry and prose of Herbert and Hopkins in line draw-
ings that accentuate Herbert's belief:

Doctrine and life, colors and light, in one
When they combine and mingle, bring
A strong regard and awe: but speech alone
Doth vanish like a flaring thing,
And in the ear, not conscience ring.

My final debt of gratitude is to Richard Wissolik, Editor and Publisher
of Eadmer Press, whose enthusiasm for this comparative study of the
poetry and prose of Herbert and Hopkins as spiritual autobiography
impelled me to seek out

> quaint words, and trim invention...
> Curling with metaphors a plain intention.

My intent is to extend the admiration and respect I have acquired for
Herbert and Hopkins by producing a text that has been a labor of love,
"a sweetness ready pennd'd:/Copy out only that, and save expense."

—Mary Theresa Kyne, S.C.

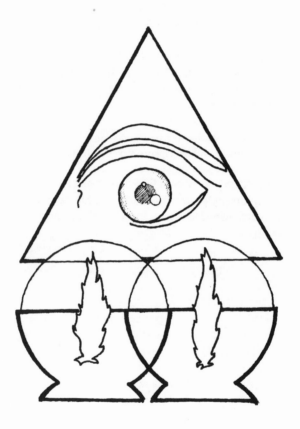

"A binding together of the whole person..."

Introduction

ALTHOUGH A TEMPORAL SPAN of almost three centuries separates the seventeenth-century English Metaphysical writer George Herbert (1593–1633) and the nineteenth-century English religious writer Gerard Manley Hopkins (1844–1889), their poetry and prose, when interpreted as spiritual autobiography, provide a means by which the journey of every person's soul is charted and offered to the "Lord of life." A comparative analysis of their poetic and prose works highlights similar themes and structural patterns, a depiction of the *agon* or (w)reckoning experience of the speakers, and a consideration of the immanent and transcendent dimensions of the Creator whom Herbert and Hopkins address in their vocations as parsons and poets. I have created the term "(w)reck" in this study to suggest both a literal wreck, such as occurs in Hopkins's *The Wreck of the Deutschland*, and a spiritual reckoning, or accounting, of the souls of Herbert and Hopkins in select poems and prose that depict their journey from sinful impulses and desolation to retribution and sanctification.

Much as the Counter-Reformation was a resistant movement in Elizabethan England, so also the Oxford Movement was a disturbing revolutionary element in Victorian England. Between the last years of the Renaissance and the mid-nineteenth century is a profound similarity in religious sensibility and spiritual awakening. I suggest that it is from this mutual, though partially independent, Christocentric sympathy that the metaphysical or contemplative strain of Herbert and Hopkins interacts and redefines the genres of poetry, prose, and spiritual autobiography.

The term "Metaphysical," applied to a group of poets who wrote under the influence of John Donne, has been used since John Dryden first employed it in his dedication to *A Discourse Concerning the Original and Progress of Satire* (1693).[1] Because the poets of the Metaphysical school "yoke together" the emotions and intellect, their contribution lies in connecting the abstract with the concrete, the remote with the near, and the immanent with the transcendent. They convince the reader that body and soul are interdependent and, thus, demonstrate the interrelatedness of life. The heightened consciousness experienced by

---

[1] Joan Bennett, *Five Metaphysical Poets* (London: Cambridge University Press, 1964) 1.

the reader of devotional works may be attributable to this "binding together" of the whole person.

This study applies the term "metaphysical" to Herbert and Hopkins and demonstrates an analysis and a correlation of these elements in the writings of both authors. Given this understanding, the metaphysical poets Herbert and Hopkins answer to Mr. Eliot's description of a poet as one who is "constantly amalgamating disparate experiences," who "is always forming new wholes."[2] Eliot himself was highly affected by the Metaphysical influence.

Each chapter of this book originates with an epigraph which excerpts lines from a poem of Herbert or Hopkins. The epigraphs provide the context in which their poems and prose, as well as the accompanying critical analyses, are to be considered. Solid justification for a comparative analysis of the poetry and prose of Herbert and Hopkins as spiritual autobiography rests with the merits and rewards the reader enjoys upon discovering the striking literary, spiritual, and biographical parallels and similitudes between these two devotional writers.

Despite the recent revival of interest and scholarship in the Metaphysical poets and in the importance of Hopkins as a modern literary figure, a thorough search for a comparative study of Herbert and Hopkins yielded surprisingly few books, articles, dissertations, or lectures. To a great extent, I was pleased that my concept of interrelating the works of these two writers was somewhat innovative and capable of expanded study; I was also curious because of the paucity of scholarly inquiry on my topic. Further study and research confirmed that a comparative analysis of Herbert and Hopkins and an intertextual treatment of their poetry and prose were, indeed, valid and useful means to pursue at length. Although I found no critical books on the poetry and prose of Herbert and Hopkins as spiritual autobiography, the theses and dissertations I consulted verified that the works of Herbert and Hopkins portray the soul's evolving relationship with its Creator. Therefore, I remained free to interrelate the poetry and prose of Herbert and Hopkins as promoting the unfinished nature and the gradual maturation of the soul: the literary and spiritual cornerstone of human existence.

Two surprises greeted me in researching this topic. First, I found no substantive studies which systematically pursued the literary and biographical elements of Herbert and Hopkins. Rather, I discovered

[2] Bennett 10.

that each critical work devoted to the authors treated them in separate chapters. Thus, my approach of continuous comparative analysis was once more confirmed as original. Second, although many critical works abound on the topic of Autobiography, I found few recent criticisms on the genre of Spiritual or Religious Autobiography; therefore, I determined to validate one of literature's little-discussed genres by establishing its genesis and evolution, outlining its principal components, and assessing its significance as literature and spirituality in the lives and works of Herbert and Hopkins.

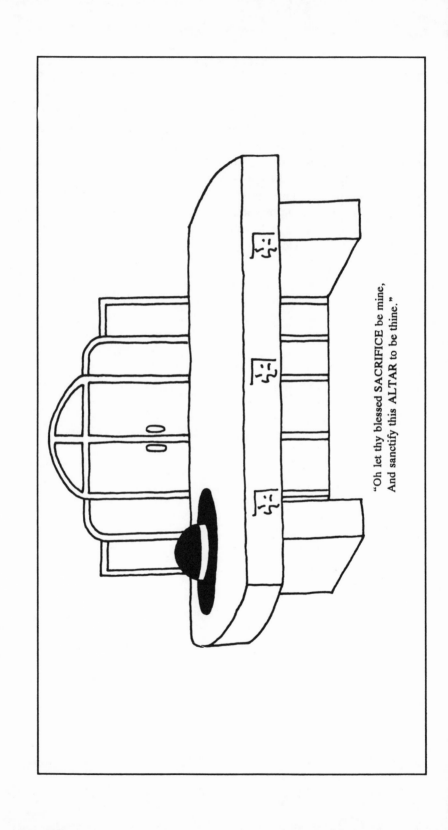

"Oh let thy blessed SACRIFICE be mine,
And sanctify this ALTAR to be thine."

Prologue

FOR THE CRITIC WHO SUSPECTS that a reading of the poetry and prose of Herbert and Hopkins as spiritual autobiography—the exercise of their faith—is restrictive in scope, T.S. Eliot provides a definition of the genre which is comprehensive, irrespective of religious orientation or personal inclination. He acknowledges the viability and validity of spiritual autobiography as the record of the poet's experience of the spiritual struggle, a setting down of "the fluctuations of emotion between despair and bliss, between agitation and serenity, and the discipline of suffering which leads to peace of spirit."[1] Works included in this genre are biographies of the human spirit. The adventures depicted may be unfamiliar to the reader, who may not share the Christian beliefs of the writers, but the reader is asked to acknowledge the writers' power to render awareness of the human condition, to order words, and to coordinate and recreate human experiences. When read as spiritual autobiography, the works of Herbert and Hopkins help the reader to define and sustain the journey of his or her life. "One need not belong to the faith or share 'the belief' of Herbert [or Hopkins] to appreciate *The Temple* [or the works of Hopkins], but the reader must possess the capacity of sympathetic entrance into the minds of great devotional poets and be willing to judge them by *their* own ethical and theological standards.... The reader should identify himself with the 'poetic self' of Herbert [and Hopkins]," even if he must temporarily suspend his disbelief.[2]

Furthermore, Eliot confirms that it is "the spiritual stamina of his [Herbert's] work that saves it from the level of the commonplace."[3] Herbert himself wrote to his mentor Nicholas Ferrar in a note accompanying his manuscript of *The Temple* (published in 1633) that "...this little book [is] a picture of the many spiritual conflicts that have passed betwixt God and my soul, before I could subject mine to the will of

---

[1] T.S. Eliot, "George Herbert: Writers and Their Work." In *George Herbert and the Seventeenth-CenturyReligious Poets*, ed. Mario A. DiCesare (New York: W.W. Norton and Co., Inc., 1978) 241.

[2] Itrat Husain, *The Mystical Element in the Metaphysical Poets of the Seventeenth Century* (London: Oliver and Boyd, 1948) 12.

[3] T.S. Eliot, "George Herbert: Writers and Their Work" 241.

Jesus my Master."[4] Hopkins, likewise, concisely conflates the nature of his priestly and poetic vocations in a letter of May 21, 1878, to his mentor Robert Bridges (1844–1930) when he says, "Stress is the life of it."[5] Hopkins defines "stress" as "the making a thing more, or making it markedly what it already is: it is the bringing out of its nature."[6] Hopkins believed that dificulty in composition was a means of achieving greater poetic value, just as difficulty in performing the spiritual exercises was productive of higher spiritual qualities. His desire that people familiarize themselves with their interior spirit and with the individuated nature of objects, events, and people is recorded in a Journal entry on July 19, 1872: "I thought how sadly beauty of inscape was unknown and buried away from simple people and yet how near at hand it was if they had eyes to see it and it could be called out everywhere again."[7] It is evident that Herbert and Hopkins acknowledge the reality of a Supreme Being with whom they interact, struggle, and ultimately embrace as "Master." The recording of this interaction and its universal and contemporaneous appeal to the reader justify a consideration of their works as spiritual autobiography.

The paradoxical nature of the Creator and the evolving spiritual state of the soul are presented with greater clarity and intelligibility when literary works and devotional works are comparatively studied, then treated as "spiritual autobiography." Although the characteristics of formal autobiography delineated by James Osborn are markedly absent in the genre of spiritual autobiography, they are noteworthy in their outlining of certain elements comprising a sustained formal autobiography. These elements include:

1.) it should be the history of a life, told by the person himself, usually in the first person;
2.) it should be written in conscious literary form of some kind, an orderly plan of narration, usually with a beginning, a middle, and an end;

---

[4] John N. Wall, Jr., ed., *George Herbert: The Country Parson, The Temple* (New York: Paulist Press, 1981) xiii.

[5] Claude Colleer Abbott, ed., *The Letters of Gerard Manley Hopkins to Robert Bridges* (London: Oxford University Preess, 1955) 52.

[6] J.C.A. Rathmell, "Hopkins, Ruskin and the *Sidney Psalter.*" *London Magazine*, 6 (1959) 60.

[7] Humphrey House, ed., *The Journals and Papers of Gerard Manley Hopkins* (London: Oxford University Press, 1959) 221.

3.) it should be a sustained attempt to delineate a whole life, albeit with selection of details.[8]

In *Design and Truth in Autobiography*, Roy Pascal clarifies that, in its ideal form, autobiography involves the attempt to depict a sincere and coherent interpretation of the self from a particular viewpoint in time in an effort to construe life as a whole.[9] Moreover, in spiritual autobiography, the individual reflects and interprets past and present experiences and thereby clarifies the development of the soul. T.C. Price Zimmermann demonstrates in "Confession and Autobiography in the Early Renaissance" that the Renaissance genre of autobiography, popularized by Petrarch, was a transmutation of the medieval practice of confession. The Christian and classical traditions, particularly the *Confessions* of St. Augustine (345–430), were blended together, enabling both laymen and priests to become familiar with the practice of the examination of conscience in a form that closely resembled the Christian confessional.[10] Since spiritual autobiography is an outgrowth of this self-consciousness, the confessions of the writers to their readers naturally follow. As Augustine's works evolved in a time when open confession was a common practice, Herbert's and Hopkins's works, when viewed as spiritual autobiography, have a decisive effect on the reader who watches the unfolding of the soul of the writers "before Thee in confession: and in my writing before many witnesses."[11] Scholars have pointed frequently to Augustine's experience of bondage to sinfulness and the liberating transformation that accompanied his conversion as significant factors in his writings.

Seventeenth-century Puritans such as John Bunyan cultivated spiritual autobiographies by recording the gradual regeneration and conversion of the Christian disciple. Works such as *Grace Abounding* treat the providence behind familiar, quotidian things in a manner that is far from trivial. "Through the introspective method, which was the great

---

[8] James Osborn, *The Beginnings of Autobiography in England* (Los Angeles: University of California Press, 1959) 3–4.

[9] Roy Pascal, *Design and Truth in Autobiography* (Cambridge: Harvard University Press, 1960) 5.

[10] T.C. Price Zimmermann, "Confession and Autobiography in the Early Renaissance." In *Renaissance Studies in Honor of Hans Baron*, ed. Anthony Molho and John A. Tedeschi (Illinois: Northern Illinois University Press, 1971) 121.

[11] Zimmermann 134.

contribution of this tradition of analysis, Bunyan has something of substance to reveal."[12] Herbert and Hopkins not only follow in this tradition, but also offer unique contributions to the genre of spiritual autobiography in their attempt to fulfill the biblical injunction: "Teach me to number my days aright, that I may gain wisdom of heart."

Eliot's essay also posits that an exact date for Herbert's *The Temple* poems cannot be determined. Moreover, he states that their order is not to be regarded as a chronological sequence, but as a record of "the order in which Herbert wished them to be read. *The Temple* is, in fact, a structure, and one which may have been worked over and elaborated, perhaps at intervals of time, before it reached its final form."[13] Helen C. White reminds us that, "In view of the fact that the manuscript to which we owe the existing form of the series was a deathbed legacy, we cannot be sure that the order in which the poems were left has any final meaning, that it in any way represents a perfected order in its author's intention."[14] Furthermore, Zimmermann points out that Petrarch regarded his essential character or ideal self as stable. "The movement of his self is from one situation to another laterally rather than forward in time. Time would then be subsumed rather than made the organizing principle of self-development."[15] The same rationale holds when reading the poetry and prose of Herbert and Hopkins as spiritual autobiography. The mechanical scrutiny implicit in a chronological analysis of the works of Herbert and Hopkins is, therefore, indefensible, given the mystical nature of spiritual experience.

This book is not concerned primarily with providing a comprehensive explication of individual poems of Herbert and Hopkins, although it fully intends to illumine individual lyrics by attempting a comparative analysis of the works of two authors who wrote within a specific spiritual tradition. It is concerned with larger patterns of religious experience and autobiographical meanings to which, in fact, poetry and prose provide a unique access to a Creator who is both immanent and transcendent.

---

[12] Roger Sharrock, "Spiritual Autobiography." In *John Bunyan*. (New York: St. Martin's Press, 1968) 61.

[13] T.S. Eliot, "George Herbert: Writers and Their Work" 236.

[14] Helen C. White, *The Metaphysical Poets: A Study in Religious Experience* (New York: The Macmillan Company, 1936) 168.

[15] Zimmermann 130, n.28.

An intertextual study of the poetry and prose of Herbert and Hopkins as spiritual autobiography reveals stylistic associations as well as spiritual parallels in the works of both writers. Hopkins shunned what he termed "the bad business" of the Victorian English language and became an experimenter in poetry and prose. In a letter of May 12, 1887, he wrote to Coventry Patmore, a fellow Catholic poet: "I have invented a number of new words; I cannot do without them."[16] The Logos and words, as well as the terms and style peculiar to the works of Herbert and Hopkins, provide associative images of the soul's construction, the birth of the poetic spirit, and the distinction of the reasoning process as it is manifested in "poetry," a word whose etymological resourcefulness—that which is "created," "built up," or "arranged"—is utilized and further enriched by Herbert and Hopkins. Indeed, poetry for both men was not only something that they took seriously; it was also the most profound expression of their personal energies and identities. With few exceptions, it is their religious experiences that move them to poetic expression. Herbert's motto "Less than the least/Of all thy [God's] mercies" ("The Poesy," ll.3-4) serves both men's unambitious regard for either secular or ecclesiastical advancement and supports the benign and humble perspective from which they view the soul's progress.

Both poets were fascinated by the intrinsic properties, musicality, and suggestive vibrations of words whose verbal affinities point to the ambiguity and paradox of life in a way that surpasses mere poetic techniques. Moreover, in many cases, Herbert and Hopkins work out the organic conflicts in the relationship with God in the very process of their works. The re-creation and unification of experience are underscored in their poetic ordering of conflict and their prosaic rendering of the human condition.

The temple as historical site and literary and spiritual symbol also undergirds the poetry and prose of Herbert and Hopkins. Bernard N. Schilling addresses the significance of building images in conveying notions of strength, order, and stability:

...building figures carry just the right persuasion toward something carefully planned as a whole.... As a literary figure, a building is simple, and clear to any understanding. Architecture becomes a familiar symbol of harmony and

---

[16] Abbott, *Further Letters of Gerard Manley Hopkins, Including His Correspondence with Coventry Patmore.* 379.

order, from the idea of God as the first architect of the world's foundations through the intricate balance of man's body, and the strength of human institutions in church and state.... As for religion, the whole structure of divinity may be shown as a complex edifice, or religious belief may become the pillar that supports, the foundation that upholds, every commonwealth. Of all religious structures the Church of England combines the ideal of order, strength, and beauty and performs its function of maintaining the edifice of public welfare.[17]

Indeed, for Herbert, the "temple" as the vehicle of his poetic and religious expression is a multivalent symbol, as Helen C. White confirms:

It might be used for the actual church building, for its ordering, its furnishing, its implications, it might be used for that Mystical Body of the Lord, the Church, with its foundation Scripture, its indwelling Spirit, its rites and ordinances, its feasts and fasts, its intercessions, its mighty commemorations, and it might be used for that recognized temple of the Holy Ghost, the spirit of the individual Christian in its struggles and its illuminations, its repentances and its confidences.[18]

In an age when religious and political reformations complicated and challenged the Renaissance milieu, Herbert presented an honest voice in his *Temple* poems, particularly those in "The Church," from which the majority of poems of Herbert in this book are cited. This voice further distinguishes itself in his prose account *The Country Parson* (published in 1652), whose title character has the responsibility to inculcate Anglican devotional practices in his parishioners. The reader of Herbert's works is impelled to acknowledge the importance of the temple of worship, the Church, as the outward visible community of believers, and daily prayer as the lifting up of the mind and heart to God in praise and thanksgiving.

All meaning for Herbert resides in the sacramental relationship between the soul and its Creator, a relationship which is strengthened by quotidian experiences as well as by biblical and patristic sources. The reader allows Herbert and the rich tradition in which Herbert situates his works to "write" on the heart the journal of a soul, with its concomitant "dark night" and eventual conversion experiences. "With

---

[17] Bernard N. Schilling, *Dryden and the Conservative Myth: A Reading of Absalom and Achitophel* (New Haven and London: Yale University Press, 1961) 252.

[18] White 168.

the exception of a few didactic poems interpreting the doctrine or ritual of the Church, all his poetry is spiritual autobiography. Herbert knows and states what he thinks, as well as what he feels, about, for example, death and immortality or the relation between God and the soul."[19] The seven chapters of this book underscore the significance of the sacramental relationship between the two writers and their God.

Like Herbert, who centers his unity of vision on the temple *topos* which joins word and sign, worship and symbol in a metaphysical strain, thereby illuminating both divine and human truths, Hopkins discovers the sacramental quality of all life in the stress and "inscape," the tension and power of nature and, primarily, of God, Who gives individuality its focus and keeps it in being. In his essay "George Herbert: Writers and Their Work," Eliot states: "If there is another example since his [Herbert's] time of a poetic genius so dedicated to God, it is that of Gerard Hopkins."[20] Indeed, Gordon Symes argues in "Hopkins, Herbert and Contemporary Modes" that "Hopkins' poetic theory and practice, no less than Eliot's, look back to the Metaphysical tradition of making a sensible whole of experience, of trying to order the acknowledged contradictions of living with a sort of sensuous logic ...as they attempt to reach behind the physical world encountered by the senses for a single justifying principle of existence.... Both poets are above all else bent on reconciling the contrarieties of existence and resolving its conflicts."[21] Ultimately, the locus of Temple for both Herbert and Hopkins is the soul, the inner dwelling place of God and the site of the soul's progress.

Hopkins's conversion from Anglicanism to Catholicism on October 21, 1866, was the fruit of a lively and determined effort to understand the condition of "rare-dear" England's soul in its severing of the bonds of Roman Catholicism and its dislike of Catholics. "We are used to thinking of Hopkins as a Roman Catholic convert and Jesuit priest, but we need to remember too that for almost exactly half his short life he was a member of the Church of England. If we can believe what most psychologists tell us, the psyche is formed early in our existence. When Hopkins was converted at twenty-two, the personality, intellect, and spiritual cast of mind that characterized him at his death were well

---

[19] Bennett 56.

[20] T.S. Eliot, "George Herbert: Writers and Their Work" 238.

[21] Gordon Symes, "Hopkins, Herbert and Contemporary Modes." *Hibbert Journal*, 47 (1948–49), 390,392.

established, and the outlines of the great poet he was to become were already implicit."[22] The close fellowship Hopkins found with Anglican Robert Bridges symbolizes Hopkins's ability to cherish a fellow poet and to temper irreconcilable religious beliefs with honesty, admiration, and poetic craftsmanship. The strong religious certitude and friendship of his mentor John Henry Newman, his peer Digby Dolben (also a close friend of Bridges), and Canon Richard Watson Dixon balanced the agnostic beliefs espoused by Hopkins's tutors T.H. Green, Walter Pater, and the liberal Benjamin Jowett, and strengthened Hopkins's vocation to the Society of Jesus.[23] Indeed, Bernadette Ward contends that

> Hopkin's conversion was more than a transfer of allegiance from one Christian communion to another; that change preceded his acquaintance with Newman. The conversion that Hopkins experienced through Newman was a transformation of heart and mind—especially of mind—that had a deep effect on the kind of poetry Hopkins wrote. Newman was Hopkin's mentor in the faith. For seven critical months while Hopkins chose his state in life, the two men lived together. During this time, Hopkins imbibed Newman's philosophy of language, which prepared him for his profound understanding of the philosophy of John Duns Scotus. The concept grew under the influence of Scotus, but it was under Newman's influence, and with connections to his linguistic theories, that Hopkins first articulated the central concept of his poetry: 'inscape.'[24]

The influence of Aquinas and Scotus on Hopkins elicited my interest in the search for the Metaphysical counterpart of Hopkins—George Herbert. In his article "Hopkins, Ruskin and the *Sidney Psalter*," J.C.A. Rathmell posits that, "during Hopkins' so-called 'silent period,' prior to his writing of *The Wreck of the Deutschland* (1875), a very remarkable amount of Metaphysical poetry was being either reprinted after a lapse of many years, or published from original manuscripts for the first time. Prior to 1870 Herbert alone had gone through several

---

[22] Robert Bernard Martin, *Gerard Manley Hopkins: A Very Private Life* (New York: G.P. Putnam's Sons, 1991) xv.

[23] Acting on the approval of Pope John Paul II, the Vatican, on January 22, 1991, declared that John Henry Cardinal Newman (1801–90) had lived a life of "heroic virtue" which was worthy of imitation. Members of the Congregation for Sainthood Causes undertook this first formal step toward the canonization of this English philosopher, theologian, and spiritual writer.

[24] Bernadette Ward, "Newman's *Grammar of Ascent* and the Poetry of Gerard Manley Hopkins." *Renascence* 43, 1990–91 (Fall-Winter) 1–2; 105.

editions."[25] Hopkins's close Oxford friend William Addis said that Hopkins's "strongest tie to the English Church" was Herbert.[26] C.A. Patrides acknowledges W. H. Gardner's belief that "Herbert's frank avowal of Christ; his passionate yet restrained colloquies with God; his vigorous and subtle expression of doctrine; his significant quaintness and happy conceits—all these elements are found, in duly modified form, in the later Hopkins." Patrides adds that Herbert's partiality for orthodox paradoxes and compound epithets like "Christ-side-piercing spear" ["Prayer (I)," 1.6] "could hardly fail to attract Hopkins."[27]

On a thirty-day retreat which began on September 16, 1868, Hopkins was introduced to the *Spiritual Exercises* of St. Ignatius of Loyola (1491-1556), who became a model for much seventeenth-century devotional poetry, including that of George Herbert. These meditations infused Hopkins's priestly and poetic vocations with "the honor and glory of God." For twenty-one years, Hopkins dedicated himself to the Society of Jesus and studied, meditated, and practiced the *Spiritual Exercises*. This spiritual text formed his perspective on life and directed his experiences, thoughts, writings, sermons, responses to nature and beauty. Shortly before he left for Manresa, the Jesuit novitiate, Hopkins's mentor John Henry Newman directed him: "Don't call the Jesuit discipline hard: it will bring you to heaven."[28] The *Exercises* informed the world of Hopkins with a religious bent in its emphasis on leaving all in God's hands to be used as He sees fit, and on detachment from personal goals and professional accomplishments, two dicta which undoubtedly dissuaded Hopkins from publishing his poems during his life. The present study suggests that the Ignatian *Exercises* influenced the form, structure, and meditative pattern of Hopkins's poems in its urging of the exercitant-reader to visualize the scene associated with the subject of the poem and to engage the five senses in evoking the setting, the significance of the event and its implications for his own life. The desolations revealed in *The Wreck of the Deutschland* reflect the major themes in the *Exercises* and their import in his priestly and poetic vocations. In this study, references from Hopkins's *Journal*,

---

[25] Rathmell 52.

[26] Wendell Johnson, "Halfway to a New Land: Herbert, Tennyson, and the Early Hopkins." *Hopkins Quarterly*, 1983 Fall; 10 (3) 116.

[27] C.A. Patrides, ed., *George Herbert: The Critical Heritage* (London: Routledge and Kegan Paul, 1983) 28.

[28] Pick 24.

Sermons, and personal letters are cited which record his reflections on Ignatian spirituality and his evolving artistic sensibilities in order to underscore the syncretism between his priestly and poetic character.

Hopkins's study of poets from Shakespeare to Keats and Herbert to Christina Rossetti, his training in patristics, Christian mysticism, and the medievalists such as St. Thomas Aquinas (1225–74), Duns Scotus (1265–1308), and St. Thomas à Kempis (1380–1471), was also balanced by a study of contemporary scientists. These studies impelled Hopkins to analysis and mechanical observation as well as to philosophical insight and metaphysical speculation, the evidence of which is borne in the poetry and prose analyzed in this book. Hopkins's knowledge of Welsh and his usage of sprung rhythm redirected the dominant pentameter line and created a counterpointed rhythm that ushered in the experimentalism of twentieth-century literature. It is this experimentalism in religious sensibility and poetic approaches that causes him to be considered a modern writer. Both Herbert and Hopkins find a religious character in shaped verse and architectonics, rhyme, and biblical typology. These techniques convey their spiritual dialectic that a holistic life involves technical as well as poetic and spiritual form in the soul's search for religious experience.

Hopkins's letters also cite the influence of John Milton, particularly of Milton's *Samson Agonistes*, on Hopkins's usage of counterpoint and sprung rhythm. Since Hopkins's admiration and emulation of Milton extends into his poetical experimentations and is admitted to in his personal writings, the opening statement in Chapter One and subsequent parallels between Milton and Hopkins demonstrate the significant influence of this Protestant post-Reformation theologian on Hopkins. Hopkins, like Milton, made use of what he terms, even in his undergraduate days, the "so-called Parallelism of Hebrew poetry," the Hebraist penchant for natural stress rather than number of syllables in an accentual line. Rathmell reminds the reader that "Hopkins and Milton were thoroughly acquainted with the form of Hebrew poetry and would have found a close approximation to its structure and sentiment in the *Sidney Psalter*, a collection of metrical psalm translations by Sir Philip Sidney and his sister, the Countess of Pembroke."[29] Many Metaphysical and Victorian writers, and certainly Herbert and Hopkins, were knowledgeable of and indebted to this work.

---

[29] Rathmell 54.

In addition to interrelating the poetry and prose of Herbert and Hopkins, then treating their works as spiritual autobiography, this book further demonstrates how a superimposing of the three Christian motifs of theodicy, colloquy, and nutriment onto a selection of Herbert's and Hopkins's works enriches the genre of spiritual autobiography and provides a more refined translation of incarnational theology for the reader. Concomitantly, this study aims at demonstrating how the selections of Herbert and Hopkins under consideration redefine the three Christian motifs and reinvigorate the three stages of classical mysticism rendered by St. John of the Cross—the purgative, illuminative, and unitive.

Dionysius, the Areopagite (circa 500) was the first to apply the term "mysticism" to the Christian experience of God in his treatise *Mystical Theology*.[30] The term implies the attempt of the soul to realize the presence of God. This definition supports a reading of spiritual autobiography in the works of Herbert and Hopkins, who sought to convey their mystical interests, insights, and experiences.[31] Moreover, Hopkins devotes a section entitled *Tres Modi* in his commentary on the *Spiritual Exercises* to the three methods of prayer. The last method—the unitive—he calls the "prayer of the affections."

Since mystical experiences vary from person to person, it is difficult to define these three stages categorically. However, the verse and prose of Herbert and Hopkins provide the salient features of their spirituality: a deep longing for God and a denial of selfish instincts which are obstacles to the will of God (purgation), a passionate expression of their love for God which allows the Light of God to fill the soul (illumination), and a seeking and gaining alliance with God (union).[32]

---

[30] Varghese Mathai, *The Evolution of the Inner Man as Seen in the Writings of Gerard Manley Hopkins and George Herbert*, diss., Baylor University, 1987, 176.

[31] Cogent summaries of the mystical doctrines, particularly of the classical authors and of St. Thomas Aquinas, St. John of the Cross, and St. Ignatius Loyola, are provided by Rev. Reginald Garrigou-LaGrange, O.P. in his two-volume series *The Three Ages of the Interior Life* (Michigan and London: B. Herder Book Co., 1951; tr. by Sr. Timothea Doyle, O.P.). In this Prologue, citations from the three stages of the mystical life and the Ignatian *Exercises* are from this text.

[32] *The Spiritual Life: A Treatise on Ascetical and Mystical Theology* by the Very Rev. Adolphe Tanquerey, S.S., provides a methodical compendium as well as devotional reading on the spiritual life. In this book, definitions and discussion of the three ways of Christian perfection are based on Tanquerey's text (Belgium: Desclée and Co., 1930; tr. by the Rev. Herman Branderis).

These experiences of longing, leaping in faith, and merging into God take place for Herbert and Hopkins within the soul. Every foundation stone that both writers put into the temple is turned into what Herbert rendered "such wealth [as] cannot be told."

In the *Spiritual Exercises*, St. Ignatius defines the initial stage of mysticism—purgation—as the soul's recognition of its place in God's creation, his awareness of sin, repentance, and submission to the divine will. He defines "illumination" as the soul's sharing in the mysteries of Christ and identifying with Christ as far as possible by attempting to attain the ideal state of *imitatio Christi*. The final stage, that of "union" with God, Ignatius defines as the condition whereby the soul is lost in God's love. Like Ignatius, St. John of the Cross, and other mystical writers, Herbert and Hopkins also experience these three significant stages of their soul's transformation, and record them in their poetry and prose. Indeed, Evelyn Underhill cites Hopkins, in particular, as "perhaps the greatest mystical poet of the Victorian era" in his "direct apprehension of the Infinite through the medium of His creation."[33]

Seen from this perspective, the works of Herbert and Hopkins emphasize that the process of *agon* or the soul's reckoning, which is the prelude to sanctification, undergirds the conditions of the mystical life, a healing gift of grace which God bestows on all those who imitate the *kenosis* of Christ. The purifications or purgations that follow are, like the cross, necessary, according to mystical and Ignatian spirituality, in order for the soul to acquire its goal: union with God. The soul's imperfections—those tendencies which inhibit charity, trust in God, and surrender of one's will to God—paradoxically lead the soul to the experience of "the dark night," defined by St. John of the Cross as "an inflowing of God into the soul to purify its habitual ignorances and imperfections, both natural and supernatural." The agony exhibited in Hopkins's "terrible" sonnets derives from a phase of spiritual progress known as *acedia*, "the dark night of the soul," a temporary "winter of discontent." The chief element of "the dark night" is that God is beginning to communicate (either intentionally or confusedly) the essence of the unitive way: the immediate awareness of God's presence in the soul. This insight, which reminded me of Hopkins's use of the word

---

[33] W.H. Gardner, *Gerard Manley Hopkins: A Study of Poetic Idiosyncrasy in Relation to Poetic Tradition* (London: Oxford University Press, 1961), II, 370.

"wreck" in his long major ode *The Wreck of the Deutschland*, impelled me to develop the concept of "(w)reck."

The Jesuit Hopkins, in a late-Victorian milieu, interprets the *Spiritual Exercises* of Ignatius in a different manner from most people in the sixteenth century when the *Exercises* originated, or in Herbert's seventeenth century; nevertheless, it is "the selfless self of self"—the act of the will or of free human decision—that Hopkins recognizes as the basic constituent of the soul. This tone of self-examination is also implicit in the penultimate stanza of Herbert's "The Church Porch," which echoes the instructional and devotional tone of the Ignatian *Exercises*, and complements Hopkins's interiority and vivid imagination:

> Sum up at night, what thou hast done by day,
> And in the morning, what thou hast to do.
> Dress and undress thy soul: mark the decay
> And growth of it: if with thy watch, that too
> > Be down, then wind up both: since we shall be
> > Most surely judg'd, make thy accounts agree
> > > ("The Church Porch, "451–56).

Herbert's lines are a remarkable parallel to the purpose and meaning of the *Exercises* as Ignatius defines it:

> For as strolling, walking, and running are bodily exercises, so every way of preparing and disposing the soul to rid itself of all the disordered tendencies, and, after it is rid, to seek and find the Divine Will as to the management of one's life for the salvation of the soul....

The four parts or four weeks into which the *Exercises* is divided are similar to the traditional stages of the spiritual life, yet the *Directory*, or book of instructions for the directors, warns:

> It would be a mistake if anyone were to suppose that having gone through the First Week he was perfectly and fully cleansed of sin; and after the Second and Third Weeks, perfectly illuminated; and at last, at the end of the Fourth Week, that he had attained to perfect union with God. For all these stages require much time and care and labour in rooting out faults, subduing passions and acquiring virtues.

The *Exercises* is a means to set the exercitant free for the pursuit of charity, which leads to the one goal of union with God through love. The ideal is to attain *contemplatio in actione* while the individual works for and with others. However, Ignatius also believed that a disciplined testing of one's feelings, emotions, and values is a necessary predisposition to proper discernment and to the development of the inner spiritual logic that assumes personal responsibility and recognizes God's action in His creation. Ignatius's, Herbert's, and Hopkins's preoccupation with detail, examination of conscience, and structured meditation bear on this discernment of spirits and result in a colloquy or a direct Person-to-person encounter. This free exchange sparks many of Herbert's and Hopkins's brighter works and all of their darker ones.

But why is such an inner spiritual journey necessary? Jesus taught his disciples that "The reign of God is already in your midst" (Luke 17:21). The follower of Christ learns that an introspection which initiates self-consciousness is essential if the soul is to live in the Kingdom of God which resides within. Yet there are many dangers that the soul encounters along the pilgrimage of faith. Self-sufficiency, scrupulosity, self-aggrandizement, and despair are pitfalls which Hopkins addresses in his "terrible" sonnets and Herbert in several matching poems.

Complementing the gift of colloquy for Hopkins is a fidelity to the essential nature of things, a concept summarized by Hopkins in the term "thisness" or *haecceitas*. Hopkins shares this view with Scotus, who also believes that the fall of man was a *felix culpa* or a "fortunate fall." Scotus and Hopkins regard the person of Christ in a way that contrasts with the belief of St. Thomas Aquinas, who considered the Incarnation to be the result of a divine decision to redeem a fallen human race. Hopkins's endorsement of Scotus's views conflicted with the traditional Thomistic doctrines upheld by Hopkins's fellow Jesuits, and contributed to his sense of alienation and desolation.[34]

The characteristic spirituality of the Counter-Reformation, embodied in *The Spiritual Exercises*, is especially evident in the Metaphysical poems of Herbert. The method of meditation with the "three powers of the soul—memory, understanding, and will"—are found in St. Augustine's treatise *De Trinitate*.[35] They devolved from the medieval meditative patterns where the Memory or Imagination was required to recall quite vividly or to create in the imagination a particular locale,

---

[34] At a Vatican meeting of July 6, 1991, Pope John Paul II officially recognized organized devotion to the theologian-philosopher Franciscan Father John Duns Scotus, thereby elevating him to the rank of beatified.

[35] Christopher Devlin, ed., *The Sermons and Devotional Writings of Gerard Manley Hopkins* (London: Oxford University Press, 1959) 344.

scene, or situation. The Understanding was then called upon to make connections and to discover points of significance, and the Will was to express its resolves in the final colloquy. The emphasis in the seventeenth-century religious poetry of Herbert is either on the individual soul's attempt to understand the mystery of God, or on the significance and subtleties of religious doctrine. Most of the paradoxes, allegorizations, and typological allusions in Herbert's poems rest upon liturgical material. As with Hopkins, many seventeenth-century religious lyrics exhibit the Ignatian influence of centering a person in prayer or meditation, or wrestling with temptation. The struggle of the individual to submit one's will to the will of God, to find freedom, not by action, but by humble submission to the Supreme Being, is at the heart of Herbert's Reformation spirituality as it is of Hopkins's Ignatian spirituality. In the meditational works of Herbert and Hopkins, there is a tremendous emphasis both on dramatic visualizations of the scene in all its sensuous detail, and on its theological and spiritual ramifications. In both writers rests the Ignatian belief that a full application of the senses enables the individual to envisage the matter at hand. Thus, both Herbert and Hopkins share the traits of classic mysticism.

The Reformation spirituality of Herbert is also evident within the Roman Catholicism of Hopkins, since the Old and New Testament prototypes, as well as St. Paul and St. Augustine, are acknowledged by Luther, Calvin, and Zwingli as the forebears in providing an understanding of salvation history. The Reformation paradigm of law, justification, and sanctification as the sequence of the Christian life offers a partial explanation of the sequencing of poems in *The Temple*, and evidences the Christian theme of theodicy in the verse and prose of Herbert. Both writers demonstrate that poetic and spiritual regeneration and growth result from the tension and stress accompanying the attempt to vindicate God's justice in allowing evil to exist. They extend the definition of the Christian motif of theodicy by inviting the reader to regard the seemingly contrary nature of God's beauty and terror by witnessing the souls of the writers in the purgative stage. As Louis L. Martz argues in *The Poetry of Meditation*, the realm of meditation is "broad enough to hold Jesuit and Puritan, Donne and Milton, the baroque extravagance of Crashaw and the delicate restraint of Herbert."[36] The suggestion is made that the meditative tradition of both Protestant and Catholic poets makes structural use of an imported Jesuit discipline of impassioned contemplation. Rathmell points out that "It is not generally realized that after the Pope's [Paul III] approval of Loyola's *Exercises* in 1548, a very large number of Catholic books and pamphlets was smuggled into Britain, thereby imbuing English protestantism with Catholic sensibility."[37]

Herbert and Hopkins direct the reader to an interpretation of the Christian theme of colloquy by portraying the soul as it is enlightened by such paradoxical similitudes as the solitude and dialogue of the illuminative stage. The Christian motif of colloquy is immediately recognized as the speakers describe and recount, primarily in nautical imagery, the voyage of the soul as it travels through the channels of "Denial" and "(Carrion Comfort)" to ultimate unification with its Creator. The more immediate "wrecking" of the soul that must occur in the speakers' quotidian experiences is evident in the poems and prose accounts that focus on the speakers' discourses with a God who seems suddenly to remove their spiritual impulses and poetic generativity.

Finally, Herbert and Hopkins invite the reader to feed on the rich literary and spiritual banquet of Lenten fasting and Paschal feasting that unite the writers with the Creator, and the reader with the Christian theme of nutriment. The biblical injunction that "He who does not work should not eat" is realized in accounts where the soul's laboring to attain union with God is depicted in sacrificial and banqueting images. The *agon*, inherent in the theme of theodicy where God's justice is vindicated, and in the (w)reckoning of the soul as it engages in a colloquy of wrestling and intense soul-wrenching, finds total justification and reward in the invitation of the soul's Master to "sit and eat" the bread, wine, and meat of eternal nutriment. This nutriment that completes the three Christian themes and the three stages of the spiritual journey is centered on the Eucharist which, as C.A. Patrides acknowledges, embodies the "marrow of Herbert's sensibility" as an

---

[36] Louis L. Martz. *The Poetry of Meditation: A Study of English Religious Literature of the Seventeenth Century* (New Haven and London: Yale University Press, 1962) 3–4.

[37] Rathmell 58. Paul III, who served as Pope from 1534–49, established the Inquisition in the Papal States and called the Council of Trent, which met intermittently from 1545–63, to reform the Catholic Church and to secure reconciliations with the Protestants.

Anglican minister as well as Hopkins's vocation as a Jesuit priest.[38]
Chapter Six is devoted primarily to the significance of the spiritual
repast in the lives and works of Herbert and Hopkins.

No autobiography—spiritual autobiography included—"can possess
wholeness because by definition the end of the story cannot be told, the
bios must remain incomplete. In effect, the narrative is never finished,
nor ever can be, within the covers of a book. Furthermore, by its very
nature, the self is (like the autobiography that records and creates it)
open-ended and incomplete: it is always in process or, more precisely,
is itself a process."[39] Chapter Seven of this book addresses spiritual
autobiography as an "Unfinished Cornerstone" that offers no finished
patterns. What Herbert and Hopkins do offer are autobiographies that
have the capacity to alter radically the reader's perspective on the truth
of life as it is experienced by the soul, and, in this respect, spiritual
autobiography assumes its claim to authentic literary and spiritual
interpretation. The poetry and prose of Herbert and Hopkins reveal,
not what the writers have done, but what they have witnessed to be
authentic, enhanced as this is by the rhetorical ingenuity of both artists.
The reader is coaxed out of systematic thought and conventional liter-
ary traditions to a confessional identification with a vision of the Word
in the context of literature and the Scriptures, as well as a heightened
self-awareness and a transformation of his or her life. An analysis of
the works of Herbert and Hopkins as spiritual autobiography helps the
reader to frame his or her experiences and to sharpen his or her aware-
ness of the endless possibilities of self-definition and self-disclosure.
Moreover, it argues for the critical importance, extreme versatility,
change, and continuity of this genre in the hallmark of literary achieve-
ment.

Religious writers in every age, according to their perspectives,
strengths, and limitations, attempt to demonstrate the correspondence
between the human soul and God. When the works of Herbert and
Hopkins are studied as spiritual autobiography, three elements become
evident: the soul is depicted in its desire to escape or transcend the
self; a scheme of religious thought emerges that is not the writers' own
invention, but is inclusive of the stages of mysticism that have been

---

[38] Patrides, *The English Poems of George Herbert* 17.
[39] James Olney, "Autobiography and the Cultural Moment." In *Autobiography: Essays Theoretical and Critical* (New Jersey: Princeton University Press, 1980) 25.

acknowledged for centuries; and the reader witnesses the use of bold and natural language which Herbert and Hopkins adapt to their subjects.

The works of Herbert and Hopkins embody the traditional belief that the soul resembles God in four ways: it is a spirit (spirituality); it is immortal (immortality); it can reason (intellect); and it can choose (free will). The conflict between the soul and God is ultimately resolved by the over-mastering intervention of the Creator, Who is the core of Reformation and Ignatian spiritualities. This book demonstrates the power that such spirituality and literature exert on the reader.

> There may be fields in which religion operates and poetry does not, as there may be areas of the mind affected by poetry and untouched by faith. But over certain areas both operate; either can quicken sensibility; either can impose an order upon scattered thoughts and feelings.[40]

A consideration of the works of Herbert and Hopkins as spiritual autobiography, and a setting down of these works side by side, help to define the tension, conflict, and resolution of the two poles of sin and love, and allow the reader to recover the experiential side of two vital traditions: the spiritual and the literary. Indeed, the emotional and intellectual responses elicited by the reader impart additional meaning and voice to the works of Herbert and Hopkins, and argue convincingly for a study of their works as spiritual autobiography.

---

[40] Bennett 142, 144–45.

Chapter One

Herbert and Hopkins:
Country Parsons and Poets

> Lord, my first fruits present themselves to thee;
> Yet not mine neither: for from thee they came,
> And must return. Accept of them and me,
> And make us strive, who shall sing best thy name.
> (Herbert, "The Dedication" to *The Temple*)

THE VINDICATION AND JUSTIFICATION of "the ways of God to men" impelled the Protestant post-Reformation theologian and writer John Milton to undertake his monumental epic *Paradise Lost*. A concomitant desire to vindicate and justify the ways of God in the human experience impelled the seventeenth-century English metaphysical writer George Herbert and the nineteenth-century English religious writer Gerard Manley Hopkins to poetic and prose accounts that invite the reader to a greater understanding of the question: "Who am I in the eyes of the Creator?" This question provides the foundation for literary works that stretch across three centuries and the life spans of two English writers in an attempt to reveal the uniqueness of the soul.

The paradoxical nature of the individual is afforded even greater substantive and spiritual value when literary works are conflated with devotional works and are considered as "spiritual autobiography." Like the poet, the spiritual autobiographer is a maker who gropes through personal inner shadows in an attempt to "write" the self and the Logos: to fashion flesh into words and words into flesh.[1]

In their *Theory of Literature*, Wellek and Warren argue that "it is best to consider as literature only works in which the aesthetic function is dominant and formally complex."[2] However, the legitimacy and relevancy of the genre of spiritual autobiography is recognized by the original manner in which it communicates the essence of one's life. "The evolution of autobiography owes much [with regard] to the orien-

---

[1] Stephen A. Shapiro, "The Dark Continent of Literature: Autobiography." *Comparative Literature Studies*, 5 (1968), 422.

[2] Shapiro 423.

tation of consciousness to concrete experience during the Renaissance, to the development of an empirical and inductive method, and to Protestant introspection."[3] Spiritual autobiography mirrors the evolution of a life in as truthful a manner as possible, recording the "successive self-images and recognitions or distortions of those self-images by the world."[4] A story results that is useful to the reader as a lesson in life experience and as inspiration.

A change in the writer's relationship with God prompts the meditation and self-examination that occurs in his or her works. Often the author doubts his or her ability to tell the story in a manner pleasing to God. While Hopkins elected some years of silence, he eventually emerged to write a prolific record of his spiritual journey. Herbert's writings impelled his congregation to a life of spiritual commitment and thus confirmed his power as poet or maker to change his world as well as that of his audience. "Questions rather than conclusions, quests rather than conquests, best characterize this genre, for the possibilities and the meaning of being human must seem like a steadily growing Everest to the climber in search of a final encompassing perspective."[5]

The term "spiritual autobiography" itself is oxymoronic and the concept almost a contradiction. Since the word "auto" suggests "self" and "bios" suggests "life," a consideration of the spiritual dimension of the individual negates any consideration of life regulated solely by the self. It is this thesis that Herbert and Hopkins successfully and incisively demonstrate in their works which, when read as spiritual autobiography, unfold the multiplicity of human paradoxes. To view a selection of Herbert's and Hopkins's works within this frame of reference is to acknowledge spiritual autobiography as a unique genre that records the journey of the soul by a speaker who transforms the crucial experiences of an individual into the objective, formal, shared experience of many readers.[6] Unlike the genre of autobiography, which is written from a specific retrospective point of view, spiritual autobiography shifts the author's attention so that it does not merely reconstruct the past, but interprets it from the perspective of the entire life, thereby

---

[3] Shapiro 425.

[4] Shapiro 426.

[5] Shapiro 431.

[6] Stephen Spender, "Confession and Autobiography." In *Autobiography: Essays Theoretical and Critical*, ed. James Olney (Princeton: Princeton University Press, 1980) 117.

ennobling experiences and events with spiritual meaning and magnitude. The writer attempts to "enact the statement of Augustine: 'I speak in your presence, O Lord, and therefore I shall say what is true.' Spiritual autobiography itself gives way ideally to the voice of God."[7] What critic Helen Vendler states in regard to George Herbert is true also for Gerard Manley Hopkins: "Ordinary narrative was usually not a suitable medium for Herbert simply because of its internal, ongoing placidity; he liked doubling-back, self-correction, revision, repentance, enlightenment, complication."[8]

Spiritual autobiography, as a literary and universal mode of self-disclosure that conjoins the immanent and the transcendent, is enriched and supplemented by autobiography's attempt at self-definition and self-justification. Rather than being considered as a continuous and chronological unfolding of the public life of the author, spiritual autobiography in the poems and prose works of Herbert and Hopkins invites the reader to be attentive to the ways by which these two men impart order and meaning to their daily experiences. Moreover, it also demands a disciplined and reflective attention to the reader's own spiritual journey.

Stanley Fish posits the analogy:

Reader: Herbert :: Herbert: God

and explains it by stating that "Herbert stands to God as his readers stand to Herbert."[9] I would advance the comparison by suggesting this reading: the reader-as-pilgrim is at the disposal of Herbert just as Herbert-as-poet is at the disposal of God. Both reader and Herbert hold the posture of anticipation and expectancy towards a being held in "benevolence" and a "supervisory intention."[10] Both the reader and Herbert intend to "read" and decipher the Logos of creation. Giving a spiritual autobiographical reading to the works of Herbert and Hopkins "amplifies the rendering of individual experience by associating it with the

---

[7] Dennis Taylor, "Some Strategies of Religious Autobiography." *Renascence*, 27 (1974), 40.

[8] Helen Vendler, *The Poetry of George Herbert* (Cambridge: Harvard University Press, 1975) 68.

[9] Stanley Fish, *The Living Temple: George Herbert and Catechizing* (Berkeley: University of California Press, 1978) 167.

[10] Fish, *The Living Temple* 167.

experience of all Christians" and with the limitations and finitude of human nature.[11] The success of the spiritual autobiographer's art lies in the response of the reader and the entire Christian community who seek communion with God.

Such a reading is relative to the writer's and reader's points of view and subordinated to the literary value of spiritual autobiography; nevertheless, it enjoins the reader to deliberate on the merits and benefits of a genre rooted in the rich tradition of the Bible, the *Confessions* of St. Augustine, the *Imitation of Christ* by St. Thomas à Kempis, and the *Spiritual Exercises* of St. Ignatius of Loyola, all part of a long line of spiritual and mystical writings that formed the cornerstone for the authors and works considered here.

The soul's experience of "turning around," which the word "conversion" suggests, demands an uprooting, an honest confrontation with the self, and an agreement to "put aside [the] old self with its past deeds" in order to "put on a new man, one who grows in knowledge as he is formed anew in the image of his Creator" (Col. 3:9-10).[12] The record of the spiritual conversion of two serious-minded Christian parsons and poets is highlighted in *The Country Parson* and *The Temple* of Herbert, as well as in *The Wreck of the Deutschland* and the "terrible" sonnets, letters, sermons, and journal of Hopkins, works which evidence the struggle of the speaker in Hopkins's "A Voice from the World": "How turn my passion-pastured thought/To gentle manna and simple bread?" (ll.174-75).[13] Although conversion brings no immunity from further spiritual (w)reckonings, it does provide a new perspective with which to face them and a renewed strength to wrestle with them.

The biblical allusion of Jacob's struggling with the angel is the analogue for the author or speaker who battles with a host of personal and spiritual deficiencies, solipsisms, and near-despair until he ac-

---

[11] George A. Starr, *Defoe and Spiritual Autobiography* (New Jersey: Princeton University Press, 1965) 17.

[12] All biblical excerpts are from *The New American Bible* (New York: P.J. Kennedy and Sons, 1970).

[13] All citations from *The Country Parson* and *The Temple* are from John N. Wall, Jr., ed., *George Herbert: The Country Parson, The Temple* (New Jersey: Paulist Press, 1981); citations from Hopkins's poems, letters, and journal are from Catherine Phillips, ed., *Gerard Manley Hopkins* (Oxford: Oxford University Press, 1986). Line references are cited parenthetically.

knowledges the mystery of the Creator who embraces him and welcomes him to the banquet of communion and salvific grace. When Herbert's and Hopkins's works are read as spiritual autobiography, the significance of the soul's conversion process is afforded universal dimensions as the reader likewise becomes engaged in the speakers' conflicts and responds in a personal manner to the experiences depicted in the works. The selections then become not merely literary masterpieces but, more importantly, artful and strategic descriptions of the soul's progress in a life of continual conversion and emerging identity. Where the genre of autobiography allows the reader to view the recorder's life in a passive and retrospective manner, spiritual autobiography demands the immediate and active engagement of the reader as both recorder and reader exchange emotional, intellectual, and theological energies. The similar literary and spiritual patterns in Herbert's and Hopkins's works permit the reader the benefit and luxury of engaging in the search for God which is grounded in the temple construction of Herbert and the *agon* or wrecking experience of Hopkins. The works of both men depict a wrestling with their respective angels or shadows, and enable the reader to participate fully in the process of spiritual awakening. Their prolific usage of literary techniques reinforces the necessity of technical form as well as poetic and spiritual re-formation in the soul's architecture.

The building elements of Herbert's temple and Hopkins's "odyssey from God back to God" are comprised of devotional practices that enhance the mutuality of love between themselves and God, their struggles in expressing the conflictive and paradoxical nature of the Christian life, and the significance that both writers attribute to a healthy dialogue and communion with God in their attempt to discern God's will in their lives.[14]

Central to a spiritual response on the part of the reader to the works of Herbert and Hopkins is an understanding of how thoroughly integrated into the lives of both men were "the conventions of prayer and praise."[15] Simply defined by St. John Damascene as "the raising of the mind and heart to God," prayer implies a dialogue with the Creator whereby the petitioner, frequently in groans and sighs, asks for

---

[14] Norman Weyand, S.J., *Immortal Diamond: Studies in Gerard Manley Hopkins* (New York: Octagon Books, 1969) 33.

[15] Terry Sherwood, *Herbert's Prayerful Art* (Toronto: University of Toronto Press, 1989) 7.

help, acknowledges his sin or distance from God, and receives reassurance of God's merciful love.[16] Praise or thanksgiving to God is the resultant activity of God's understanding and undertaking of human experience. As St. Ignatius states in his *Spiritual Exercises*: "Man is created to praise, reverence, and serve God our Lord, and by this means to save his soul."[17] The inseparability and mutuality of prayer and praise are evident in Herbert's "The Altar" and Hopkins's "My prayers must meet a brazen heaven."

One of the distinctions of spiritual autobiography is its explication of the Christian motifs of theodicy, whereby a justification of the call is detailed; of colloquy, whereby the exchange that occurs between the petitioner and God is explicated; and of nutriment, whereby the spiritual sustenance that God provides to those who listen to His call is spread out for the reader. Herbert's "The Altar" and Hopkins's "My prayers must meet a brazen heaven" incorporate these themes structurally and theologically.

The petitioner's conviction that God will listen to him is evident in these poems which begin as humble disclaimers of personal holiness and integrity. In Herbert's shaped verse "The Altar," the "broken heart" is cemented by contrite tears and "meets in this frame" to praise its Creator. The ultimate praise of God results from the struggle to locate the Divine Architect and to fashion a life of ministerial service and sacrifice. The promise of communication between the soul and its Creator which this poem exhibits is stated in the Acts of the Apostles where salvation is promised to those who "call on the name of the Lord" (2:21). F.E. Hutchinson regards Herbert's lyrics as "colloquies of the soul with God or self-communings which seek to bring harmony into that complex personality of his which he analyses so unsparingly."[18]

The necessity of preparing the groundwork for God's call to each individual and then responding to the particular calling for which each soul is fitted is a Christian commonplace that underlies the works of Herbert and Hopkins. To deny the call is to refuse this basic Christian responsibility and to jeopardize the soul's fitness for the Kingdom of

---

[16] Sherwood 7.

[17] Louis J. Puhl, S.J., *The Spiritual Exercises of St. Ignatius* (Chicago: Loyola University Press, 1952) 12.

[18] F.E. Hutchinson, *The Works of George Herbert* (Oxford: Clarendon Press, 1964) xxxvii.

God. The struggles of both Herbert and Hopkins solicit periods of rejection and denial of the call, as well as confirmation and affirmation of its significance.

Herbert credits God as being the Great Poet and attributes personal triumphs and spiritual growth to God's justice, mercy, and reconciling love. Since the Church is the common ground in which his calling is nurtured, Herbert begins "The Church" section of *The Temple* by offering the "first fruits" of his life on the Altar on which he intends to fashion a sacrificial heart. As he progresses in "The Church," "his emphasis is on encounter with his audience: 'None goes out of Church as he came in, but either better or worse.'"[19] Herbert assumes his Christian responsibility with a seriousness of purpose that inspires an outreach to the particular reader as well as to the wider audience. Realizing the uniqueness of each soul, he shifts his literary and spiritual strategies to include both direct and subtle approaches in the explorations of the Christian life. "Herbert does not see, as did John Cotton, his older contemporary, any distinctions between any members of his congregation in terms of their ultimate destiny before God; all are called, equally, to the same Church and the same altar. The task of the priest, in Herbert's terms, is to find each parishioner where he is and move him from that place toward fuller involvement in the Christian life."[20] Moreover, the opening of *The Country Parson* begins with a definition of "A Pastor [as] the Deputy of Christ for the reducing [bringing back from error] of Man to the Obedience of God."[21] The function of the Parson as physician and healer is evident in most of Herbert's works. In "A Priest to the Temple," Herbert states that the country parson will be able to act as physician to his flock. He even shares with his elder brother Edward, Baron of Cherbury, an interest in the curative properties of herbs. "Home-bred medicines are...familiar for all men's bodyes."[22] Likewise, *The Country Parson* describes in prosaic form the pastor's duties, the operation of his household and his parish, his personal prayer life as well as the conduct of public worship. Both Herbert and Hopkins as spiritual physicians con-

---

[19] Wall 36.

[20] Wall 31.

[21] Wall 55.

[22] Margaret Bottrall, *Every Man A Phoenix: Studies in Seventeenth-Century Autobiography* (London: William Clowes and Sons, Ltd., 1958) 72.

sider the progress and relapse of the soul in its various stages of development.

Since human beings are embodied creatures, the exterior space they occupy and the interior space out of which they operate assume chief literary and spiritual significance in Herbert's *The Temple* poems where architecture and space serve as metaphors for the soul. Reformation members of Herbert's congregation considered themselves as temples constructed by the hand of God Who placed them in a certain space on earth reserved exclusively for them. *The Temple* is filled with such architectural allusions as windows, floor, church porch, and such monuments as altar and church. In "The Altar," Herbert reinforces his appeal to the reader's eye, first, by constructing a poem in the shape of the topic under consideration and secondly, by capitalizing words (ALTAR, HEART, SACRIFICE, ALTAR) which outline the poetic and spiritual calling to which he has adhered and to which he enjoins his reader. In this poem, therefore, the reader actually sees the truth of the recorder's experience "framed spatially as well as linguistically."[23] The physical and the spiritual are each afforded significance in the life of this Anglican minister, often misrepresented as a pious dogmatist who preferred the transcendent to the commonplace. This claim is, no doubt, rooted in Izaak Walton's *Life of Herbert* which paints him as "a Saint, unspotted of the World, full of Alms-deeds, full of Humility, and all the examples of a vertuous life" and by Nicholas Ferrar who, in his Preface to *The Temple* in 1633, describes Herbert as "a companion to the primitive Saints."[24] Conversely, Douglas Bush terms Herbert "a lover of music and of 'mirth.' Sometimes, happily, he feels his shrivelled heart recover its greenness, and then he can smell the dew and rain 'And relish versing.'"[25]

Typological poems in *The Temple* appeal to the reader's spiritual insight as well as to the physical eye and dramatize the viability and mutuality of spiritual and spatial form. Indeed, by providing a shape for the topic it signifies, Herbert allows the reader the opportunity to participate not only in the unfolding of a verbal argument, but also to form "a mental image of the place," an Ignatian method of meditation

---

[23] Sherwood 77.

[24] C.A. Patrides, "A Crown of Praise: The Poetry of Herbert." In *The English Poems of George Herbert* (London: J.M. Dent and Sons, Ltd., 1975) 6.

[25] Douglas Bush, *English Poetry: The Main Currents from Chaucer to the Present* (New York: Oxford University Press, 1963) 61.

commonly portrayed in devotional poetry in the seventeenth century.[26] Indeed, the Ignatian *Exercises*, brought to England by missionaries, had a significant impact on English literature and became a model for many treatises on meditation during the Counter-Reformation.[27] Louis L. Martz also suggests that this spirit of meditation began with Robert Southwell and extended to the Metaphysical Poets and to Milton. Indeed, "the seventeenth century was an age which favored and fostered introspection, and an emphasis upon spiritual development."[28]

Most importantly, this framing device reveals the likeness between God the Divine Architect and the poet-builder, both of whom are concerned with capitalizing on the form and function of God's dealings with His servants. "The Altar" is emblematic or, as Joseph Summers terms it, "hieroglyphic."[29] "It develops a visual argument but also presents a visual embodiment for that theme in the shape and structure of the poem itself."[30]

Albert C. Labriola supports Robert Shaw's belief that "The Altar" is in the shape of an upper-case "I," and makes an even richer contribution to this poem as a work of spiritual autobiography in his detailed treatment of the poem as a work that suggests both "the sinful egoism of the speaker...and the hieroglyph of the sacred name."[31] He maintains that the speaker in "The Altar" moves from stubborn and vainglorious impulses and pride toward sanctification in a poem that visually enacts both Old and New Testament analogues to yield a rewriting of the old dispensation and a fashioning of the new heart of humankind into "a living sacrifice of praise" to the Creator.[32]

The form of "The Altar" beckons the reader to an observation of linear symmetry where a quatrain begins and ends the poem and an indented octet comprises the middle portion. Edmund Miller makes some cogent observations on the pictorial significance of "The Altar"

---

[26] Richard Strier, *Love Known: Theology and Experience in George Herbert's Poetry* (Chicago: University of Chicago Press, 1983) 12.

[27] Martz 2.

[28] Bottrall 4.

[29] Joseph H. Summers, *George Herbert: His Religion and Art* (New York: Center for Medieval and Early Renaissance Studies, 1981) 123.

[30] Barbara Lewalski, *Protestant Poetics and the Seventeenth-Century Religious Lyric* (New Jersey: Princeton University Press, 1979) 204.

[31] Albert C. Labriola, "The Rock and the Hard Place: Biblical Typology and Herbert's 'The Altar.'" *George Herbert Journal*, 10 (1986–87), 68.

[32] Labriola, "The Rock and the Hard Place" 62.

by contrasting Herbert's poem with the Greek altar poem of Dosiadas
and the Christian and English Protestant poem "ARA Christianæ re-
ligioni."[33] He observes that Herbert's altar omits the slab or altar
proper and is, therefore, "symmetrical top to bottom as well as side to
side" to emphasize "both the symmetry of the Old Dispensation and the
New and the contrast between them."[34] When the temple was de-
stroyed according to Christ's prediction, the Altar was broken forever,
but Herbert reminds the reader of the biblical injunction that "Christ
Jesus himself [is] the capstone" (Eph. 2:20). "There is no external
stone or altar anymore because Christ has brought the sacrifice within
and raised an altar in the heart."[35]

When the reader treats this poem as spiritual autobiography, he or
she becomes aware of the discipline and uniformity of the lines where
the initial two lines and last two lines of the quartets are a decameter,
lines 3 and 4 of the opening quartet and 13 and 14 of the concluding
quartet are in octameter, and the middle section is a tetrameter. Such
regularity replicates and duplicates the Divine Architect's perfect form;
it also reinforces the value of the Logos in describing the justice and
power of the Lord of all creation Whose mysterious nature sanctifies
the human temple of stone into the sacrificial altar of the heart.

Critic Alan Heuser notes Herbert's and Hopkins's fascination "with
numbers and proportion, a mathematical bias evident in their verse
architecture. While Herbert employed the counterpoint of short lines
against long lines, Hopkins exploited the stress counterpoint of abrupt
and outriding feet within long lines. Both poets observed rigid
patterns—Herbert rendering physical arrangement of the poem on the
page significant, but Hopkins depending almost entirely on the ear to
render dynamics of syntax intelligible."[36]

Herbert's major contention is that the story of humankind's salva-
tion is ultimately not an individual's story, but God's story; the attempt
to explain how salvation occurs is the responsibility of Herbert whose
particular calling as parson and poet is to reveal God's love for His

---

[33] Edmund Miller, "Drudgerie Divine: The Rhetoric of God and Man in George
Herbert." In *Elizabethan and Renaissance Studies*, ed. Dr. James Hogg (Austria: Uni-
versität Salzburg, 1979) 113.

[34] Miller 114.

[35] Miller 116.

[36] Alan Heuser, *The Shaping Vision of Gerard Manley Hopkins* (London:Oxford
University Press, 1968) 115, n.1.

creatures. Whatever glory is achieved, therefore, is not his, but God's. As he states in the "Dedication" to *The Temple*: "Lord, my first fruits present themselves to thee;/Yet not mine neither: for from thee they came,/And must return." The speaker in "The Altar" has acquired the responsibility of priest in offering the sacrifice of praise, "which is the antitype of the Old Testament bloody sacrifice. The focus on praise [here] also inaugurates the theme of the special responsibility of the Christian poet to find fit ways to praise, relating that theme also to the typological paradigm of the Old Testament altar of stone, and New Covenant temple in the heart."[37] This convention is contained in the *schola cordis* tradition where the synecdoche of the heart is used to portray the Christian himself and to incorporate the reader into this devotional practice. The technique of synecdoche of the heart is used extensively in *The Temple* where Herbert frames the soul's journey to its Creator in metaphors suggesting engagement, dissociation, and return. Like the speaker in "The Altar," the reader, too, is "cut, framed, re-arranged, inscribed [into] a set of speaking stones."[38] He is "built into this temple, to become a dwelling place for God in the Spirit" (Eph. 2:22).

"The Altar" alludes to and restates Psalm 51:19, "My sacrifice, O God, is a contrite spirit; a heart contrite and humbled, O God, you will not spurn." Herbert as a Christian David petitions and praises God through his lyric works and invites the reader to enter into the temple framed by the poet and the Divine Architect. "Like David's heart, this heart-altar is broken and contrite but it is still a 'hard heart' cemented in stone. It must be shaped by God and not by man into a fitting altar of praise."[39] "The human heart is the *locus* where man's changing relationship with the Lord is understood and experienced.... For the reader such instruction in vision, voice, and feeling is both learned and experienced in the school of his own heart."[40]

The opening poems of *The Temple* present the relationship between the interlocutors in a rather formal and distant manner. A progression from the lord-servant relationship to a variety of relationships is devel-

---

[37] Barbara Leah Harman, *Costly Monuments* (Cambridge: Harvard University Press, 1982) 196.

[38] Harman 189.

[39] Lewalski 310.

[40] Labriola, "Herbert, Crashaw, and the *Schola Cordis* Tradition." *George Herbert Journal*, 2 (1978), 20,23.

oped through a series of experiences which comprise the Christian journey, experiences that underscore the significance and viability of biblical typology. The Old and New Testaments, therefore, mark the story of humankind's redemption and uncover the truth that Christ died for each person, not in spite of, but because of, his or her faults. "The fundamental situation of the speaker as a Christian everyman is thus posed in typological terms in this first poem: the need for his Old Testament stony altar-heart to be hewn by God's power and wholly transformed into its New Testament antitype, a heart of flesh, a temple not built with [human] hands."[41] The sanctification of the sacrifice is what the reader recognizes as the recurring motif in *The Temple*: "The Sacrifice is the beginning, middle, and end of man's redemption."[42] God's love and justice accompany yet override the individual's struggles with limitations and elicit an emotional response in both the speaker and the reader. "The self-sacrificing Lord arouses pity, gratitude, and contrition in the sinner's 'hard heart.'"[43]

In order to understand the ideas and beliefs that shaped Herbert's self-definition, it is important to situate his works in the theological, social, and political milieux out of which they emerged. The Elizabethan theater presented "the problems and contradictions of the human spirit in terms of action rather than as subjects for meditation."[44] Unlike the Elizabethan Age whose literary works, such as Spenser's masterpiece *The Faerie Queene*, were overtly didactic and were concerned with affixing a social context to the Christian life, the Stuart Age refined its theological position by turning inward and by attempting doctrinal and liturgical uniformity in the person of Archbishop Laud.[45] "Herbert's stress on the role of the visible Church represents to some extent a shift within Anglicanism away from a focus on society as the arena for Christian living and toward a greater emphasis on the value of corporate religious life for its own sake."[46] The Church, therefore, becomes for him the spiritual realm in which he chooses to live out the Christian life, having been disappointed and disillusioned with the neglect of social reform by the political realm, particularly the Parlia-

[41] Lewalski 312.
[42] Stanley Stewart, *George Herbert* (Boston: Twayne Publishers, 1986) 97.
[43] Labriola, "Herbert, Crashaw, and the *Schola Cordis* Tradition" 68.
[44] Bottrall 14.
[45] Wall 10.
[46] Wall 11.

ment of 1624 in which he had a seat.[47] His taking of Holy Orders shortly after this session of Parliament confirms his decision to serve the Church as an ecclesiastic rather than as a lay man. Herbert is situated, then, at the juncture of Elizabethan and Stuart rules and inhabits modes of conduct in keeping with each dynasty.

The Elizabethan or Tudor dynasty regarded all of English society and service to the crown as appropriate contexts for the Christian life; Herbert, likewise, reflects in his works the outreach such a context implies. Even the shape of his poems—altar, wings—suggests an active involvement in and concern for his surroundings, and his usage of the colloquy motif where he addresses the Lord reinforces the Tudor belief that God is as present in English society as in the church building. Similarly, Stuart England's emphasis on daily prayer and Bible reading finds a home in Herbert's personal life and works. Even before his stay at Bemerton, he recited the Office and grew increasingly familiar with the Bible and other devotional prayers which serve as sources for his poems and prose accounts.

It is fortunate that the Parliament of 1624 was a disappointing and disillusioning experience for Herbert. The event led him to return to the Church from which he had allowed himself a brief absence, and to embrace a life of ministerial responsibility and devotional service. His works evidence both the on-going dialogue between God and His servants, and the quotidian life of the Christian community. The synthesis of both strains is the material used to forge the prayer life of his congregation and the matter of his writings. Herbert welcomes and confronts the reader as he does his own congregation, drawing him or her into the doors of the temple to discover a richer self and a just but generous God through Whom "the whole structure is fitted together and takes shape as a holy temple in the Lord" (Eph. 2:21).

The significance of *The Country Parson* and *The Temple* as works of spiritual autobiography lies in their positing of the Church as both an ecclesiastical and social structure and as the primary means whereby the individual acquires self-definition. Such a reading of the works allows the reader to confront himself or herself, to judge himself or herself against the high standards stated in the works, and to acknowledge the shift in focus from the individual to the Creator as Herbert engages in direct address with his Lord. "We can speculate on what

---

[47] Wall 12.

cultural conditions promote an emphasis upon individual identity, but conceptions of individual identity are articulated, extended, and developed through an institution like autobiography."[48] Understandably, a consideration of Herbert's works as spiritual autobiography minimizes a mere introverted or solipsistic reading of the nature of the soul. Herbert's poems "explore a very wide range of emotions and spiritual states; such poems are once deeply personal self-probings, an 'anatomy of the soul,' and at the same time presentations of everyman's spiritual autobiography. [They] portray in general terms a movement from penitence and conversion to some higher plane of spiritual life.... They also reflect the Protestant meditative emphasis upon soliloquy, expostulation with the self and with God, self-examination, and self-questioning."[49] Indeed, as Barbara Harman suggests in *Costly Monuments*, typological poems such as "The Altar" "make representation [of the reader] possible by making the speaker's enduring account the story of others rather than the story of the self."[50]

Through hieroglyphic or typological poetry the reader is able to personalize the Pauline reminder that "you are the temple of God and the Spirit of God dwells in you.... For the temple of God is holy, and you are that temple" (1 Cor. 3:16). Summers points out that Herbert establishes "the first poems within 'The Church' (the central section of *The Temple*) [on] the altar upon which the following poems (Herbert's sacrifice) are offered."[51] In "The Altar," Herbert modifies the traditional shape of the Old Testament altar of sacrifice by using it to signify, not only a communion table, but more so his beliefs concerning the relationship between the heart, the work of art, and the praise of God. Perhaps two of the most convincing proofs for the involvement of the reader in the works of Herbert lie in the fact that "The Altar" was rendered into musical form in 1671 by John Playford and is contained in his "Psalms and Hymns in Solemn Musick" edition, and that it is transcribed by Louise Schleiner.[52] There are various ways by which

---

[48] Elizabeth W. Bruss, *Autobiographical Acts* (Baltimore and London: The Johns Hopkins University Press, 1976) 5.

[49] Lewalski 51; 171.

[50] Harman 196.

[51] Summers, *Geroge Herbert* 142.

[52] Schleiner's transcription occurs in her article "The Composer as Reader: A Setting of George Herbert's 'The Altar'" in the *Musical Quarterly*, LXI (1975), 426. Patrides, *George Herbert: The Critical Heritage* (London: Routledge and Kegan Paul, 1983) 366.

the Logos is translated into discernible form. That the musicality of Herbert's verse finds a consonance in the spirit of classic John Playford and contemporary Louise Schleiner attests to its universality, its attempt to vindicate the ways of the Creator, and, most importantly, its insistence on subordinating human life and history to this Creator.

Like Herbert, Gerard Manley Hopkins's voice also celebrates the revealed world and demonstrates the call of the Christian disciple by addressing the struggles that the soul encounters in arriving at its spiritual goal. The voice in Hopkins's works also subordinates his will to God, but not before a total engagement in the wrestling process strains the speaker as well as the reader in an intensely dramatic encounter. Both Herbert and Hopkins depict the *agon* experience of the soul in a more overt and confrontational manner than did previous devotional writers. The writing of the experience is rooted, nonetheless, in the face-to-face directness evident in "the dialogue of the Elizabethan stage, which was composed in intimate contact with vernacular colloquialism as well as with classical rhetoric. The sixteenth-century and seventeenth-century religious poetry of Herbert's time furthers the confrontational ways of treating the self [and] suggests Hopkins' later stark self-confrontation."[53]

While Hopkins's dates (1844–89) suggest his placement among the Romantics and Victorians, his rejection of "the major tenets of Romanticism [and] the whole complex variety of Romantic themes of imagination, perception, and creation...enacts a decidedly post-Romantic religious ontology."[54] Furthermore, his expansive religious thought prevents him from enjoying an affinity with the Victorians. He refuses to give poetry the power, as does Matthew Arnold, to be substituted for religion, and he denies the Victorian morality, declared by such critics as Benjamin Jowett, Greek professor and tutor at Balliol, that "A man is not a man who does not control his passions."[55] For Hopkins, the words of a poem are not enough to serve God or humankind. The struggle to fit finite words to the infinite Logos leads him, as it does Herbert, to a continual discovery of God in the physical world. Both

---

[53] Walter J. Ong, S.J., *Hopkins, the Self, and God* (Toronto: Toronto University Press, 1986) 137–38.

[54] Marylou Motto, *"Mined with a Motion": The Poetry of Gerard Manley Hopkins* (New Jersey: Rutgers University Press, 1984) 1.

[55] Paddy Kitchen, *Gerard Manley Hopkins* (Massachusetts: West Hanover and Plympton, 1979) 33,35.

men's works explore the spiritual life in highly conscious and inventive forms. "The two poets trace their moments of grace and desolation within a framework of believed truth; both canons are conspicuous in their experimentation with the word and with the poem. Finally, both poets make significant use of the senses to aid in their assent, relying on the world for revelation of God's word."[56]

It is evident from his letters that Hopkins knew and admired Herbert's work. In one of his letters, Hopkins compares Herbert and Henry Vaughan and says that, while Vaughan "has more glow and freedom than Herbert [he has] less fragrant sweetness [and is not] Herbert's equal."[57] In *The Shaping Vision of Gerard Manley Hopkins*, Alan Heuser observes that "Influence on Hopkins of the baroque verse of the seventeenth century began with his reading of Herbert.... [M]uch of Hopkins' imagery may be understood through study of baroque emblem-literature and the repository of classical and biblical symbols."[58] As Hopkins underwent his religious conversion from Anglicanism to Catholicism, he wrote in a manner that echoed in substantive fashion the biblical language, allusions, and constructions of Herbert, who came to represent for Hopkins "the most attractive aspects of English religious art and life."[59] In a letter frequently cited and printed initially by G.F. Lahey, Hopkins's close Oxford friend William Addis states that "love of Herbert was [Hopkins's] strongest tie to the English Church."[60] It follows that, as the time for Hopkins's conversion approached, he examined and re-echoed the biblical imagery and poetic diction of Herbert, along with and in contrast to that of his contemporaries.

Although Herbert and Hopkins wrote in relative obscurity and chose not to publish during their lives, "one has the sense that Herbert, much more than Hopkins, consciously intended his work to be published. He shaped the volume [*The Temple*] carefully and left it to a friend [Nicholas Ferrar], asking that he decide whether it was worthy of publication. Hopkins may have had a similar plan in mind as he looked over the copies of his poems [Robert] Bridges had made.... Furthermore, Hopkins left his papers to the Society of Jesus, but the

---

[56] Motto 8.
[57] Motto 170, n.16.
[58] Heuser 117.
[59] W. Johnson, "Halfway to a New Land" 116.
[60] W. Johnson, "Halfway to a New Land" 116.

poetry went to Bridges."[61] While the writings of both men are situated in the world, it is Hopkins who tries to seize the world with particular conviction and portray it in a voice that captures the struggle with the words and with the world in a manner that challenges the deceptively simple messages of Herbert. Nevertheless, both poets impugn the elevation of the self and the reliability of the poet's voice in depicting the meaning of life. "Unlike the Romantic visionary who would create the world, the Hopkins speaker goes out to observe and respond to God's creation in the world" and so resembles the Herbert speaker in finding God in creation.[62]

The speakers in the works of Herbert and Hopkins reflect the gap of two centuries that separates the authors themselves and recounts the difference of emphasis between Anglican and Roman Catholic traditions. Herbert merges the "I" with the eternal Godhead to whom he relegates all experience and existence; Hopkins uses the "I" to portray the depth of feeling—the in-stress—that eventually unites with the Godhead. The response of John Henry Newman, Hopkins's mentor, to the world confirms Hopkins's belief in the primacy of human nature, "which disbelieves logical proof at times, yet at other times believes wholeheartedly although it has no scientific basis for belief." [63]Newman, whose own conversion from the Anglican to the Roman Catholic priesthood significantly altered his outlook and goals, became one of the most influential men in the nineteenth century. At the end of Discourse Five in *The Idea of a University* (1853), Newman declares that "We attain to heaven by using this world well, though it is to pass away; we perfect our nature, not by undoing it, but by adding to it what is more than nature, and directing it towards aims higher than its own."[64] Perhaps this incarnational view of existence accounts for Hopkins's lively description of things, of their inner nature, their embodied life which he terms "inscape," in a writing that welcomes both the natural and the supernatural.

Most of Hopkins's poems, therefore, employ the seasons as the basis for a depiction of life. The tone of "My prayers must meet a brazen heaven" (1865), written at age twenty-one, is a foreshadowing

---

[61] Motto 171, n.17.

[62] Motto 12.

[63] Motto 13.

[64] John Henry Cardinal Newman, *The Idea of a University*, ed. Martin J. Svaglic (New York: Holt, Rinehart and Winston, 1962) 93.

of the "terrible" sonnets of twenty years later in its usage of harsh, cacophonous diction to suggest an inaccessible and rather inhospitable heaven.[65] This speaker is overwhelmed by his sin and so meets with the consequences of sin which are, as Milton writes in Book IX of *Paradise Lost*, "distance and distaste,/Anger and just rebuke" (ll. 9–10).[66]

The hardness of heaven's gates prohibits the speaker from gaining the attentive ear of God, and reminds us of the heart of the speaker in Herbert's "The Altar" which is "cemented with tears." Images of cementing in Herbert and of molding in Hopkins show the reader how both writers merge the earthly and the transcendent in grounding their prayer experience, an encounter that often begins as a "Battling with God" (Hopkins) and ends as an altar of sacrifice (Herbert) where the heart and the Victim become one. Here Hopkins engages in two battles simultaneously: the seeking of entrance into "a brazen heaven," the failure of which only confirms his "long success of sin," and of engaging in a "warfare of my lips in truth," the failure of which leads to the prayer of desire. More substantial than an outpouring of "tears," the "warfare" produces "a fortified city, a pillar of iron, a wall of brass," which God promises to His servants. Rather than viewing this as a poem of total darkness, the reader senses the speaker's growth in perseverance and spiritual transformation.

Hopkins entered "My prayers must meet a brazen heaven" in his collection of poetry on September 7, 1865.[67] Paul Mariani suggests that the tone of self-loathing which dominates the poem might have resulted, in part, from "his refusal to accept Catholicism outwardly, for it is clear that he had already, probably since the preceding March, seen its validity for him, although it took a year more to make the assent outwardly."[68] The speaker in the poem confesses his own uncleanness and inability "to buoy my heart above," to transcend the heaviness of his heart. The experience of "the dark night of the soul," which will continue to accompany Hopkins in his spiritual journey, has its antecedents in early poems such as this one whose structure and

---

[65] Gardner 82.

[66] John T. Shawcross, ed., *The Complete Poetry of John Milton* (New York: Doubleday and Co., Inc., 1971).

[67] Paul L. Mariani, *A Commentary on the Complete Poems of Gerard Manley Hopkins* (New York: Cornell University Press, 1970) 31.

[68] Mariani, *A Commentary on the Complete Poems of Gerard Manley Hopkins* 31.

stanzaic pattern underscore the weightiness of his heart and the severity
of his religious experience.

"My prayers must meet a brazen heaven" is comprised of two oc-
taves in iambic tetrameter. Images of brass, iron, and clay in the sec-
ond octave render concrete and severely control the personal desolation
in the first octave. The diction is extremely direct. There is no experi-
mentation or playfulness in literary techniques, language, or rhythm.
In spite of the popular misconception that Hopkins's poetry is extreme-
ly esoteric and abstruse, experimental and sophisticated, "when he
experiences a religious depression, as here in his sense of sin and
damnation or in his heroic effort in his last years to seal his will totally
to God, Hopkins without exception employs a severe style in which
each word is weighed, like chiseled stone fitted into place."[69]

The very act of "Battling with God" and of wrestling with his own
angel or shadow now becomes the prayer of the speaker. It is evident
from this treatment of Herbert's "The Altar" and Hopkins's "My
prayers must meet a brazen heaven" that prayer is not solely what St.
John Damascene defined as "the lifting up of the mind and heart to
God." A consideration of these two poems as spiritual autobiography
amplifies this definition to preclude a spiritual battle waged in the
schola cordis tradition of a "harden'd" heart that is alternately "ce-
mented with tears" and "mingled with clay." This type of prayer at-
tempts articulation but meets instead a "hold[ing of] my peace" as well
as "A warfare of my lips in truth." Active and deep personal involve-
ment, underscored by the usage of the personal pronoun in both poems,
and by colloquy, whereby the speaker addresses God directly as he
struggles to find a logical answer to God's ways to humankind, are
apparent in these two corresponding poems of Herbert and Hopkins.

The difficulty Hopkins experiences in his spiritual growth is like-
wise recorded in Herbert's "The Quiddity," a poem composed of three
quatrains written in iambic tetrameter, as is Hopkins's "My prayers
must meet a brazen heaven." "Quiddity" is a scholastic term for the
true nature, or essence, of a thing.[70] This term is comparable to Hop-
kins's "inscape," which is similarly defined as the intrinsic "thisness"
or haecceitas that distinguishes one element of being from another,
"the inimitable and distinctive 'design' or 'pattern' of a particular

---

[69] Mariani, A Commentary on the Complete Poems of Gerard Manley Hopkins 31–32.
[70] Wall 186, n.147.

thing. Like [Duns] Scotus before him Hopkins' concern was with the individualistic differences in things."[71] The term "inscape" suggests "'shape' and 'creation' so that Hopkins designates the 'scapes' of the world as emblems of God's dynamic creativity. This facet becomes an important link with his Ignatian spirituality in his later thinking. The accompanying term, 'instress,' is a term that appears many times in his writing. It is a principle of being which keeps a thing in existence."[72]

"The Quiddity," like "Misery," and "A True Hymn," is a self-conscious poem that continues the prayer-praise motif, reinforces the significance of the common and the ordinary in the quotidian life of the Christian community, and treats the writing of poetry as an exercise that is critical to spiritual awareness. The poem begins with a direct address to "My God" and proceeds, through a series of negations, to catalogue what "a verse is not": a crown, a point of honor, or gay suit, hawk, banquet, renown, good sword, lute. By applying the *via negativa* method, Herbert qualifies the role of poetry, and in the final two lines states what a verse is: that which unites the writer and the Author of life. "Since, through verse, the speaker is with God, poetry thus is seen to excel all other goods or human activities."[73] Images of struggle and warfare are interspersed with banqueting and ludic images to depict the embracing of contraries that Herbert aligns with poetic and spiritual regeneration. Despite the deceptively simple definition of the nature of his poetry, "Herbert's direct identification of his poetry with [the word] 'use' [in the penultimate line—'But it is that which while I use/I am with thee, and *Most take all.*'—] has gone both unannotated and unexplicated" until Heather A.R. Asals's study *Equivocal Predication.*[74] Asals alludes to Augustine's *De Doctrina* where he states that "Some things are to be enjoyed, others to be used, and there are others which are to be enjoyed and used."[75] Poetry for Herbert, as well as for Hopkins, is a vessel that will lead them to God. The journey motif reinforces the *homo viator* and strongly cautions the reader

---

[71] Samuel John Hazo, "An Analysis of 'Inscape' in the Poetry of Gerard Manley Hopkins." Master's Thesis. Duquesne University, 1955, 25.

[72] David A. Downes, *Gerard Manley Hopkins: A Study of His Ignatian Spirit* (London: Vision Press Ltd., 1960) 28.

[73] Wall 186.

[74] Heather A.R. Asals, *Equivocal Predication: George Herbert's Way to God* (Toronto: University of Toronto Press, 1981) 57.

[75] Asals 57.

that many shipwrecks and turmoils accompany the wanderer *en route* to God. Poetry aids in articulating these experiences and unites the speaker and reader with their Creator: "while I use/I am with thee." Poetic diction and literary techniques accompany the Christian disciple on the journey home but, as the closing line suggests, verse is only one passage the soul uses in arriving at its destination to God. "[Language] finds no fixed harbour in single definition—for it only 'uses' the oneness of earthly sound to convey the totality of God."[76] The "totality of God" is what Herbert and Hopkins seek to describe in their works; however, both writers are also fully aware that "the enjoyment of poetry in and for itself" is an inferior and abusive strain which hinders the true depiction of the Logos.[77]

One of the chief sources of the Christian's and the poet's desolation is his inability to praise God properly. Yet the attempt must be made, for this is "the portion" or the proper end of humankind. In "Misery," the speaker also begins with a direct address to God and continues by negating the ability of the "clay heart" to "praise thy name.... How shall infection/Presume on thy perfection?" (ll.31;35–36). The progress of the soul from complaint to repentance to praise is the itinerary that leads to ultimate communion with God. Writing furnishes the argument or justification—the quiddity—of the spiritual experience.

"A True Hymn" is "Herbert's most direct and extended treatment of the relative values of sincerity and art."[78] This religious lyric is a clear demonstration of Herbert's intention to devote his writings to "the fineness which a hymn or psalm affords" and to accord the highest value to those works that attempt to fit the lines to the composition of the soul. If the words merely rhyme, and individual engagement of mind and soul are missing, God "justly complains." "This poem is not itself put forth as a 'true hymn' but rather as a piece defining the term. The heart's few words are the true hymn in the poem."[79] "The inability to praise is a source of grief because praise is the only mandated sacrifice after the cross of Love abolished the eternal sacrifices of

---

[76] Asals 60.
[77] Asals 58.
[78] Strier 201.
[79] Strier 205.

propitiation under the Law."[80] In "The Parson's Library" of *The Country Parson*, Herbert writes that "the chief thing, which God in Scriptures requires is to worship him in truth, and spirit" (John 4:24).[81] The speaker assures the reader that "God doth supplie the want" of the "scant verse" and accepts what appears to be, by worldly standards, an artistic failure. The stamp of God's approval on the tablet of the heart is signified by Herbert's usage of anthropomorphism where God writes "Loved." This action does not imply that God completes or perfects the task of the speaker; such a view would deny the free will of the Christian disciple and remove the dignity God had primordially bestowed on him or her in declaring that "whatever the man called each of them [created beings] would be its name" (Gen. 2:19).

This selection of Herbert's and Hopkins's works combines prayer and poetry in the hope expressed by Herbert in Chapter IV of *The Country Parson*, titled "The Parson's Knowledge," that the Parson serve as "a commerce in knowledge between the servants of God, for the planting both of love, and humility."[82] Herbert's and Hopkins's dual vocations as parson and poet enrich and ennoble the genre of spiritual autobiography. By utilizing the Bible, their private meditations, as well as their literary and theological scholarship, these two country parsons and poets lead the reader into "the secrets of God" that they articulate with design and intent.

---

[80] John R. Mulder, "George Herbert's *The Temple*: Design and Methodology." *Seventeenth-Century News*, 31 (1973), 38.

[81] Wall 105.

[82] Wall 59.

Chapter Two

"Ah!" Creation: The Sacrament of the Soul's Encounter with God

> All things counter, original, spáre, strange;
> Whatever is fickle, frecklèd (who knows how?)
> With swíft, slów; sweet, sóur; adazzle, dim;
> He fathers-forth whose beauty is pást change:
> Práise hím.
> (Hopkins, "Pied Beauty")

BOTH HERBERT AND HOPKINS view commonplace realities and nature, in particular, as the "outward signs instituted by Christ" that grace the life of the Christian disciple and provide the means by which he or she apprehends permanence. The works of these two writers reflect their theological belief that a disciplined and evolving vision allows the reader to see through the life of things into the life of God. Their nature poems, in particular, enact the Pauline doctrine: "Since the creation of the world, invisible realities, God's eternal power and divinity, have become visible, recognized through the things He has made" (Rom. 1:20).

This sacramental outlook finds a correspondence in the ordinary occurrences of daily life that reject any dualism between matter and spirit. Jerome Bump suggests that Hopkins denied the heretical Manichean split between matter and spirit that was popular during his age and that Hopkins's "conversion to Catholicism was part of his revolt against this antithetical view of reality."[1] Hopkins's idea of poetry as an attempt at portraying opposites that unexpectedly come together is reminiscent of a passage in the fourteenth chapter of Samuel Taylor Coleridge's *Biographia Literaria* (1817) in which he describes Imagination as a power which:

> reveals itself in the balance or reconciliation of opposite or discordant qualities: of sameness, with difference; of the general with the concrete; the idea

---

[1] Jerome Bump, *Gerard Manley Hopkins* (Boston: Twayne Publishers, 1982) 58–59.

with the image; the individual with the representative; the sense of novelty and freshness with old and familiar objects; a more than usual state of emotion with more than usual order.[2]

Likewise, Herbert had the capacity to conjoin the seemingly disparate elements and to recognize their inner worth and uniqueness, qualities that undoubtedly attracted Hopkins and amplified his theories of *haecceitas* or "thisness," inscape, and instress. The embracing of the contraries of human experience and the ability to allow the discordant phenomena of life to nourish the inner spirit further appealed to Hopkins in his struggle to find a way of thinking, living, and praying his faith amid the complexities of his contemporary society. "That universe which, in an earlier period, had been an intelligible metaphor for God's sustaining and governing power changed into a metaphor that hides its analogy, that is to say, a symbol of hieroglyph—it was no longer unambiguous."[3] Like Herbert, Hopkins's revolt against simplistic dualisms reinforces an "Anglo-Catholicism that transcends such dualisms as heaven vs. earth and life vs. death."[4]

Herbert's attempts "to convey God's presence and his grace, his active but invisible participation in the Christian life," is frequently accomplished "in the natural world and in the Christian speaker's claims of divine participation in his inner life."[5] The speaker in Herbert's poems, therefore, much like the speaker in Hopkins's poems, allows nature to serve as the intermediary between divinity and humanity. The natural world becomes "a medium that expresses God, a means God uses to communicate with mankind."[6] Often natural occurrences and the resultant spiritual condition are depicted as causal in the providential scheme, leading the reader to an immersion of himself or herself in the particular essence of the natural world as it reveals the nature of God. Like Herbert, Hopkins firmly believes that the "dearest freshness deep down things" ("God's Grandeur," 1.10) contain and manifest the splendor of God as comprehensively and benignly as do

---

[2] Bernard Bergonzi, *Gerard Manley Hopkins* (New York: Macmillan Publishing Co., Inc., 1977) 178.

[3] Mulder 45.

[4] Mulder 45.

[5] Diana Benet, *Secretary of Praise: The Poetic Vocation of George Herbert* (Columbia: University of Missouri Press, 1984) 48.

[6] Benet 48.

those enjoying the beatific vision. For Hopkins, nature's finery distills God's unfallen, protective, omnipresent nature and beckons a posture of adoration and awe ("ah!", 1.14). Since the Holy Ghost broods over it, "nature is never spent" (1.9). Peter Milward posits that Hopkins's use of "Oh" and "Ah," while determined by considerations of contextual euphony, is also nuanced by the quality of enthusiasm, of that "instress" or inner energy "which the poet delighted to observe in things and in which he recognized the operation of the Holy Spirit. And so the outcome of all his poetry may be seen as an elaboration on the fundamental hymn of praise in the Judeo-Christian tradition."[7]

Although as refined a critic as T.S. Eliot calls Hopkins a "nature poet," influenced as Hopkins was by a reading of John Ruskin and an absorption in the designs of nature, nature observation is not an end in itself for Hopkins as it was for many Romantic writers. "For Hopkins, the central fact of the world is the mystery of the Incarnation, Christ the Word (the Logos or Idea) become flesh by assuming matter. The Incarnation is operative in time and space, in Hopkins' time as in Christ's, in Wales as in Galilee. Therefore, God's workings can be discerned in the phenomenological world; there is spiritual meaning, news of God everywhere for those who are properly receptive."[8]

Hopkins's sonnets, of which "God's Grandeur" (1877) is paramount, demonstrate the influence of Milton on Hopkins's "rhythmical experiments" with sprung rhythm as it embodies the "charged" emotion of the speaker in an attempt to free his rhetoric.[9] "He was attempting to employ in his sonnets a rhythm which would smoothly yet precisely capture the stress of his personal poetic voice."[10] In a letter to Robert Bridges of February 15, 1879, Hopkins admits that "No doubt my poetry errs on the side of oddness. I hope in time to have a more balanced and Miltonic style. But as air, melody, is what strikes me most of all in music and design in painting, so design, pattern or what I am in the habit of calling 'inscape' is what I above all aim at in

---

[7] Peter Milward, S.J., "Exclamations in Hopkins's Poetry." *Renascence*, 42, 1989–90 (Fall-Winter); 1–2, 118.

[8] Mariani, *A Commentary on the Complete Poems of Gerard Manley Hopkins* 91.

[9] Mariani, *A Commentary on the Complete Poems of Gerard Manley Hopkins* 86.

[10] Mariani, *A Commentary on the Complete Poems of Gerard Manley Hopkins* 89.

poetry."[11] Two years previous, in a letter of August 21, 1877, he explained to Bridges his usage of sprung rhythm as "the nearest to the rhythm of prose, that is the native and natural rhythm of speech, the least forced, the most rhetorical and emphatic of all possible rhythms, combining as it seems to me, opposite and, one wd. have thought, incompatible excellences."[12]

The 1877 sonnets are successful in revealing to the reader the presence of Christ in nature. These poems were written "when Hopkins was studying theology in Wales, 'always to me a mother of Muses.' It was the time of immediate preparation for the reception of the priesthood. He was happy at the time and the countryside buoyed him up. His study of Scotus deepened [as did] his admiration and love of the inscapes of this world, which were to him news and word of God."[13] Indeed, in "God's Grandeur" and "Pied Beauty" he explores his priestly vocation by celebrating creation. The speaker in these sonnets finds himself out-of-doors, in the pastoral setting where God is readily accessible. His nature poems seem to parallel the growth in nature with the vibrant and youthful spirit of humanity. "Often posed as superlatives, an absolute and universal statement begins these poems, seeming to anchor the images which follow in the certitude of cognition: 'Nothing is so beautiful as Spring-'in "Spring"; 'The world is chárged wíth the grandeur of God' in "God's Grandeur"; 'Glory be to God for dappled things' in "Pied Beauty"; 'Look at the stars! look, look up at the skies' in "The Starlight Night." Although [these poems are] shaped by design and offer dogma at the outset, the reader's experience of the poems centers in the accumulated empirical evidence gathered from the world,

---

[11] Abbott, *The Letters of Gerard Manley Hopkins to Robert Bridges* 66. W.H. Gardner in his *Gerard Manley Hopkins: A Study of Poetic Idiosyncrasy in Relation to Poetic Tradition* (rep. 1966) states that "While professing to imitate Milton [in one of Hopkins's Letters] [Hopkins] acknowledges Shakespeare's ascendancy by being, in effect, more like him" (107). John R. Mulder's parenthetical sentence in "George Herbert's *The Temple: Design and Methodology*"—("Shakespeare's Sonnets XXIII, XXIV, and XXVI are apt descriptions of the Poet's progress, the use of perspective, and the typological method of *The Temple*.")—merits recognition and further exploration. [*Seventeenth-Century News*, 31 (1973), 43].

[12] Abbott, *The Letters of Gerard Manley Hopkins to Robert Bridges* 46.

[13] W.A.M. Peters, S.J., *Gerard Manley Hopkins: A Critical Essay Towards the Understanding of His Poetry* (Oxford, London: Alden and Mowbray Ltd., 1970) 41.

the lyricism that the poems then proclaim a manifestation of the absolute."[14]

In addition to demonstrating how a reading of poetry as spiritual autobiography can exhibit the wrestling of the soul and the colloquy between the human and the divine, Hopkins's advances in diction and poetic techniques also include significant contributions to the Petrarchan sonnet tradition and its careful balance between the octet and sestet. For example, the octet of "God's Grandeur" provides a justification for the creation of the world. The double stress on the words "chárged with" underscores the Jesuit motto "Ad majorem Dei gloriam," "to the greater glory of God." God's grandeur is manifested in the simple but rhythmical objects of life—shook foil, oil, toil, and soil—and penetrates the world as with an electric charge. It is present in and through the phenomena of nature, but most pointedly in those persons who are prepared to receive this epiphany. Although the marks of the previous and current generations have "seared," "bleared," and "smeared" the sensibilities and sensitivities of humankind and the glory of the environment, "nature is never spent" (1.9), as the sestet establishes. The inscaping of the fact that the present as well as the previous generations share the guilt of ignoring the epiphany by having trod down the soil occurs with Hopkins's placing the word "then" next to the word "now" in line four of the octet, anticipating the superimposition of the Holy Ghost "over the bent/World" at the poem's conclusion. The Holy Ghost with its warm breast and bright wings grounds God's love with a certitude of wonder and awe, renewal and regeneration. The power of the sestet lies in its assurance of nature's and humankind's survival.

Although many generations have followed their own "bent" and have ignored the Light that beckons to be recognized, the heavens will continue "to declare the glory of God and the firmament [to] proclaim his handiwork" as is demonstrated by Psalm 19, one of the biblical analogues for this poem.

Particularly in this poem and in "Pied Beauty," Hopkins's belief in the blending of the incarnational and sacramental vision is clearly marked. In "God's Grandeur," Hopkins writes of how God's grace and grandeur work through nature and renew all of creation while the Holy Ghost presides over the bent world, a world that is enslaved by original sin and the primordial injunction of earning its bread by the sweat of

---

[14] Motto 53, 54.

its brow, but also a world bent, perhaps, in adoration and praise of its Creator. When viewed in this way, Ruskin's critical term "landscapes" is helpful in defining "the matrix of images artists use to express their paradisal or demonic dreams of human life."[15] In his sacramental sonnets, Hopkins uses sonnet divisions—an octet of two quatrains and a sestet of two tercets—to allow the reader to imagine a scene, to apply each of the five senses, and to glean from this meditative exercise a personal or moral lesson.

W.H. Gardner comments on the significance of what is considered the most important image in the poem—the exact meaning of "foil"—by referring to one of Hopkins's letters to Bridges wherein he explains the term. Hopkins writes:

> I mean foil in the sense of leaf or tinsel, and no other word whatever will give the effect I want. Shaken gold-foil gives off broad glares like sheet lightning and also, and this is true of nothing else, owing to its zigzag dents and creasings and network of small many cornered facets, a sort of fork lightning too.[16]

Gardner maintains that "God's Grandeur" "presents a factual antimony and then, in the sestet, tries to remove the contradiction and balance the account."[17] The sestet echoes Milton's belief, stated in the zoomorphic image at the outset of *Paradise Lost*, that, despite the worst efforts of humanity, the Spirit of God continues to speak through nature:

> ...and with mighty wings outspread
> Dove-like satst brooding on the vast Abyss
> And mad'st it pregnant
>   I. 20–22.

Gardner is quick to point out that, although Hopkins seems to echo Milton, there is a "set purpose and a significant change of tense" in Hopkins. "The process of creation is still going on" in "God's Grandeur."[18] The creative Spirit of Love that was present at the creation

---

[15] David A. Downes, "Beatific Landscapes in Hopkins." *Hopkins Quarterly*, 1 (1974), 142.

[16] Gardner 230.

[17] Gardner 232.

[18] Gardner 233.

of the universe still hovers over it, providing it with beauty, light, and protection. The realization of the direct instress or place of God in the world of nature awakens the alert reader to a response of wonder and "ah!" in the "deep down things" of the quotidian experience.

For Hopkins, the universe serves as a bond linking God and humanity. "God's Grandeur" is a poeticizing of St. Ignatius's "Contemplation to Obtain Love" in the *Spiritual Exercises* where he "urges man to look on the sacred world about him as an effort of God to communicate His love to man, as a vision of God's love."[19] Hopkins writes in a commentary on Ignatius: "All things therefore are charged with love, are charged with God and if we know how to touch them give off sparks and take fire, yield drops and flow, ring and tell of him."[20] The entire universe is charged with the grandeur of God because all is a part of His Mystical Body. As the reader enjoys the lyricism of the Milton counterpointed rhythm of this piece, the spiritual world breaks through and the value of reading the poem as spiritual autobiography is realized. The reader is challenged "to inscape (the Greek *scope* for 'look') by finding in the earth a tabernacle of the divine dwelling."[21] "God's Grandeur" reminds the reader that God turns all things, even humankind's abuse of nature and refusal of redemption, to the good. "The interstices of physical and human nature are filled with his presence through the *kenosis*. The very rod of chastisement has been turned against himself and is now a staff of leadership held in the hand of the Good Shepherd."[22] Subsequently, the image of the rod becomes the "lashed rod" in *The Wreck of the Deutschland* and assumes greater substantive value in the "terrible" sonnets. Therefore, through the very process of writing these poems, Hopkins invites his readers to the advanced scope of meditative silence.

The *kenosis* or self-emptying of Christ finds further signification in Hopkins's "Pied Beauty," one of his experimental "curtailed or 'Curtal-sonnets' of ten and one-half lines."[23] The imperative dictated at the outset—of glorifying God for "dappled" or diverse things—finds

---

[19] John Pick, *Gerard Manley Hopkins: Priest and Poet* (New York: Oxford University Press, 1966) 63.

[20] Devlin 195.

[21] James Finn Cotter, *Inscape: The Christology and Poetry of Gerard Manley Hopkins* (Pennsylvania: University of Pittsburgh Press, 1972) 172.

[22] Cotter 172.

[23] Mariani, *A Commentary on the Complete Poems of Gerard Manley Hopkins* 113.

its analogue in the Pauline tradition where the author kneels "before the Father from whom every family in heaven and on earth receives its name" (Eph. 3:14–15). This poem reinforces the Christian motif of theodicy by justifying the creation of the universe and of humanity posited in "God's Grandeur." Moreover, it exemplifies how humankind's purpose is "to inscape reality, to unify it through his encounter with Christ the Son of God and Son of Man. The final 'Praíse hím' of the sonnet counterpoints and climaxes the whole descending movement of the poem from the 'skies of couple-colour,' down to the landscapes and mundane trades. All things opposite and individual at last coalesce in an abrupt command to ascend to the Father."[24]

"Pied Beauty" begins and ends with an exhortation to give honor and glory to God, a Being of infinite variety, creativity, energy, and stability. In his *Confessions*, St. Augustine describes God as "most ancient Beauty, ever-old and ever-new," and the world's beauty as being "composed of contraries, not in figure, but in nature."[25] The two-word coda concluding the sonnet—"Praíse hím"—reinstates and amplifies the first line of the sestet ("Glory be to God for dappled things–") by "throwing the ten-line sonnet off balance in a most satisfactory way, even while they introduce the listeners to a world of changeless values beyond the world of 'fickle' sensible things."[26] That Hopkins rejoiced in variety and multiplicity, in things that are "counter, original, spáre, strange" (1.7), is evident in this poem which demonstrates his belief and reinforces his Jesuit training that the more distinctive an object is, the more unique and personal a revelation of God it manifests. This is, undoubtedly, why he felt particularly grateful for "dappled things," for "couple-colour skies," for "rose-moles all in stipple" upon the bellies of trout, for all the landscapes that show forth the contrast of black wings on golden finches, for variegated pastureland and meadowland, and for the distinctive "gear and tackle and trim" of all the existing trades. This poem demonstrates the influence of Duns Scotus in its intense particularity and distinctiveness of natural things: in the thisness of things. It is also a "search for a beatitude in

[24] Cotter 185.

[25] Donald McChesney, *A Hopkins Commentary: An Explanatory Commentary on the Main Poems, 1867–89* (New York: New York University Press, 1968) 71.

[26] Alison G. Sulloway, *Gerard Manley Hopkins and the Victorian Temper* (New York: Columbia University Press, 1972) 107.

the landscape of a culture...that often fails to examine aesthetic expression for spiritual meaning."[27]

"Pied Beauty" serves as a paean, a hymn of praise, in honor of the Creator of "dappled things." "This epithet 'dapple' is one of Hopkins's favorites, and a perpetual delight in varicolored beauty is a striking characteristic of his poetic interests. The falcon in 'The Windhover' is described as 'dapple-dawn-drawn' and in *The Wreck of the Deutschland* (st.5), [the speaker] cries, 'I kiss my hand to the dappled-with-damson west.'"[28] The verb tense describing the act of creation here, as in "God's Grandeur," remains in the present, the continuous present signifying God's presence in the world: "He fathers-forth whose beauty is past change" (l.19). "The world's pied beauty is constant through time; beauty's imperative demand on man is equally so. In fact, the force of the poem's final line makes us recognize the poem's opening line—'Glory be to God for dappled things-'—as the imperative it is," an injunction directed also toward the speaker's profound duty and the author's priestly responsibility.[29]

His technical genius allows Hopkins to describe the uniqueness and wonder of all things. "By creating a linguistic unit such as 'fresh-firecoal chestnut-falls' out of an adjective, noun, and verb, he suggests that what he saw could not be simply classified, that some of its individuality resided in the intersections of our categories."[30] The rich variety and mutability of nature are revealed through the diction and poetic techniques to suggest the ever-evolving and dynamic relationship of a God Who is both immanent and transcendent in His dealings with His creation and His creatures.

The plans of the Original Architect for the creation of the world and of humankind are curiosities for the inquisitive Herbert and Hopkins that beckon to be treated with poetic imagination and scriptural certitude. When considered as spiritual autobiography, the following poems enlighten the reader and stimulate his or her intellectual and theological perspective to a theodicy or justification of God's ways to His people: Herbert's "The Pulley" and "The World" and Hopkins's "The Starlight Night," "As kingfishers catch fire," and "Spring."

---

[27] Downes, "Beatific Landscapes in Hopkins" 142.
[28] Weyand 287.
[29] Motto 83.
[30] Bump, *Gerard Manley Hopkins* 154.

In St. Paul's first letter to the Corinthians, he conveys to his readers two important spiritual lessons on the idea of a building. He instructs them that they are to build the structure of their lives as a quality, indestructible building to be aligned with Christ's life. He also assures them that each person is a holy temple of God by posing a rhetorical question to them: "Are you not aware that you are the temple of God, and that the Spirit of God dwells in you?... For the temple of God is holy, and you are that temple" (1 Cor. 3:16-17). The indwelling of God that constitutes the *schola cordis* tradition finds significance for Herbert and Hopkins in the inner nature of the Christian disciple as well as in the external world of nature. Both writers see in their own written attempts to praise God the connection between praise and song that King David found when he commanded his soul to "Awake" so as to "chant your praise among the nations" (Ps. 57:9-10). By analogizing the soul to a "stately house" as Herbert does in "The World," and by giving it a restless disposition as he does in "The Pulley," he succeeds in conveying its ambiguous and contradictory nature. Since all the works comprising *The Temple* are frames which support the human soul, the temple of God is afforded the dignity it deserves as each poetic and prosaic construction addresses the building of a spiritual edifice within the human heart.

The inward presence of God is a reality so keen to Herbert's apprehension that he uses simple poetic diction and linguistic expression as well as familiar colloquy between the soul and God. "There is no doubt that such a composition was, in its own day, reckoned one of the most successful and persuasive of the Author's appeals to all classes, to induce them to put their trust in the Almighty, who had bestowed so much upon them."[31] The predominant tone is one of quiet joy and peace in the midst of the doubts, hesitations, and distractions that preoccupy the Christian disciple.

In "The Pulley" and "The World," Herbert suggests that any "restlessness" or discontent which the soul experiences is a positive attempt by a seemingly distant God "with a divine plan to bring the soul to felicity" and to Himself.[32] "The Pulley" represents God as endowing "man" with "strength, beauty, wisdom, honor, pleasure" (ll.1,6-7) reserving, as the divine gift, "rest" (l. 10) or peace. In this poem, as in

[31] Patrides, *George Herbert: The Critical Heritage* 202.
[32] Patrides, *George Herbert: The Critical Heritage* 322.

many of his poems, Herbert celebrates the munificence of God's grace. God says, "Let us...pour on him all [the blessings] we can" (l.3). "The Pulley" witnesses to the moral creation of humanity and reminds the reader, as C.A. Patrides suggests, "of the legend of Pandora's box which released Sickness, Old Age, Vice, save that Hope remained to comfort man so afflicted."[33] Edmund Miller explains the analogy of the pulley by suggesting: "One side of a pulley does not go up unless the other comes down, but two may use a pulley to ascend together by climbing on opposite ropes and keeping pace. [Likewise] Christ does not simply pull man to Heaven; man can ascend because Christ ascends on the other rope in an act of friendship."[34] Helen Vendler further assigns the term "'explanation-poem,' one that creates a myth to answer the riddle: 'Why is man full of ennui and restlessness, though rich in blessings?'"[35] In order that "Nature" not be the total recipient of humankind's favor, thereby causing a rupture in the close relationship God wants with His people, a spirit of "repining restlessness" (l.17) and dissatisfaction with the created universe is annexed on to the Temple where the Original Author dwells. For Herbert, "rest" is to be found only with God. Behind Herbert's use of the term is the profound corollary of justification by faith. According to Calvin, "Christ died and rose again that we might have eternal Sabbath...that we might rest from our own human works and allow the spirit of God powerfully to work within us."[36]

Whether the soul attains its destination of God by pure goodness or by the alternate way of weariness of the world is inconsequential. What is of consequence is the generosity and imagination of a Creator who provides so many blessings and "alternative motivations for man."[37] God's love and generosity abound in "The Pulley," a poem that exhibits paradox, irony, and paronomasia within a spiritual frame. "What might seem imperfection in his creature is paradoxically supreme evidence of God's artistry and love: restlessness is 'The Pulley' that draws man to God."[38] God desires that all people return to Him;

[33] Patrides, *The English Poems of George Herbert* 166–67.
[34] Miller 67.
[35] Vendler 32–33.
[36] Gene Edward Veith, Jr., *Reformation Spirituality: The Religion of George Herbert* (Lewisburg: Bucknell University Press, 1985) 78.
[37] Benet 94.
[38] Benet 95.

He alone will provide "the rest" at journey's end. This poem is unique
in its proffering an explanation by God of the suffering imposed on
humanity as well as an alleviation of this anxiety. Here God's voice is
presented directly as an interlocutor or commentator on the human
condition. Since humankind is made in the image of God, Heaven is
the natural resting place for the Christian disciple.

"The World" is another poem of creation. "Since some of the
biblical synonyms for temple are house, habitation, and palace, we are
in the presence of this complex of ideas when we read that 'Love has
built a stately house.'"[39] "The World" is one of many "definition
poems" in *The Temple* that, while not demonstrating "The Pulley's"
intimate colloquy of God with the soul of the Christian disciple, never-
theless concerns itself with the community of believers. Indeed, like
many poems in *The Temple* collection, "The World" engages in a four-
fold colloquy among the writer, his audience, the reader, and God.
While the term "colloquy" and the tone of many Herbertian poems
suggest humankind's desire for communication and communion with
another individual, "The World" makes clear Herbert's consistent
belief that a part of the individual still yearns for a closed and dark
space where he or she may be "shelt'red from drought and dew"
(1.12). "Repining restlessness" is the design of life in "The Pulley" and
"The World" because in both poems "the values and characteristics
associated with structured selves and structured scenes—the preserva-
tion of boundaries, the projection and fulfillment of desire, the develop-
ment of character, the interest in psychic coherence and in the relation
of part to whole—have necessarily been abandoned.... All access to
closure and to the narrative and psychic stability closure brings has
been abandoned or relinquished, overturned or overcome."[40]

The seemingly good things—*Fortune, Pleasure*—are counterbal-
anced by the gifts of prudence—*Wisdom* and rev'rend *laws*. The Tem-
ple of the Holy Spirit, restated in this poem as "a stately house" (1.1),
is overcome "slyly" by Sin and Death which attempt "To raze the
building to the very floor" (1.17) and would succeed were it not for the
generous Love and omnipresence of the Divine Architect who contin-
ues the process of creation He initiated in "The Pulley" by building an

---

[39] Chana Bloch, *Spelling the Word: George Herbert and the Bible* (Berkeley: Univer-
sity of California Press, 1985) 125.
[40] Harman 149-50.

even "braver Palace than before" (1.20). This Palace is the soul of the
Christian disciple which becomes increasingly unafraid of the false
fancies and "fine cobwebs" (1.3) that attempt to undermine its frame
while it is in a state of Grace, and to disguise its very structure. The
temple *topos*, so dominant in Herbert's spirituality, bears a direct rela-
tionship to the body of religious poetry and prose that informed so
much of the seventeenth century. "One of poetry's greatest potential
values [throughout the seventeenth century] was that God could employ
it as a means through which man might perceive his relationship with
God."[41] That relationship is strengthened in the reader's realization
that, although the heart of the Christian disciple is weak and heir to
temptations, sin, and death, the structure built by God is strong and is
sustained by the love and providence of the Original Architect. Indeed,
The Temple includes and embodies its own poetic. "Underneath the
Poet's varied readings of Salvation and Creation lies a steady Chris-
tocentric meaning that gives a focus to the Poet's career."[42]

The same Architect who endowed humankind with the Herbertian
"glass of blessings" visited Hopkins, particularly in his nature sonnets
considered in this chapter which are, like Herbert's "The Pulley" and
"The World," hymns of creation and praise, joyful expressions of his
sacramental vision. "God's Grandeur" and "The Starlight Night" were
the first sonnets Hopkins had written since his elected silence of nearly
twelve years.[43] They serve as reminders "in a directly autobiographi-
cal way, of Hopkins's happiness during his years in North Wales,
despite the pressure of his studies."[44] A journal entry for August 17,
1874 reveals a positive exaltation of spirit and anticipates the poem
"The Starlight Night": "As we drove home the stars came out thick:
I leant back to look at them and my heart opening more than usual
praised our Lord to and in whom all that beauty comes home."[45]

Hopkins issues the imperative of observation frequently in this
poem and underscores its significance by employing clear and brilliant
light images that symbolize the need of an inner vision. Geoffrey Hart-
man has commented that in Hopkins "the act of sight has become a

---

[41] Summers, *George Herbert: His Religion and Art* 78.
[42] Mulder 43.
[43] Kitchen 73.
[44] Bergonzi 88.
[45] House 254.

moral responsibility."[46] Indeed, in "The Starlight Night," the word "look" is inevitably followed by an exclamation point (there are sixteen exclamations in the poem's fourteen lines), and serves as the call to inscape (the Greek *scope* for "look"). Furthermore, it is an indicator of the speaker's compelling emotionalism and desire to convince the reader to participate in the speaker's own experience of what St. Ignatius in his *Spiritual Exercises* termed "God's being in every creature by essence, presence and power."[47] Ignatius also issues the imperative to his readers to "Look at the author and achiever of our faith (Heb. 12:2); *mira, mira,* look at him."[48]

Hopkins's spiritual growth and maturity in writing impel him to move from the sensuous religious love seen in his earlier poems to a contemplative love that is at the root of Ignatian spirituality. Where "God's Grandeur" laments humankind's failure to connect to God through the grandeur of His creation, "The Starlight Night" is an explicit exhortation to buy and bid for "Prayer, patience, alms, vows" (1.9) in order that "Christ and his mother and all his hallows" (1.14) may find a "home" in the "withindoors house" (1.12) of the Christian disciple. Robert Bridges suggests that stanza 29 of Herbert's "The Church Porch" serves as an analogue and a companion poem to Hopkins's "The Starlight Night":

> What skills it, if a bag of stones or gold
> About thy neck do drown thee? raise thy head;
> Take stars for money; stars not to be told
> By any art, yet to be purchased
>   (ll.170–73).[49]

The biblical analogue for both of these poems is the Lucan passage where Christ exhorts his "little flock" to "Sell what you have and give alms. Get purses for yourselves that do not wear out, a never-failing treasure with the Lord which no thief comes near nor any moth destroys. Wherever your treasure lies, there your heart will be" (Luke

---

[46] Motto 24.

[47] Daniel A. Harris, *Inspirations Unbidden: The "Terrible Sonnets" of Gerard Manley Hopkins* (Berkeley: University of California Press, 1982) 34.

[48] Todd K. Bender, *Gerard Manley Hopkins: The Classical Background and Critical Reception of His Work* (Baltimore: The Johns Hopkins Press, 1966) 147.

[49] Catherine Phillips, ed., *Gerard Manley Hopkins* (Oxford: Oxford University Press, 1986) 348.

12:33-34). Since "The Church Porch" poem (subtitled "Perirrhan-terium," a Greek term for the holy water sprinkler) precedes "The Church" section of Herbert's *The Temple*, the suggestion is made that this poem "is a preparatory ritual of cleansing or 'setting-apart' before entering 'The Church.'"[50] In like manner, the light of Hopkins's "fire-folk sitting in the air" in "The Starlight Night" cleanses and puri-fies the catalogue of nature—farmyard, orchard boughs, barn, and, most importantly, the observer himself who is preparing his heart for Christ, the spouse. "The stars, then, creation's beauty itself, provide a means, a bright currency, not for hoarding up but for freely spending to buy eternal beauty—heaven, of which the heavens themselves are but a reflection. The stars cannot be bought, nor do we want them; they are like husks, Hopkins says. What we do want, rather, is the beauty they reflect, the grain within, Christ."[51]

Christ is so present to the speaker in "The Starlight Night" that the speaker engages in a colloquy with the reader, directing him to pay particular attention, not only to the created world, but also to the Ori-gin of creation and to the spiritual emblems and sacramental symbols the speaker loves. Hopkins acts as a spokesperson as he "bids" his readers to a greater religious consciousness and to an ownership of the earth. He had written to his mother in a letter of March 1, 1870: "no one is ever so poor that he is not (without prejudice to all the rest of the world) owner of the skies and stars and everything wild that is to be found on the earth."[52] This tone of "spontaneous, sensuous apper-ception of the exterior world and Christ's immanence therein" domi-nate the poems of Hopkins considered here.[53] Conversely, *The Wreck of the Deutschland* and the "terrible" sonnets, treated in the following three chapters respectively, demonstrate the internal anxiety and con-flict that eventually overtake the soul of the speaker, resulting in the perceived disappearance of Christ from nature and from Hopkins's life.

Hopkins's creation poems reveal an eternal aspect to nature that is due to God's presence and protection. Humankind's return to the Cre-ator in heaven is represented by the conventional place just above or behind the stars, thereby elevating the temporal order to the spiritually

---

[50] Wall 121.

[51] Mariani, *A Commentary on the Complete Poems of Gerard Manley Hopkins* 99-100.

[52] Abbott, *Further Letters of Gerard Manley Hopkins* 111.

[53] Harris 75.

transcendent. Now "the sense of how all things resemble each other, rhyming and chiming, is as exciting to Hopkins as the sense of how each thing is different, unique in itself."[54] The creation poems of Hopkins describe the dynamism of earthly nature—the nature of land, sky, and humankind's physical form—through imagery that expresses the inner moral and spiritual qualities of the Christian disciple.

All the beauty of the created world "is only an outward sign of an inner and spiritual Beauty; in Hopkins's own words, it is a 'barn' which houses the Heaven of Christ and his 'hallows,' a medieval word for 'saints.'"[55] The mere repetition of the word "all" in Hopkins's "The Starlight Night" is representative of the vast expanse of creation and underscores the yearning for union with the one thing desired which, for Herbert and Hopkins, is union with the Beloved. Both writers envision the attainment of this union by living a life of sacrifice and *kenosis*. Paradoxically, this descent moves them toward the prize of fullness of being; it is not a falling away into nothingness but, rather, a winning of the world by losing it. The works of Herbert and Hopkins, therefore, when read as spiritual autobiography, translate Christ's imperative "to store up heavenly treasure, which neither moths corrode nor thieves break in and steal" (Matt. 6:20).

In reading Herbert's and Hopkins's works as spiritual autobiography, one is awed by their deep reverence and respect for life in its multifaceted and unique forms as well as by their ascribing of the physical beauty of nature and humanity to the loveliness of God the Creator. Hopkins's sonnet "As kingfishers catch fire" (1881) is a re-telling of the creation story in synoptic form, using once more the images of fire and light in the kingfishers and dragonflies respectively, and continuing with how "Each mortal thing" (l.5) resembles its natural counterparts as it bespeaks the Logos. The sestet conveys the enthusiasm of the self-conscious speaker in his determination to communicate with the reader through the medium of language: "I say more" (l.9). "Throughout Hopkins, we are encouraged to believe that the speaker is 'real,' a presence before us, just as all his namings of his own physical gestures would have him."[56] Hopkins clearly delineates his belief that the

---

[54] W. Johnson, *Gerard Manley Hopkins: The Poet as Victorian* (New York: Cornell University Press, 1968) 130.
[55] McChesney 57.
[56] Motto 79.

vocation to write is as valid a means for the creation of his inner self
as is the priestly vocation.

The self of the speaker ultimately is viewed through the eye of God
whose scope is vast enough to envision "Christ play[ing] in ten thou-
sand places/...To the Father through the features of men's faces"
(ll.12,14). As Hopkins writes in one of his sermons, "It is as if a man
said: 'That is Christ playing at me and me playing at Christ,' only that
is no play but truth; That is Christ *being me* and me being Christ."[57]
This thought recalls the description of Wisdom in the Book of Prov-
erbs: "Then was I beside him as his craftsman, and I was his delight
day by day, playing before him all the while, playing on the surface of
his earth; and I found delight in the sons of men" (8:30-31).

"Hopkins had focused on creation and the self during his Liverpool
retreat in late August 1880."[58] In "As kingfishers catch fire," Hopkins
is concerned with humankind's coming into being—"Selves-goes its
self"—(l.7) and with the accession of God's will, completed in the
kenosis of Christ, for Christ embodies all the individual degrees and
distinctions of nature, and is "the way, truth, and life" of all. Hop-
kins's opening commentary in his journal regarding the *Spiritual Exer-
cises* expresses "the touchstone of his Ignatian spirituality: 'I consider
my self-being, my consciousness and feeling of myself, that taste of
myself, of I and *me* above and in all things.'"[59] These lines re-echo
"Selves-goes its self; *myself* it speaks and spells" (l.7) of "As
kingfishers catch fire." The Ignatian sensuousness implicit in the *Spiri-
tual Exercises* is apparent in this poem where there is "a kind of psy-
cho-immersion into the self to find Jesus abiding and then the plunging
of that Jesus-self into the world of natural beings to see the transcen-
dent Christ.... This gives an aesthetic dimension to personal faith...and
reveals a special sacral quality to all existence."[60]

---

[57] Devlin 154.

[58] Mariani, *A Commentary on the Complete Poems of Gerard Manley Hopkins* 178.

[59] Downes, "Beatific Landscapes in Hopkins" 152-53.

[60] Downes, "Beatific Landscapes in Hopkins" 141. A Miltonic parallel is readily
apparent. John T. Shawcross points out in a footnote to line 68 of "On the Morning of
Christ's Nativity" that the "Birds of Calm [that] sit brooding on the charmed wave" are
the halycons or kingfishers, symbols of Christ. Shawcross also cites lines from *Paradise
Lost* (I.19-22) as further Miltonic allusions to the "brooding wings [of] the Spirit of God
outspread," and thus confirms the usage of zoomorphic images in both Milton and
Hopkins. Shawcross 66.

The theme of ascent and return to the Father is particularly domi-
nant in Hopkins's works; "as a biographical structure it gives Augus-
tine's work [*Confessions*] its shape and direction and additionally un-
derlines the value Hopkins always stressed and found in experience....
A major point of the *Confessions* is that man does not ascend directly
through exterior creation to the Father, but turns within and discovers
him in the inner self; then man mounts back through creatures to the
creator, or, rather, all reality becomes his potential field of knowledge
of the One."[61] From a variety of options concerning what the speaker
can do with his life, he must, like Christ, choose one thing to do and
be, so that he can say definitively: "What I do is me; for that I came"
(1.8). This line recalls the biblical passage stating Christ's reply when
Pilate asked, "So, then, are you a king?" Christ responded: "The rea-
son I was born, the reason why I came into the world, is to testify to
the truth" (John 18:37). "The simple singleness of 'What I do is me'
was later denied [Hopkins] as he tried to deal with its bitter converse
and cope with a self cabined and confined. His letters from Dublin
stand in direct opposition to the joy so evident in this sonnet. The
harmony of being and doing which we have in 'As kingfishers catch
fire' had left him."[62]

This poem, in particular, displays the incarnational aspect of spiri-
tual autobiography as a literary genre which continually fills the uni-
verse with its ever-renewing creativity of expression, spiritualization
of meaning, and unification of immanence and transcendence. "A con-
sideration of the 'world within' ourselves is by far a more powerful
means of realizing God participating in creation through the Incarnate
Christ."[63] The Word or Logos becomes enfleshed in the writer and
the reader who, in turning to their daily responsibilities, praise God as
best they can according to their own inscape. In fulfilling their distinc-
tive natures in union with their Creator, they give glory back to the
Origin of life, and become truly "the just man" who "justices;/ Keeps
grace" (ll. 9-10). They not only perform acts of fairness but are them-
selves persons who are truly, justly, themselves. They are the entire,
the real, "man," receptacles of the divine grace that created them. The

---

[61] Cotter 116.

[62] John Robinson, *In Extremity: A Study of Gerard Manley Hopkins* (Cambridge:
Cambridge University Press, 1978) 52.

[63] Downes, "Beatific Landscapes in Hopkins" 153.

praise in this poem then, extends to the just one who "justices" and "keeps grace," as well as to the Lord of creation.

When considered as spiritual autobiography it is evident that the "more" that Hopkins expresses culminates in a poetic vision that depicts with intense excitement and fervor the mystery of who he is in the eyes of the Creator. This excitement impels him to dedicate his life to expressing the Inexpressible: "for that [he] came."

"Spring" is, perhaps, one of the most idyllic of Hopkins's 1877 sonnets. "May was always a special month for Hopkins, even before he became a Catholic and it took on the special significance of being Mary's month. The May of 1899 was no exception."[64] It was the culmination of what Hopkins described to Bridges in a letter dated November 26, 1882 as "my Welsh days, my salad days, when I was fascinated with *cynghanedd* or consonant-chime," and during it he wrote "Spring."[65]

The octet in "Spring" celebrates its subject in brilliantly descriptive sensual imagery. The sestet continues to praise the edenic innocence which earth's "sweet being [possessed] in the beginning" (1.10), but which clouded and turned sour with humankind's sinning. As in the other creation sonnets of Hopkins considered in this chapter, "Spring" shifts to the imperative mood in lines 11–12 of the sestet as the speaker engages in a colloquy with Christ, invoking Him to "Have, get before it cloy,/Before it cloud...and sour with sinning." "In these urgent commands, Hopkins seems to be reversing the familiar convention of the *carpe diem*, 'gather ye rosebuds,' directing it towards the preservation rather than the loss of innocence."[66]

When Hopkins wishes to portray the ideal nature of the Christian disciple, he centers on the strength of youth and the beauty of spring. In this poem, he exhorts Christ to claim for Himself the "Innocent mind and Mayday in girl and boy" (1.13) before it becomes "sour with sinning" (1.12). In an 1879 sermon, Hopkins was to say regarding the giving of one's youthful life to Christ:

> ...the man or woman, the boy or girl, that in their bloom and heyday, in their strength and health give themselves to God and with the fresh body and joy-

---

[64] Kitchen 176.
[65] Abbott, *The Letters of Gerard Manley Hopkins to Robert Bridges* 163.
[66] Bergonzi 181.

ously beating blood give him glory, how near he will be to them in age and sickness and wall their weakness round in the hour of death![67]

Since Hopkins sees the Fall re-enacted in every person's life, he invokes Christ, the "maid's child," on behalf of that vulnerable innocence.[68]

One of the most significant leitmotifs of Hopkins's works is the free will of the Christian disciple that permits him or her to choose sin and thereby refuse to view nature sacramentally. Hopkins's "persistent theme is a calling back of mankind [to what he was in his prelapsarian state], never a vision of some future wholly different from past or present. There is a simple kind of conservatism in this grand and extensive view, as well as a moral concern."[69]

Christ is once more the "principle of relation" for Hopkins. "Spring" begins with a "secular vision of natural fecundity" and moves to a vision of the "Eden garden" that eventually encompasses the Christian universe.[70] "This typological transfiguration emanates from the assumption that an analogy between finite and eternal is intrinsic to the particularities of the landscape itself."[71]

Indeed, the way Hopkins describes this landscape causes the reader to shift his attention very rapidly from one image to another, thereby supplementing the poem with a dynamism that revitalizes, even when the speaker is not directly exclaiming to the reader to "look up at the skies!" as does the speaker in "The Starlight Night." The reader quickly becomes sensitive to the propelling force of Hopkins's diction, and becomes conscious of the fertility and momentum of the language itself, of its power to influence and direct both the conscious state and the spiritual state. The alliteration, assonance, and consonant chimes carry the reader forward as he or she comes to recognize first the sounds of the words and afterwards the symbolic significance of the immanence of their Origin.

Hopkins initiates the sestet by interjecting a question: "What is all this juice and all this joy?" This technique splendidly achieves a twofold purpose: it allows the reader to step back from the exuberant

---

[67] Devlin 19.
[68] Gardner 352.
[69] Robinson 89.
[70] Harris 42.
[71] Harris 43.

description of the natural world in the octet, and to attempt an answer as to what constitutes the nature of creation and his or her own involvement in it. By redirecting the sestet in this way, Hopkins helps the reader to discover the internal spring that will provide the sustenance and nourishment of a life "worthy the winning." (l.14). "The questions in Hopkins may not stand out in the reader's mind in the way that the exclamations or interjections do probably because the questions rarely remain real questions—they rarely hang unanswered.... Whether his speaker poses his questions to man, God, or self, the answer is soon forthcoming."[72]

However, the deceptively simple and direct response contains within it the conflict between the speaker's love for beauty and created things and his love for God, a conflict he expresses with a multiplicity of questions in *The Wreck of the Deutschland* and the "terrible" sonnets.

For Hopkins and Herbert, the seeming contraries of creation and destruction, growth and decay, are embraced as vital and particular elements in the cyclic pattern of life, as they were in the medieval tradition of their predecessor Duns Scotus.

The selection of Herbert's and Hopkins's works considered in this chapter combine prayer, poetry, and prose in depicting God's grandeur as it "gathers to a greatness" in the written expression.

Thus the spiritual and literary artists George Herbert and Gerard Manley Hopkins are at the same time parsons true to heaven and poets true to earth.

---

[72] Motto 99.

"Love built a stately house..."

Chapter Three

"The Dark Night of the Soul": A (W)Reckoning of the Spiritual Life

I did say yes
O at lightning and lashed rod;
Thou heardst me truer than tongue confess
Thy terror, O Christ, O God;
Thou knowest the walls, altar and hour and night:
The swoon of a heart that the sweep and the hurl of thee
    trod
    Hard down with a horror of height:
    And the midriff astrain with leaning of,
    laced with fire of stress.
                        (Hopkins, *The Wreck of the Deutschland*)

THE RENAISSANCE WITNESSED a renewed interest in men and women by endowing them with moral worth, dignity, and the opportunity of realizing personal dreams. The Reformation carried this individualism further into matters of faith; it was instrumental in defining the term "vocation" or calling, and in assigning responsibility of the individual soul to God. In the theology of Calvin and Protestant believers, "vocation" became the mark of human eternal destiny, the call by which God summoned His chosen to eternal life.[1]

This interiorization of consciousness also penetrated the Victorian era and contributed to a more refined understanding of the will and the concept of selfhood. As products of their respective eras, Herbert and Hopkins reckoned with the stresses of a ministerial and poetic vocation. Their call impelled them to approach hesitantly, and later embrace, the ecclesiastical ministry, to remain poets upon becoming priests, and to align the stresses of English verse with the stresses of their personal experiences. Both Herbert and Hopkins share Augustine's theory "that the creative agent of metrical order in poetry is not the poet but rationality (the Logos) itself, working through the poet's ear."[2] This point is crucial to an acceptance of the frequent claims of Herbert and Hop-

---

[1] Robert B. Shaw, *The Call of God* (England: Cowley Publications, 1981) 1.

[2] William H. Pahlka, *Saint Augustine's Meter and George Herbert's Will* (Ohio and London: Kent State University Press, 1987) 90.

kins that God, not they, is the "true maker" of their poems. When the poetry and prose of Herbert and Hopkins are interpreted as spiritual autobiography and God is recognized as the subject of these works, the works become imprints of the authors' spiritual (w)reckonings and imitations of the divine form impressed on the soul.

Herbert and Hopkins view their vocations as the common ground upon which they and all the faithful meet, and also as that which set them apart for unique forms of service. As ministers and writers, they fulfill a sacramental function, a sacrifice of praise. As Ignatius states in the first Principle and Foundation (the Fundamentum), and Herbert and Hopkins readily endorse: "Man is created to praise, reverence, and serve God our Lord, and by this means to save his soul.... We should not prefer health to sickness, riches to poverty, honor to dishonor, a long life to a short life.... Our desire and choice should be what is more conducive to the end for which we are created."[3] Vocation, as these writers experience it, is not merely an intellectual assent to doctrine, but a spiritual awakening that expresses itself in their poetic and prosaic arguments. The ministerial and poetic vocations of Herbert and Hopkins are tried by a demanding Master Who initiates a covenant and anxiously awaits the soul's calling of "O Christ." The "fire of stress" accompanying the personal and vocational commitments of Herbert and Hopkins produces literary works that underscore the significance of self-doubt and religious incertitude in the life of the Christian disciple.

Hopkins's poetry follows a movement from an appreciation of diversity contained in a total unit, as in his nature poems, to the works of consolation and desolation, especially *The Wreck of the Deutschland* (1875) and the "terrible" sonnets (treated in Chapters Four and Five), where ambiguity and duality provide the stress of poetic and spiritual form. In the latter poems, Hopkins records the soul as an imitator of Christ, but not as having completed this process of imitation. Thus, there appears to be a duality in this relationship, a separateness between the soul and God. For the Christian disciple, this stage is not the end but, rather, a significant part of the journey of the soul to its Creator. It is this *kenosis* or self-emptying of the soul in order that it may be filled with God that Hopkins treats in *The Wreck* and Herbert in "Bitter-Sweet," "The Storm," and "Affliction (II)." Initially, an intertextual study of "Part the First" of Hopkins's *The Wreck* (stanzas 1–10)

---

[3] Puhl 12.

and Herbert's "Bitter-Sweet" and "The Storm" is pursued, followed by a study of "Part the Second" of *The Wreck* (stanzas 11–35) and "Affliction (II)."[4] The biblical injunction "Deep calls unto deep in the roar of many waters" is realized in these poems as a colloquy occurs between the soul and God in circumstances that overwhelm the ordinary and hasten the transcendent. These poems share an incarnational and sacramental view of the world that grounds their Christian realism and provides a fresh impact on the reader.

Deep intensity and mysticism in both Herbert and Hopkins find a most creative and original outlet in these select works where the refinement of the soul by the process of purgation is portrayed emblematically through images of physical and spiritual (w)reckonings. Here, both body and soul unite in rendering an account of what St. John of the Cross (1542–91) and the mystics termed "the dark night of the soul." This spiritual phenomenon is rooted in the biblical address of James "to the twelve tribes in the dispersion" in which he exhorts them to "count it pure joy when you are involved in every sort of trial. Realize that when your faith is tested this makes for endurance. Let endurance come to its perfection so that you may be fully mature, lacking in nothing," in contrast to "the doubter [who] is like the surf tossed and driven by the wind" (James 1:2–4,6). The works analyzed in this chapter contain images of literal and figurative (w)reckonings implicit in the spiritual life.

Herbert and Hopkins are not alone in bringing "individual experience and emotion to the great subject of God's dealings with humankind. They follow in the tradition of long religious lyrics such as the fourteenth-century 'Pearl' and Milton's ode 'On the Morning of Christ's Nativity.'"[5] By recording the very personal search for God in the midst of the soul's arid wasteland, Herbert and Hopkins depict the struggle of the soul for self-sufficiency to its ultimate submission of "Thou mastering me/God!" (*The Wreck*, I.1.1–2), a spiritual process which redefines the life of the Christian disciple.

The Wreck "dramatizes the opposition between a soul almost lost in despair and a seemingly absent God, where the bond between them is reduced to dry and anguished assertion."[6] The "elected silence" that

[4] *The Wreck of the Deutschland* is hereafter cited as *The Wreck*.
[5] W. Johnson, *Gerard Manley Hopkins: The Poet as Victorian* 24.
[6] Bergonzi 179.

visits Hopkins from 1868–1875 is broken with the writing of this lengthy poem, now among the most famous and complex poems in the English language. *The Wreck* reveals how a news event may be turned into a personal and theological narrative of spiritual autobiography as it incorporates the themes and strains of Hopkins's conversion experience. Hopkins's first major work as well as his longest poem, *The Wreck* was inspired by *The Times* newspaper account of a shipwreck, an event which "made a deep impression on me, more than any other wreck or accident I ever read of."[7] In this letter of Christmas Eve, 1875, to his mother, he acknowledges clippings she sent him about the disaster and reports that he is already "writing something on this wreck."[8] He explained the poem to the Canon at Highgate School whom he befriended, Richard Watson Dixon:

when in the winter of '75 the Deutschland was wrecked by the mouth of the Thames and five Franciscan nuns, exiles from Germany by the Falck Laws, aboard of her were drowned I was affected by the account and happening to say so to my rector he said that he wished someone would write a poem on the subject.[9]

The obvious effect of this event on Hopkins is further heightened by the fact that the poet's father, Manley Hopkins, was an expert on the protection and safety of shipping.[10] "His professional interest in nautical situations [he wrote many highly technical publications on shipping law and marine insurance, in addition to other books of poetry] may have predisposed his poet-son to treat, on two occasions [*The Wreck of the Deutschland* and *The Loss of the Eurydice* (1878)] the subject of shipwreck."[11] Mr. Hopkins's keen interest in nature was inherited by his eldest son Gerard Manley Hopkins, whose poems on nature and creation provide the imagistic counterparts for the personal revelations in *The Wreck* and the "terrible" sonnets. Perhaps Hopkins also inherited from his poet-father, who was Welsh, the consonant chimes he

[7] Abbott, *Further Letters of Gerard Manley Hopkins* 135.

[8] John E. Keating, *The Wreck of the Deutschland: An Essay and Commentary (Ohio: Kent State University Bulletin*, 1963) 13.

[9] Abbott, *The Correspondence of Gerard Manley Hopkins and Richard Watson Dixon* 14.

[10] Kitchen 19.

[11] Gardner 7.

inserted into *The Wreck*.[12] The process and the result of this experiment he continues to explain to Dixon:

> I had long had haunting my ear the echo of a new rhythm which now I realized on paper [sprung rhythm]...much more flexible, and capable of much greater effects. However I had to mark the stresses in blue chalk, and this and my rhymes carried on from one line to another and certain chimes suggested by the Welsh poetry I had been reading (what they call *cynghanedd*) and a great many more oddnesses could not but dismay an editor's eye, so that when I offered it to our magazine the *Month*, though at first they accepted it, after a time they withdrew and dared not print it.[13]

Hopkins succeeds in conveying the mystery of God and nature over the powerless human by using sprung rhythm and consonant chimes as well as poetic rhymes and analogues to depict the terrifying forces occurring in the drama of God, nature, and humanity.

Structurally, *The Wreck* is a two-part Pindaric ode composed of thirty-five eight-line stanzas. "Among the most successful features of the 'Deutschland' stanza is the long six-footed eighth line. This shares with the Alexandrine at the close of a Spenserian stanza the contemplative prolongation of sound followed (almost always) by a reflective pause."[14] Raymond Schoder's essay, "Hopkins and Pindar," demonstrates the close affinities and parallels between these "towering poetic giants" in style, thought, and use of language. He notes the

> over-arching device in Pindaric structure [as] the technique of raising the individual event which occasions the victory ode into the plane of universal truth and significance.... Hopkins 'inscaped' his language in the Pindaric pattern by native instinct. But he found in Pindar and in Greek tragic choral lyric a kindred way of speech which encouraged him to maintain his own remarkable style, so different from most English usages, especially in the Victorian Age. Hopkins, like Pindar, uses exclamation, often in conjunction with personifica-

---

[12] Gardner 2.

[13] Abbott, *The Correspondence of Gerard Manley Hopkins and Richard Watson Dixon* 14-15.

[14] Norman H. MacKenzie, *A Reader's Guide to Gerard Manley Hopkins* (Ithaca: Cornell University Press, 1981) 59.

tion; archaic and newly-coined words, sprung rhythm, repetition of metrical pattern.[15]

In a letter of April 2, 1878, Hopkins points out to Bridges the influence of the Pindaric ode structure on *The Wreck*:

> The Deutschland would be more generally interesting if there were more wreck and less discourse, I know, but still it is an ode and not primarily a narrative. There is some narrative in Pindar but the principal business is lyrical.[16]

Since, as Hopkins states, *The Wreck* is an ode, not a prosaic treatise, it is not required to provide explicit or sequential development of thought. Consequently, the unity is contingent on the imagination of the reader rather than on logic.

The ballad-like qualities of *The Wreck* are confirmed by Jerome Bump's synopsis of the poem. "Part the First," which consists of ten stanzas, "is autobiographical, recalling how God touched the speaker in his own life. The second begins with seven stanzas dramatizing newspaper accounts of the wreck and the sufferings of the crew and passengers. Then fourteen stanzas narrow the focus to a single passenger, the tallest of the nuns, who was heard to call to Christ before her death. The last four stanzas address God directly and culminate in a call for the conversion of England."[17]

This poem is, as Bridges termed it at the beginning of his edition of Hopkins's poems, a "dragon in the gate" for many readers and critics who have difficulty reconciling a view of nature and of God that is both terrifying and sacramental.[18] Hopkins told Bridges, justifying the poem in the face of his friend's dislike: "I may add for your greater interest and edification that what refers to myself in the poem is all

---

[15] Raymond Schoder, S.J., "Hopkins and Pindar." In *Gerard Manley Hopkins: New Essays on His Life, Writing, and Place in English Literature*. ed. Michael E. Allsopp and Michael W. Sundermeier (Edwin Mellen Press, 1989) 117, 119, 121.

[16] Abbott, *The Letters of Gerard Manley Hopkins to Robert Bridges* 49.

[17] Bump, *Gerard Manley Hopkins* 94.

[18] Bergonzi 157.

strictly and literally true and did all occur; nothing is added for poetical padding."[19]

Naturally, critics posit a variety of scholarly opinions and readings of *The Wreck*, many confirming a reading of *The Wreck* as spiritual autobiography. David Downes acknowledges that "the poetic impulse of this work derives its power from a new, intense, transforming, touching ('stressing') of self and things through which Hopkins came to an overwhelming realization of God participating in his being. A new realization of immanence leads to a new recollection of transcendence" for the poet.[20] Downes finds the great achievement of *The Wreck* to be Hopkins's "ability to find appropriate concrete images to convey the passion and the power of religious realization, the movement from the discovery of the masterhood of God through terror and majesty, violence and love."[21] Critical opinion also confirms the influence of George Herbert on Gerard Manley Hopkins. Jerome Bump, for example, cites *The Wreck* as Hopkins's "most Metaphysical poem" wherein Hopkins "realized that if, as Herbert suggested [in line 47 of "The Size"] 'These seas are tears, and heav'n the haven,' a Christian must accept the seas and tears in imitation of Christ before there could be any talk of 'heaven-haven'" (*The Wreck*, II.35.275).[22] Indeed, the *Deutschland* is the vessel that leads the poet and the nuns to God.

This acceptance of the spiritual struggle is a natural result of Hopkins's personal and vocational commitment to the soldierly Ignatian ideals. The soldier is trained to obey unquestioningly. In His *Notes*, Hopkins underscores Ignatius's *Exercises*:

> whatever is commanded, permitted, or accepted, is justified.... It must have its positive rightness or justification...to which the subject has given consent or obedience.[23]

Evidently, the obedience of the soldier justifies itself, as Hopkins demonstrates in his verse and prose. "The ideal need to imitate the 'hero

[19] Elisabeth W. Schneider, *The Dragon in the Gate: Studies in the Poetry of Gerard Manlley Hopkins* (Berkeley and Los Angeles: University of California Press, 1968) 38-39.

[20] Downes, "Beatific Landscapes in Hopkins" 155.

[21] Downes, "Beatific Landscapes in Hopkins" 156.

[22] Bump, "Hopkins, Metalepsis, and the Metaphysicals." *John Donne Journal*, 1985; 4(2), 317.

[23] Devlin 157.

of Calvary' constantly in the walk of faith and the zealous awareness of the Ignatian vocation to achieve that end help Hopkins justify the ways of God to himself."[24] The ways in which God interacts with Hopkins are incorporated in the three appellations that Hopkins assigns to his Lord in the penultimate line of *The Wreck*: "prince, hero of us, high priest."

The critical attacks on *The Wreck* as a technically artificial and obscure "occasion" poem are countered with Hopkins's own defense of Metaphysical poetry. As an admirer of this school of poetry, he saw no faulty artificiality in the "exquisiteness, farfetchedness" of the Caroline age, nor in the "chimes suggested by the Welsh poetry," nor in the folk poetry whose effects he uses quite often in *The Wreck*.[25] In a letter to Bridges in May 1878, Hopkins admits that *The Wreck* is obscure, that he was "not over-desirous that the meaning of all should be quite clear."[26] *The Wreck* reflects the ambiguity and paradox of life, particularly that of the Christian disciple whose life is rooted in the suffering, death, and resurrection of the Master.

The Wreck begins as one of the most direct and personal literary accounts of the speaker's address to God, continues with a violent depiction of the great forces of nature and the overwhelming power of the Creator to delve into the recesses of the heart, and concludes with a petition that "heaven-haven" be the reward of the soul's (w)reckoning with the Lord. Jude V. Nixon contextualizes Hopkins's usage of "heaven-haven" by suggesting that the storms of "heaven-haven" allude to the liberal climate of the 1860s from which Hopkins desired to escape:

> When Hopkins enrolled at Oxford in 1863, some eighteen years after the culmination of the Tractarian Movement of Keble, Pusey, Newman, and other notable High Churchmen, the city was still feeling the aftershocks of that great Movement. The Tractarians attempted to counteract the growing liberalism and to check the threat of German Higher Criticism, both of which led to the defection of many young Oxford undergraduates from what appeared to them as a theologically compromising Anglicanism into the relatively safe religious haven of Roman Catholic theology.[27]

---

[24] Mathai 135-36.
[25] Keating 46.
[26] Abbott, *The Letters of Gerard Manley Hopkins to Robert Bridges* 50.
[27] Jude V. Nixon, "Gerard Manley Hopkins and Henry Parry Liddon: An Unacknowledged Influence." *Renascence* 42, 1989-90 (1-2); 94.

Considered in this light, a reading of *The Wreck* as spiritual autobiography provides a fresh perspective from which to view the conversion process, and enjoins the Christian disciple to contemplate the three Christian themes of theodicy, colloquy, and nutriment.

When read as a colloquy between the speaker and God, the poem exhibits the gradual submission of the soul to the Master. Furthermore, a reading of *The Wreck* as a depiction of theodicy—a vindication of God's justice—reinforces Hopkins's and the reader's acknowledgement of the constant immanence of God. The fact that the verbs are in the present tense at the outset of the poem confirms the "Over again" (I.1.8) presence of this God Who also provides the body's vitality and the soul's sustenance—"giver of breath and bread" (I.1.2)—and thus supports a third reading of the poem as an explication of the Christian motif of nutriment.

A consideration of how the three stages of meditation direct *The Wreck* provides a focus for the three Christian themes. For example, the reader witnesses the theme of theodicy—the justification of God's nature—and the theme of colloquy or dialogue with God in Hopkins's praising and honoring the King and Master of the universe, Whose sovereign nature calls forth a host of paradoxes in the human heart: mastery and mercy, pain and beauty, suffering and peace, lightning and love, winter and warm (I.9). Even the natural elements present a contradiction: they are ready to minister to a person's well-being and enjoyment, and they are equally ready to destroy him, as does the weather that occasions the main event of this poem. "The mysteries of our inner and outer lives point back to a God who, to human intelligence, must remain endowed with a paradoxical combination of opposing attributes. God's justice is his mercy, his chastisements are his blessings" as he uses evil to effect good.[28]

A shipwreck provides the occasion for this poem, as well as the symbol which translates the soul from a posture of prayer and praise to a realization of the dreadfulness and terror of God's grandeur and the diminution of humanity. As F.R. Leavis states, Hopkins "realizes [the shipwreck] so vividly that he is in it, and it is at the same time in him."[29] How the speaker finds a reconciliation between the horror of the shipwreck and the loving omnipotence of God is the *tour de force*

---

[28] Keating 20.

[29] Philip Martin, *Mastery and Mercy* (London: Oxford University Press, 1957) 28.

in "Part the First" that brings the speaker and the reader to a recogni-
tion of God's omnipresence and constant attempts to "touch me afresh"
(I.1.7) with "touches" that are frequently "astrain with leaning of,
laced with fire of stress" (I.2.16). The poem is filled with cacophonous
diction and poetic irregularities that convey the "stress" of the soul and
the "hurtle" of hell and that anticipate the six "terrible" sonnets of
1885–89. "There is a tendency today to discount the terrible aspect of
the Christian God, and to deprecate the use of such language as this as
being inconsistent with a doctrine of a loving God, and of Christ the
Lover of men. But 'love' in the sense in which the word relates to God
is not the soft emotion which the word connotes so often in everyday
speech. The 'love' of God is a devouring flame, strong, pure, holy,
and it is in his love as well as in his judgment that God's mastery of
men is to be seen."[30]

To the soul who stands in an attitude of prayer and praise to God,
the entire universe bespeaks the Creator's beauty and becomes
"chárged wíth the grandeur of God," as was demonstrated in the select
poems and prose in Chapters One and Two of this book. But the per-
son who continues his pilgrimage to "heaven-haven" undergoes a fur-
ther purging, one that causes the soul to become "sóft síft/In an hour-
glass," "mined with a motion, a drift" (I.4.25–27) as it converts or
turns to the "Lord of life." This purgation, a vital stage in mystical and
Ignatian spirituality, opens the soul to new-found dimensions of "the
heart of the Host"(I.3.21) and creates a new life that stirs into flame
"His mystery" and His glory. However, the speaker realizes that the
beauty of God's revealing Himself to the soul comes "Not out of his
bliss" (I.6.41). "This healing beauty, this loveliness which gives new
life to men, is not an accidental overflow from a blissful God in an
untroubled heaven; its power and its healing issue from the pain of
God. This is the deepest mystery of the Faith: 'here [even] the faithful
waver, the faithless fable and miss'" (I.6.48).[31]

Now the speaker's realization is twofold. He becomes aware that
the world's grandeur and beauty issue from a God Whose only Son
underwent a passionate incarnation and diminution to acquire human-
kind's redemption in a sinful and suffering world. Moreover, he recog-
nizes that this salvific action continues as it "rides time like riding a

---

[30] P. Martin 33.
[31] P. Martin 36-37.

river" (I.6.47). A reading of *The Wreck* as spiritual autobiography confirms that a true and intimate knowledge of "the Lord of Life" is acquired only through personal suffering and the process of *kenosis* whereby the soul enters into Christ's Passion, Death, and Resurrection. Spiritual and physical loss and suffering provide an added *scope* or insight into the nature of God and help the soul to respond to God's call with yet another "I did say yes" (I.2.9). Conversion, then, implies a flooding of the soul with an understanding of both the terror and might, as well as the power and joy, of God's love.

This conversion occurs at various times for the Christian disciple. "Hither then, last or first...Never ask if meaning it, wanting it, warned of it—men go" (I. 8.62,64). The mastery and the mercy of God as He claims the soul for Himself occur sometimes suddenly and strongly, as it did for St. Paul, or softly and gradually as it did for St. Augustine: "Whether át ónce, as once at a crash Paul,/Or as Austin, a lingering-out sweet skill" (I.10.77–78). Sometimes God's will is forged "With an anvil-ding/And with fire" (I.10.73–74); other times it comes "stealing as Spring" (I.10.75) and "melts" the soul to Itself. For example, Hopkins's mentor Newman wrote that his own conversion process included both "anvil-ding" and "sweet skill." After his ordination as deacon, Newman wrote: "I feel as a man thrown suddenly in deep water," whereas his previous reception into the Roman Catholic Church on October 8, 1845, was "like coming into port after a rough sea."[32] Many Pauline statements confirm that, for the Christian, suffering is not a dreaded thing to be avoided at all costs; rather, it is when Christian disciples are persecuted, slandered, and suffering loss that they are nearest to understanding the mystery of the strong love of God for His creatures. The faith which is victorious in *The Wreck* is not one that eliminates difficulties, but, rather, one that lives in the face of them. "To the non-Catholic," Hopkins tells Bridges, "a mystery is an interesting uncertainty; to the Catholic, an incomprehensible certainty." In embracing Catholicism, Hopkins definitely rejects such images of God as are suggested by even a few random phrases from current Victorian literature —"the stream of tendency by which all things fulfill the law of their being," "the President of the Immortals," "the grand Perhaps."[33]

---

[32] Kitchen 18.
[33] Keating 18.

The Wreck attests to Hopkins's inscape of the Infinite, particularly during times of religious and personal stress. In "Part the First," Hopkins addresses himself to a recurring spiritual crisis. In lines 7–8 of *The Wreck*, for example, the speaker says: "...and dost thou touch me afresh?/Over again I feel thy finger and find thée." "Over again" suggests a recurrence of the crisis, of the "dread" that serves as a transition from purgation to illumination.[34]

In writing discursively of the attempt to find in seemingly remote and disparate elements an imaginative and spiritual relationship with a God who is both just and merciful, Hopkins joins forces once again with Milton. "In *Lycidas*, the ratio of the parts to one another is also remote—the drowning of Edward King, recollections of student life at Cambridge, the attack on the clergy, the future of John Milton—yet the diverse elements are imaginatively fused. The same kind of fusion can be discovered and defended in the *Deutschland*."[35] Both Milton and Hopkins attempt "to justify the ways of God to men" by using ordinary experiences to depict God's immanence and transcendence.

For a poet preoccupied with inscape—with the specific and essential quality of all things—all paradoxical and baffling aspects of God as the poet knows them through experience and revelation must be considered and included in his theodicy. "Action under stress or by stress is not only a particular in Hopkins's universe, but the one condition showing forth the *resilience* of things, their inexhaustible individuality."[36] Had Hopkins subscribed to the Thomistic outlook, he might have emphasized the mystery of a Deity Whose attributes are largely a human description of what is ineffable. Adopting the Scotist doctrines, however, Hopkins prefers to emphasize the mystery of a God in whom disparate and seemingly contradictory attributes actually co-exist. Since Scotus and Hopkins view the Deity as being immediate in

---

[34] On p.22 of *The Wreck of the Deutschland: An Essay and Commentary*, John E. Keating finds proof of the significance of the wording "in the 1918 text, lines 6-7, stanza 1, [which] reads, 'And after it álmost únmade, what with dread,/Thy doing; and dost thou touch me afresh?' But before revision, the reading was, 'And after at times álmost únmade me with dread,/Thy doing; and dost Thou touch me afresh?' The words 'at times' are crucial; here we have Hopkins' own authority for saying that the experience with which the *Deutschland* opens was a recurrent one." Hopkins later addressed these recurring spiritual crises in his "terrible" sonnets and the Dublin poems.

[35] Keating 48.

[36] Geoffrey H. Hartman, *The Unmediated Vision: An Interpretation of Wordsworth, Hopkins, Rilke and Valéry* (New Haven: Yale University Press, 1954) 55.

human experience, cosmic terror is yoked with cosmic loveliness; moreover, the loveliness becomes an assurance that the soul can accept the terror that is yoked with it.[37]

The profound influence of Duns Scotus on Hopkins's thought is clearly evidenced in a journal entry of July 19, 1872:

> At this time I had first begun to get hold of the copy of Scotus on the Sentences in the Baddely library and was flush with a new stroke of enthusiasm. It may come to nothing or it may be a mercy from God. But just then when I took in any inscape of the sky or sea I thought of Scotus[.][38]

The Scotist philosophy of the uniqueness of each individual, of perception, and of being bears directly on Hopkins's poems, which are experiences of perception and understanding. "'He haunted who of all men most sways my spirits to peace" ('Duns Scotus's Oxford,' l.11) is much quoted when Hopkins's metaphysics are explained, for in Duns Scotus Hopkins found the confirmation he wanted for the system he had already largely constructed to explain his own perception of reality."[39] Like Scotus's works, Ignatius's *Spiritual Exercises* refines Hopkins's understanding of a God who is both lightning and love, a Creator close to his creatures. Scotus, however, explored these mysteries; in the summer of 1872 when Hopkins studied his works, Scotus provided "the exstasy of interest," which, as Hopkins says in a letter to Bridges, leaves the mind "swinging; poised, but on the quiver."[40]

Against this background of spiritual and physical turmoil and contraries, a theophany occurs, rendering dignity to "the dark night of the soul" as it is experienced by the speaker. With this assurance, the speaker anticipates another manifestation of God as the restorer of faith to England in "Part the Second." Hopkins concludes "Part the First" as he began it: with emphasis on "master" and "mastery." As complete as the speaker's submission to God is at this point, it takes on a new perspective and a more profound obeisance in the nun's confession of the "Master" in the tempest and shipwreck in "Part the Second."

---

[37] Keating 42-43.

[38] House 221.

[39] James Olney, *George Herbert and Gerard Manley Hopkins: A Comparative Study in Two Religious Poets*, diss., Columbia University, 1963, 128.

[40] Abbott, *The Letters of Gerard Manley Hopkins to Robert Bridges* 188.

The paradoxes and contraries of the soul are also expressed by the Metaphysical Herbert, who uses the succinct phrase "bitter-sweet" in an eight-line poem (the stanzas of *The Wreck* are also eight lines) that bears the same title and which contains further oxymoronic phrases such as "dear angry" (1.1) and "sour-sweet days" (1.7). Nearly every phrase in this condensed statement of Christian resignation amplifies the oxymoron of the title. Like the speaker in *The Wreck*, the speaker in "Bitter-Sweet" also engages in a colloquy with "my dear angry Lord" (1.1) who has struck at and cast down the heart of the speaker. These seemingly violent actions accompany a paradoxical love of which the speaker is confident the Lord has for him and he has for the Lord. This love elicits complaints and lamentations and, ultimately, approval and refinement. "It is his understanding of sacramental theology which enables Herbert not only to endure suffering but to experience joy."[41] For Herbert, as for Hopkins, God's love and wrath are intimate and related experiences. "Three elements—the hyperbolic account of distress, the argument with God and the certainty of a hearing—furnish the substance of Herbert's complaints."[42] The soul's progress from purgation and illumination to union with God is evident in this poem of Herbert whose absence of imagery, so dominant in Hopkins's *The Wreck*, is itself a spiritual exercise whereby the reader may examine his or her relationship with this contradictory and complex God.

The poetic techniques that Herbert uses in "Bitter-Sweet" to depict the anguish and turmoil of the soul's conversion experience are in contradistinction to those of Hopkins. Where *The Wreck* uses a lengthy two-part ode, a multiplicity of nature images, and a rich variety of biblical, patristic, and current sources to convey the soul's (w)reckoning, Herbert turns from his typical sonnet-length (or lengthier) practice to an eight-lined hexameter to delineate the characterization of the speaker's days as both sweet and sour. "Bitter-Sweet" is a poem that renders, not the host of images of *The Wreck*, but "one carefully and imaginatively rendered image, suggestive of an abundant range of experience, slight only in number of lines."[43] This strophic brevity in Herbert's later poems witnesses to the "landmark of formal variety"

---

[41] Shaw 79.

[42] Bloch 262.

[43] Mary Ellen Rickey, *Utmost Art: Complexity in the Verse of George Herbert* (Kentucky: University of Kentucky Press, 1966) 121.

that undergirds *The Temple*.[44] Herbert chooses simple diction when, like Hopkins, "he is concerned with the most profound issues and is engaged in the most searching exploration of the spirit. It is not uncommon for [Herbert's] whole poems to contain only monosyllables and disyllables, and for those to be words which might crop up in casual speech."[45] Although Herbert's diction in "Bitter-Sweet" appears simple and commonplace, its intention is not to convey a kind of simplistic spirituality but to suggest, rather, that metaphysical topics of meditation are as familiar as any quotidian item. The ease with which the speaker in Herbert's poems engages in a colloquy with God strengthens Herbert's intention "to divest Heaven [and celestial matters] of any shred of exoticism, [and to describe] them in terms remarkable only for their earthliness."[46]

Like the speaker in *The Wreck*, the speaker in "Bitter-Sweet" realizes that the "sour-sweet days" (1.7) are given for his correction. However, as "The Sacrifice," "The Rose," and other poems by Herbert confirm, the bitterness contains a sweetness. "In the bitterness of remedy can be found the sweetness of God's love, which reclaims his sinful creatures. To participate in the bitter cross is to find love's sweet sacrifice; it is to find the sweet rose that purges, the love expressed in the pattern of suffering that purges man's sin."[47] In Chapter 34 of *The Country Parson*, titled "The Parson's Dexterity in Applying of Remedies," Herbert echoes the soldier Ignatius in acknowledging the purging that is necessary in order for the soul to acquire union with God when he writes of the

> double state of a Christian even in this Life, the one military, the other peaceable. The military is, when we are assaulted with temptations either from within or from without. The Peaceable is, when the Devil for a time leaves us, as he did our Savior, and the Angels minister to us their own food, even joy, and peace; and comfort in the holy Ghost.[48]

Hopkins's works also emphasize this belief. For example, in his notes "On Personality, Grace, and Free Will," Hopkins uses the word

---

[44] Rickey 135.
[45] Rickey 166.
[46] Rickey 168.
[47] Sherwood 65.
[48] Wall 105-06.

"pitch" to describe the purgation by which God's grace invites the soul. "God's grace allows man to taste the degree of goodness above the one in which he is already living."[49] When he writes in *The Wreck*: "To flash from the flame to the flame then, tower from the grace to the grace" (I.3.24), Hopkins describes his priestly and poetic vocations as invitations from God to a new "pitch" and as opportunities for further illumination and union with his Creator.

In "Bitter-Sweet," Herbert, like Hopkins, uses language in a new and vigorous way. He places his words in divine contexts and employs the formal elements of his verse which are seen in other *Temple* poems—sound, metrics, structure, juxtaposition, oxymoron—to reveal two truths firmly maintained by Herbert: that God spans heaven and earth, and that His role as Divine Physician urges him to reprove as well as heal. "What we from our limited perspective have taken to be opposites, separated as earth from heaven, are in Herbert's poems bound together by line and syntax, which parallel the binding force of God's grace, and by paradox and oxymoron, which reveal unity beneath our narrow view of antithesis."[50] The speaker in "Bitter-Sweet" advances from viewing the Lord as a Being who "dost love, yet strike[s];/Cast[s] down, yet help afford[s]" (ll.2-3), to One who is able to join "lament, and love" (l.8). The speaker progresses from the opposition implied in the word "yet" to the healthy tension of "and" that conjoins "lament" and "love." "'Bitter-Sweet' gradually collapses the distinction between joy and grief by changing the conjunctions between them."[51] The speaker, therefore, lives, "not in the midst of a contradiction that would destroy him, but within a paradox that chastens and gives life."[52] As with the sequence of conjunctions, the poem exhibits a movement toward unity, away from fragmentation and multiplicity, and suggests the creative act of God which is, itself, a blend of opposites. "Bitter-Sweet" suggests how divine grace transforms the soul from complaint to praise, from wailing to approval and acceptance, just as the entire *Temple* reveals to the reader the reality beneath appearances, the life-giving view from eternity.[53]

---

[49] Phillips 336.

[50] Sharon Cadman Seelig, *The Shadow of Eternity: Belief and Structure in Herbert, Vaughan, and Traherne* (Kentucky: University of Kentucky Press, 1981) 35.

[51] Pahlka 190.

[52] Seelig 35.

[53] Seelig 35.

It is evident that Herbert's intentions to grow spiritually mature and to fashion his own heart into a Temple wherein the Divine Architect may reside are inseparable from his desire to advance his artistic powers of expression as he struggles to describe accurately and succinctly his relationship with God. "Bitter-Sweet," like *The Wreck*, conveys the poet's laboring in God's presence to overcome the isolation and aridity of "the dark night of the soul." That God rewards this struggle to make art a prayerful event is apparent in the restored self-image of the speaker, whose familiar and honest expressions yield the conjoining of "lament, and love" (1.8). Like the Davidic psalmist, the speaker is convinced that God is listening, and is determined to order his laments so that Love will have the final word.

A reading of "Bitter-Sweet" as spiritual autobiography strengthens a definition of theodicy that depicts a God who is associative and inclusive rather than contrastive and superior. This definition is reinforced by the alliteration of "lament" and "love," a construction also utilized by Hopkins who alliterated contrastive elements—"lightning and love," "winter and warm"—to insist on their fundamental identity.[54] Both Herbert and Hopkins convey "God's benevolent intent by sequentially positioning God's attributes in this way: the bad aspect is always followed by a good one canceling the bad one out."[55]

A further constitutive element of theodicy occurs in Herbert's poem "The Storm" where the speaker learns that the tension of the "tempestuous times" (1.5) is both purgative and necessary to a cleansing of "the air without, within the breast" (1.18). The setting of the sea in both "The Storm" and Hopkins's *The Wreck* provides the speakers with an image and symbol around which to focus their "sighs and tears"("The Storm," 1.3). The "winds and waters" (1.1) in "The Storm" are made agents of divine worship, designed to test or to please the soul and to induce it to contemplation. As in "Bitter-Sweet," the speaker in "The Storm" trusts that God will respond to the assaults and sieges of his conscience at the door of heaven, irrespective of the manner in which these genuine needs are expressed. "Essential to his entire theological framework is the belief that this [apparent] rudeness is not an offense to God. In one of the most terrifying moments of *Grace Abounding*, Satan tells Bunyan [that] God 'hath been weary of you

---

[54] Vendler 296, n.4.
[55] Vendler 242.

these several years...your bawlings in his ears hath been no pleasant voice to him.' The regenerate Christian [in Herbert's poems] cannot believe this. Herbert presents God as putting aside all the concerns of His majesty in order to give the 'throbbing conscience' ["The Storm," l.9] what it needs."[56] Through the Christian motif of colloquy, the voice of the psalmist is conveyed in "Bitter-Sweet" and "The Storm," and resounds through tones of urgency, boldness, coaxing, remonstrating with God in the face of despair, daring "to assault, and besiege thy door" (1.12). "In *The Temple* this feature of the Psalms coincides with what is commonly called the rhetorical mode of [M]etaphysical poetry. One is impressed by the variety and ingenuity of the strategies used by the speaker to advance his own interests."[57] As a *figura* of the biblical Psalmist, the speaker in Herbert's poems reveals "The Church" as a compendium of religious lyrics in the poems' variety of forms and kinds.[58] Yet "even more than the Psalter, 'The Church' is the record and the dramatization of a single I-thou relationship."[59] Herbert's use of simple, religious diction acknowledges the sacramentality of daily life. Only one who knows God well can speak to Him in such familiar terms. "The only meane too persever," Calvin writes, "is when being furnished with Gods promises, wee appeale untoo him." Herbert insists that God must help because his very nature of justice, mercy, and love demands it.[60] The light that results from this familiar exchange between the soul and God dignifies the purgative experience and strengthens the illumination of faith.

In "The Storm," Herbert deduces that, in his case, storms would be salutary. In line five of "The Bag," he claims that "Storms are the triumph of his art," and in "Affliction (I)," that he is "blown through with ev'ry storm and wind" (1.36). In Chapter IX of *The Country Parson*, titled "The Parson's State of Life," Herbert writes of the need "to be clothed with perfect patience, and Christian fortitude in the cold midnight storms of persecution and adversity."[61] By assaulting and besieging God, Herbert finds what he terms in his letter to Nicholas

---

[56] Strier 187.
[57] Bloch 266-67.
[58] Lewalski 301.
[59] Strier 166.
[60] Bloch 269.
[61] Wall 66.

Ferrar the "perfect freedom."[62] The tempests themselves remind and accuse "poor mortals" of their "crimes" (1.6) and need of repentance. "In 'The Storm,' the speaker assumes that the weather has a directive for him—and for all others."[63] The directive which the storm holds for him is that, without strife, there will be no peace; without discord there can be no concord or spiritual refinement. The soul's suffering from divine (w)reckoning is as important a part of God's providence as is the joyous praise recorded in the earlier poems. Because these natural elements convey a divine message and set in motion a significant spiritual process, they merit the praise of the speaker in the final two lines of "The Storm": "Poets have wrong'd poor storms: such days are best;/They purge the air without, within the breast." "Herbert's decreasing production of explicitly church-centered poem [in 'The Church'] is accompanied by an increase in the number set within the purview of everyday life. In 'The Storm,' he muses on the disturbance before him."[64] "The natural occurrence and the spiritual condition it inspires are smooth cause and effect in the providential scheme. Thus the speaker of *The Temple* treats the natural world as the Creator's eloquent countenance."[65]

The Christian life for the speaker in "Bitter-Sweet" and "The Storm" centers on the search for God in the personal and the communal, the particular and the typical, the immediate and the timeless, much as it does for Ignatius and Hopkins. God participates in the speaker's life as much in His seeming absence as in His immanent presence. Herbert's conception of God and God's relation to the soul impel Herbert to blend institutional and mystical elements in his writings.[66] Herbert's verse and prose remind the reader that the spiritual powers of prayer, praise, and dialogue accompany the soul on its journey to the "door" of the heavenly Father.

Thus, the natural occurrence of the tempest serves Herbert and Hopkins as an emblem of spiritual regeneration. The tempest also serves as a symbol of God's nature, the condition of the soul, and the sacramentality of the natural world. In the ocean Herbert and Hopkins find a symbol that is immense and sweeping enough to join the external

---

[62] Vendler 233.
[63] Benet 62.
[64] Rickey 131.
[65] Benet 49.
[66] Husain 150.

and internal manifestations of God, and to unite them with the inner experience of the Christian disciple. In their description of the (w)reckoning experience of the Christian disciple, these select works of Herbert and Hopkins yield quite readily to a classification of spiritual autobiography.

"Part the Second" of Hopkins's *The Wreck* and "Affliction (II)" of Herbert shift the attention from the (w)reckonings of the speakers to the "Lord of life," as Herbert addresses Him (1.2), and to "the Master,/Ipse, the only one, Christ, King, Head," as Hopkins names the Figure who accompanies the soul on its maritime voyage (II.28. 220–21). However elaborate and difficult the wording, the twofold structure and duality in *The Wreck* are easily apprehended. The two parts of the poem fit structurally, as William York Tindall observes, like the parts of an equation: "...the relation of Hopkins to God is that of the principal nun to God. Her shipwreck is a metaphor for his spiritual trouble and its relief." For both the poet and the nun, the relief is a new understanding, a clearer inscape, achieved in very different ways, of the nature of God revealed in Christ. The poet's concern and prayer that the same illumination may come to all people, especially to the citizens of England, is a natural corollary.[67] The personal encounter with Christ evoked in Part the First is both paralleled by and contrasted with the figure of the tall German nun in Part the Second.

The theodicy evident in "Part the Second" of *The Wreck* depicts the darkness which the "master of the tides" (II.32.249) confers on the soul who immerses itself in the meaning of Christ's Passion. Geoffrey Hartman writes: "Christ, a corporeal Christ, Ipse, is for Hopkins the manifest of man, as ringing is of the bell, fire of kingfishers, hurl and gliding of the windhover."[68] How such identification occurs and how the soul engrafts itself onto Christ until it achieves union with Him is portrayed through the five Franciscan nuns whose German steamship, while taking emigrants from Breman to Canada, was overtaken by an icy snow gale on the Kentish Knock at the mouth of the Thames River.

The number five takes on religious significance in its parallel to the number of wounds Christ acquired in the crucifixion. To Hopkins, "even their number is a symbolic mark of their imitation of Christ,

---

[67] Keating 47.
[68] Lyle H. Smith, Jr., "Beyond the Romantic Sublime: Gerard Manley Hopkins." *Renasccence* 34 (3), 1982; 176.

charged with divine mystery."[69] Five becomes a cipher for Christ, as stanza 22 states: "Five! the finding and sake/And cipher of suffering Christ" (ll.169–70). The lines continue with the revelation that these marks of suffering and humiliation are "of man's make/And the word of it Sacrificed" (ll.171–72). The "Stigma, signal, cinquefoil token" (l.175) are marks of an innocent lamb, recalling the Old Testament topos of Abraham leading his only son Isaac to Moriah where he was to offer him up as a holocaust until the Lord's messenger intervened, and the New Testament figure of Christ the Good Shepherd who lay down His life for His sheep. "Predestined, and most precious to Christ, are those who [like St. Francis, the founder of the religious community to which the five nuns belong] wear his wounds—that is, transform the hurts reflected by men into the marks of Christ—and so share his sufferings, and are themselves united to his redemptive sacrifice."[70] What appears to the world to be pitiful wounds becomes in God's eyes the means and the sign of mystical union with Him. The five nuns become, in their own persons, "the device and index and seal" of the suffering Christ as each one represents a wound of Christ's passion.[71] The account of *The Wreck* is translated as a case of providential gain as the nuns, considered a flock, are called back to the fold in the evening as Christ "royally reclaim[s] his own" (II.34.271).[72]

Such fellowship with the sufferings of Christ enables the speaker, the five nuns, and the reader, to become so swept up in the voyage that they acquire a special intimacy with God and an assurance of His providential care. The appellative "Sister" at the outset of stanza 19 carries a twofold significance: it is the conventional title for a member of a religious congregation, but in this context it also expresses a deep affinity between the speaker and the nun, both victims and victors in the struggle of "the dark night of the soul." "All of the religious powers attributed to the nun were really those of the poet who was inscaping 'the unshapeable shock night' (II.29.227). The tall nun was the foil for Hopkins' new faith. [Both nun and poet] had a common meaning in Christ."[73] The epithets "lioness" and "prophetess" (II.17.135–36) applied to the nun in *The Wreck* reinforce her courage and spiritual

---

[69] Mathai 129.
[70] P. Martin 49.
[71] P. Martin 49.
[72] Mathai 130.
[73] Downes, "Beatific Landscapes in Hopkins" 157.

insight as she becomes one with Christ in prevailing over the disaster
and in revealing the mysteries of God's dispensations.[74] Although the
actual circumstances admit of impending disaster and seeming doom,
of "widow-making unchilding unfathering deeps" (II.13.104), the
"Orion of light" (II.21.165) rides the torment and transforms "ship-
wrack" to "harvest" and "tempest" to "grain" (II.31.248–49). The nun
who calls out, "'O Christ, Christ, come quickly'" (II.24.191) achieves
a closeness to Christ and an identification with Him as a result of her
extreme situation. Her aspiration—"'O Christ, Christ, come
quickly'"—parallels the Ignatian prayer of self-abandonment:

Take, O Lord, and receive all my liberty, my memory, my understanding, and all
my will, all that I have and possess. Thou hast given it to me. To Thee, O Lord,
I return it. All is Thine, dispose of it wholly according to Thy will. Give me Thy
love and Thy grace, for this is sufficient for me.[75]

When the elements of Christian mysticism, as well as all that Hopkins
and the nun possess, are taken away, it is God's favor that remains.
Their acts of total self-giving demonstrate the paradox of the soul
gaining God within the human temple, which Herbert also addresses in
The Temple and *The Country Parson.*

This member of the "coifèd sisterhood" identifies also with St.
Gertrude and Luther (II.20.157). All three belonged to the small town
of Eisleben in Germany (Deutschland), "double a desperate name"
(II.20.154).[76] By placing the nun, St. Gertrude, Cain and Abel, and
Luther in the same stanza, Hopkins once again demonstrates how the
best and worst co-exist in a world devoid of simplistic dualisms. In a
letter of January 6, 1865, Hopkins wrote to E.W. Urquhart, curate of
SS. Philip and James in Oxford. In that letter, Hopkins made similar
use of Luther as an example of the mysterious course of events: "How
strangely different is the fate of two reformers, Savonarola [a 15th-
century Dominican monk] and Luther! The one martyred in the
Church, the other successful and the admired author of world-wide
heresy in schism!"[77] Once again, the parallel to Milton's *Lycidas*
where Milton denounces the clergy is noteworthy. "In the poet's mind,

[74] Keating 76-77.
[75] Puhl 102.
[76] P. Martin 47.
[77] Abbott, *Further Letters of Gerard Manley Hopkins* 18.

the nuns, as exiles under the Falk Laws, were contemporary victims of
the movement which Luther had initiated. Moreover, Hopkins believed
that Luther had destroyed the unity of the Church and had prepared the
way for England's defection from Catholicism. For Hopkins, the con-
sequences of the Reformation would be a major and enduring tribula-
tion of the Church."[78] The "desperate name" of the Deutschland is,
therefore, intensified in its additional signification as the name of Lu-
ther's homeland as well as the site of the shipwreck.

In "Part the Second" of *The Wreck*, Hopkins provides an inclusive
view of Christian theodicy or justification of innocent suffering that
reverses merely human values by encompassing the suffering and pain
of God Himself and the crucifixion of His Only Son, the Logos. Al-
though Christ's Passion, Death, and Resurrection do not change events
or deny pain, the Christian disciple's acceptance of the events and pain
causes a transformation and a healing process to occur which give
substantive value and meaning to the "sorrowing heart" (II.27.212).
Hopkins integrates the theme of theodicy and the mystical stage of
union with God by crediting the suffering of the nuns, crew, and pas-
sengers to their vocation to be imitators of their Master, Christ. The
"inscaping" of Hopkins's soul with Christ's self involves suffering and
"pitch" and what in his mystical perspective Hopkins calls "sacrifice."
The Christian disciple shares in the sufferings of Christ by becoming
"selved" in or united to Him.

Hopkins points out that the traditional view of Christ as being pres-
ent primarily to worshippers in the chancel of a church is overturned
in this experience where Christ is "unchancelling poising palms"
(II.21.166) and opening all barriers which screen off His presence.
Similarly, Herbert asserts that the "throbbing conscience" "Dares to
assault, and besiege thy door"("The Storm," ll.9,12). The biblical
analogue to these lines is the Song of Songs, which is traditionally
applied to the religious life: "My lover is like a gazelle or a young
stag. Here he stands behind our wall, gazing through the windows,
peering through the lattices" (Song of Songs 2:9). Both Herbert and
Hopkins depict a God Who is accessible in the sacrificial extremity of
those who love Him, suffer with Him, and identify with Him. The nuns
in *The Wreck* achieve this unitive state through a spiritual and physical
test of faith in which even the natural elements overtake them. God's

---

[78] Keating 81-82.

presence is revealed, not only in the sheltered seclusion of a church chancel—a place such as a convent chapel with which the nuns would be familiar—but also wherever "Surf, snow, river and earth/Gnashed" (II.21.164–65) occur. Fortunately for the "poor mortals," such storms "are best;/They purge the air without, within the breast" ("The Storm" ll.17–18). In *The Wreck*, God removes the nuns from their sheltering screenwork or chancel in order to measure their heroism in a dangerous public task.[79]

It is not the intention of Hopkins to explain suffering; rather, *The Wreck* is an odyssey which the nun and the Christian undergo in "christen[ing] her wild-worst Best" (II.24.192). "Through her faith in Christ the nun makes her ordeal the opportunity for the best experience of her life."[80] The nun knows that Christ is present and she appeals in her extreme situation to His advent as she holds "the cross to her" (II.24.192). To the nun, the storm is Christ, and she welcomes Him, though His approach means a sort of crucifixion. The disjointedness of stanza 28 mirrors the inadequacy of the poet and the nun to articulate the vision of Christ which the nun witnesses. Like Simon Peter, she, too, sees Christ on the waters and realizes His mastery, power and control. Christ "cure[d] the extremity where he had cast her" (II.28.222), and in this transforming of a calamity into a victory and a triumph, the soul of the nun fulfills the purpose of its creation. In the shipwreck, God's mastery and mercy stated at the conclusion of "Part the First" are documented and fulfilled. The nun's ability to see "beneath and behind the horror of storm and shipwreck the Lord, the Lover, to see 'shape' in what seemed 'unshapeable,' and meaning in what was apparently meaningless tragedy [provides the] crux of the whole poem."[81] Taking a Christ-centered view of her surroundings, she renames ("christens") physical disaster a spiritual victory and conveys a spiritually literate reading to the storm.[82]

Hopkins's essential concern is not with the precise number of the victims or their external appearance and history, but with the state of their souls and their acceptance of a God who is all justice and all mercy.[83] The *Deutschland* carried passengers like the nuns who came

---

[79] MacKenzie 44.
[80] Phillips 340.
[81] P. Martin 58.
[82] MacKenzie 46, 50.
[83] Keating 72.

to accept and embrace God's will, as well as passengers who attempted suicide. There were many aboard the *Deutschland* who were of "a bitterer vein for the/Comfortless unconfessed of them-" (II.31.243–44). "Many of the voyagers were not gathered to God; others were quite irreligious, for *The Times* of December 11 reports that one man hanged himself, another hacked at his wrist with a knife. The words 'not under thy feathers' (II.12.93), then, express Hopkins' distressed concern for those who he fears were not in the way of salvation."[84] Nevertheless, Hopkins is quick to point out that they are "not uncomforted," that "lovely-felicitous Providence" (II.31.245) maintains His tender finger on them. "Through the self-givingness of one soul it may well have been that those 'poor sheep' on board the stricken ship were herded back to the Shepherd of whom they were themselves unaware. 'All souls lost' holds within it the potential of 'All souls saved.'"[85] Those who, like the nuns, offer their pain for the sake of Christ and for the redeeming of the world's sins reenact in their own lives the *kenosis* of Christ and the redeeming love and mercy of God Himself, and thus fulfill the "dangerous public task" with which they have been charged. The deep union with Christ that ensues is one that no (w)reckoning can annihilate.

Although the life of Hopkins is vastly different from that of the five German nuns, he seeks a peace and union with God by living the Ignatian discipline and undergoing the faith cycle of consolation and desolation. Trusting in a "lovely-felicitous Providence" that will leave the "Comfortless   unconfessed   of   them-/No   not   uncomforted" (II.31.244–45), he depends on God's outriding mercy to provide "an ark" of salvation (II.33.258), even for the "last-breath penitent spirits" (II.33.262). Hopkins is caught up, not only in a spiritual transformation, but in a self-revelation as well. He undergoes a change from his declaration at the beginning of "Part the First" that "I am sóft síft/In an hourglass" (I.4.25–26) to a movement away from the self to the whole English nation and, indeed, to the entire society. Initially, he addresses God as "Thou mastering me" (I.1.1), but in the concluding stanza of the poem, he addresses God as "Our King," "hero of us," and his homeland as "rare-dear Britain." The shift in the personal pronoun from the first-person singular to the first-person plural signifies

---

[84] Keating 72-73.
[85] P. Martin 64.

the gradual union of Hopkins with the "Énglish sóuls" and his God. It also confirms "a pattern of ascent" which constitutes Hopkins's vision of reality and spirituality, and confirms the Ignatian meditative pattern.[86]

Thus, a reading of *The Wreck* as spiritual autobiography suggests answers to the question on which the genre is centered—who am I in the eyes of the Creator? By depicting a speaker who enters into the experiences of other persons, Hopkins characterizes a Christian disciple whose life is an instressing of the soul with God. Hopkins's skill in taking a tragic news event and imbuing it with an Ignatian meditative pattern allows him poetically to bridge the "wreck" of the *Deutschland* and of the lives on board the ship with his own spiritual (w)reckoning. The poem describes his particular hope that God will continue to rule providentially over "the English souls" of his "rare-dear Britain" (II.35.277-78) so that they may convert to Catholicism. Likewise, it underlines his universal conviction that Christ will "easter in us, be a dayspring to the dimness of us, be a/crimson-cresseted east" (II.35.78). The wreck of the *Deutschland* provides the occasion for a virginal telling-forth of how one poet envisions God working in the world "among our shoals" and "in the roads" until he meets God in "the heaven-haven of the reward" (II.35.274-75) at the end of the spiritual journey.

While the experience of "the dark night of the soul" is not the preferred one for Herbert or Hopkins, it is crucial to spiritual regeneration. Herbert's five "Affliction" poems convey this developing spiritual maturity. "Affliction (II)," in particular, marks the speaker's spiritual and intellectual awakening to the ontology of exegesis itself and the idea that he himself is the text: "Thy cross took up in one,/By way of imprest, all my future moan" (ll.14-15).[87] Herbert's theology, then, suggests that the pain of trying to love God has its compensations. His belief, however, like that of Hopkins, is that spiritual difficulties recur. Indeed, the initial line of "Affliction (II)" is an enjoinder to the Lord that He not "kill" the speaker "ev'ry day." "However symmetrical the ideal state of the Christian at any one moment, the pilgrimage of the [seventeenth-century] Christian in time was not a broad and straight

---

[86] Boyd Litzinger, "The Pattern of Ascent in Hopkins." *Victorian Poetry*, 2 (1964), 43,47.

[87] Asals 45.

highway from the vales of sin to the Heavenly City. Most of the men
of the seventeenth century did not believe that sorrow was totally ban-
ished or that man could achieve continuous beatitude on this earth."[88]
Rather, it is the presence of the Lord here and now, in the daily expe-
riences, that Herbert apprehends with quick intimacy and expresses
with the simplicity of one who has found his center beyond himself.[89]
"Affliction (II)" concerns not so much self-knowledge as an under-
standing of the nature of reality and of the paradoxes, reversals, and
emotional fluctuations through which the spiritual life evolves.

The speaker's awareness of his unworthiness is treated in "Afflic-
tion (II)" by the use of legal tropes—metaphorical diction that translates
the "broken pay" (l.4) of the speaker into the cost of discipleship that
the speaker, like his Lord, is willing to take up, "since thy one death
for me/Is more than all my deaths can be" (ll.2–3). The immediate
need of the speaker here, as in *The Wreck*, inspires a blunt conversa-
tion with God. Herbert's resolve to conform to the incarnate Word who
is "All my delight" (l.13) leads him through the same "common sewer,
sea, and brine" (l.7) of human experience as Hopkins undergoes in *The
Wreck*. The God who provides delight concomitantly provides "my
smart" (l.13) in the same spirit of contraries evident in "Bitter-Sweet,"
"The Storm," and Hopkins's *The Wreck*. The movement toward uni-
fication with God involves the gradual collapsing of these contraries,
much as it does in Herbert's "Bitter-Sweet." "Christ's specific attention
to the individual convinces the speaker that his own suffering is less
paltry than it first seems and thus explains affliction and grief as a 'bait'
that draws man to God."[90] The speaker is assured of God's favor and
so is able to engage in a colloquy with the "Lord of life" (l.2) with
compelling directness as he complains of but, ultimately, accepts God's
chastisement and discipline. "Self-giving becomes self-enriching be-
cause in the commerce of divine love, the eliminated self gets sublimat-
ed, converting the human into the divine."[91] Christ's grief becomes
the speaker's grief and, paradoxically, his salvation and "All my de-
light" (l.13). Herbert's "poems modulate into a defense of God's ways;
it is from that movement of argument, not merely from vivid emotional

---

[88] Summers, *George Herbert* 87.
[89] White 200.
[90] Sherwood 115.
[91] Mathai 221.

coloring, that the poems derive their effectiveness" and the Christian theme of theodicy is realized.[92]

The Christian life for Herbert and Hopkins is a cyclic process of desolation and consolation, not a static mode of being. The process is primarily one of a spiritual unfolding in which external factors and events are assigned a "catalytic significance." "The world of external fact [of storms, circumstances of affliction] is important insofar as it releases in Herbert and Hopkins a motion in the direction internally set."[93] A reading of their works as spiritual autobiography recognizes the authors' selections of various incidents as paradoxical, meaningful, and redemptive in relation to the pattern of reality in their lives. "Elements of past experience are wrenched loose a little bit from the context in which they originally stood; they are singled out because they are now seen to have a symptomatic meaning they may not have had before."[94]

A study of the poetry and prose of Herbert and Hopkins as spiritual autobiography offers the reader an account of God's grandeur and mastery in the thunder and lightning, as well as in the beauty and sacramentality of nature. Furthermore, it records the process by which these two authors learn to "say yes" to the literal and spiritual (w)reckonings (even when the river of circumstances seems to ride the way of "terror" and "horror") that empower them to become God's landscape upon which is "imprest" the nature of the soul and the God of "All [their] delight."

---

[92] Shaw 77.

[93] Karl J. Weintraub, "Autobiography and Historical Consciousness." *Critical Inquiry*, 1 (1975), 831.

[94] Weintraub, "Autobiography and Historical Consciousness" 826.

Chapter Four

The Cost of Discipleship:
An Audit of the Soul's Account

> With witness I speak this. But where I say
> Hours I mean years, mean life. And my lament
> Is cries countless, cries like dead letters sent
> To dearest him that lives alas! away.
> (Hopkins, "I wake and feel")

AS HERBERT AND HOPKINS advance in their ministerial and poetic vocations, they wrestle with circumstances and events that seem to impede spiritual progress and to deny the three stages of Christian mysticism. Herbert and Hopkins pay a high price—emotionally and physically—in responding to the vocation of Christian discipleship as their souls undergo a reckoning or an audit of the salvific but painful chastenings by God. This process of sanctification involves the "breaking" of the self in order that the soul may receive Christ more fully. As the *Spiritual Exercises* states, the ministerial vocation demands a sacrifice of everything that is held dear, "for the glory and praise of God our Lord and for the salvation of [the] soul."[1] What Paul Mariani states so convincingly when referring to Hopkins is merited also by Herbert: "it takes an incredibly heroic strength to follow to their logical conclusions the dictates of a position as ascetic and unwestern as the one [Herbert and] Hopkins found [themselves] in and to alter, in the process of altering [their] consciousness, [their] very muse for something like 'the greater glory of God.'"[2] This sacrifice is addressed in select poems of Herbert and six "terrible" or "dark" sonnets of Hopkins.

The *agon* experience initially described by Hopkins in *The Wreck* and by Herbert in "Bitter-Sweet," "The Storm," and "Affliction (II)" finds further intensity and dramatic depiction in an interrelated study of the matching poems in this chapter: Herbert's "The Cross" and Hopkins's "To seem the stranger"; Herbert's "Denial" and Hopkins's "I wake and feel"; Herbert's "Complaining" and Hopkins's "No

---

[1] Puhl 75.
[2] Mariani, "Hopkins: Towards a Poetics of Unselfconsciousness" 49.

worst." These poems depict the soul's descent into the emptiness within. Chapter Five treats Herbert's "The Collar" and Hopkins's "(Carrion Comfort)"; Herbert's "Affliction (IV)" and Hopkins's "Patience, hard thing"; Herbert's "Justice (I)" and Hopkins's "My own heart," poems that evidence the soul's ascent to God.[3] In analyzing these poems as spiritual autobiography, I use the order to suggest, not the order of their composition, but their depiction of the gradual desolation and consolation of the soul, which follows the classical descent and ascent of the Ignatian *Exercises*. Moreover, such a comparative analysis reveals a spiritual progression summarized in a statement Hopkins once made about himself: "me, the culprit, the lost sheep, the redeemed."[4] In these poems, Herbert's and Hopkins's usual consciousness of nature and creation, their intelligence about poetry, and their theological formation are joined by a new element: the mark of their daily relations with God, relations that are clearly not without frustration and combat. Both Herbert and Hopkins learn that alternating periods of consolation and desolation are germane to the cyclical pattern of the Christian experience and to the literary *corpus* of both writers. Louis L. Martz's term of "argumentative evolutions" is an apt description of the select works of Herbert and Hopkins considered in this chapter and in Chapter Five, all of which, when considered as a unit, "first compose the problem, then analyze its parts, and end with resolutions and patterns in colloquy with God."[5] When considered as spiritual autobiography, these poems translate the devotional content of the writers' emotional disturbances and emphasize the human cost of discipleship which Herbert and Hopkins elsewhere express with greater serenity and gentler submissiveness. Furthermore, they demonstrate the willingness of these two writers to pay the price of Christian discipleship.

In line nine of *The Wreck*, Hopkins foreshadows the ambiguity of the terrible nothingness of self and the overwhelming power of God depicted so categorically in the "terrible" sonnets: "Thou art lightning and love, I found it, a winter and a warm." He now returns to the experience of "the dark side of the bay of thy blessing" *(The Wreck*

---

[3] Mariani, *A Commentary on the Complete Poems of Gerard Manley Hopkins* 212.

[4] Patricia A. Wolfe, "The Paradox of Self: A Study of Hopkins' Spiritual Conflict in the 'Terrible' Sonnets." *Victorian Poetry*, 6 (1968), 85.

[5] Martz 61.

I.12.95) and finds himself, like Jacob struggling with the Angel, wrestling even with God. "Only now the wrestling is more lingering, longer drawn out. God is absent to him and strongly silent."[6] The theme of personal and national conversion that dominates *The Wreck* is further developed in the "sonnets of desolation" that Hopkins wrote in the next decade.

Reformation and Jesuitical thought fully sounds the experiences of Herbert and Hopkins in three ways, clearly evidenced when a selection of their works is analyzed as spiritual autobiography. First, the works depict how the soul must be broken of its tendency to depend upon its own merit; second, how the soul must face physical and emotional suffering in order to increase its dependence upon God; and third, how the soul must be faithful to "the Hidden God," the *deus absconditus*, so that one walks by faith and not by sight (2 Cor. 5:7), submitting one's will to God's will even when it seems God is absent.[7] A comparative analysis of six of Herbert's poems and six of Hopkins's "terrible" sonnets demonstrates how these two Christian disciples undergo spiritual warfare: the seeming disappearance and silence of God, a sense of abandonment, an awareness of futility, a period of spiritual instability, the eventual rejection of the self, and the resolution of the spiritual crises through an identification with Christ. The poems also serve as *de profundis* orisons uttered by two ministers whose souls, like the soul of the writer of Psalm 130, sound the depths of spiritual misery, contrition for sins, and a trust in God's mercy and reprieve.

It is important to note that, despite the seeming absence of God and the intense spiritual and emotional conflict depicted in these poems, neither Herbert nor Hopkins doubts the existence of God. There is a gap in the relationship between God and the speakers, brought about by God's seeming withdrawal from their souls, yet there is also an assurance that God will inevitably return and sanctify their souls. "We cannot apprehend a work of literature," says Mr. Middleton Murry, "except as a manifestation of the rhythm of the soul of the man who created it. If we stop short of that, our understanding is incomplete."[8] The selections of poems considered in this chapter and in Chapter Five

[6] Peter J. Milward, S.J., and Raymond V. Schoder, S.J., *Landscape and Inscape: Vision and Inspiration in Hopkins's Poetry* (London: Paul Elek Ltd., 1975) 84.
[7] Veith 145.
[8] Pick 138.

are deeply expressive of the souls of Herbert and Hopkins during times of keen self-criticism as they cast about to find a reason for their spiritual desolation. "Christian readers will see in these poems an expression of a very traditional theme in spiritual writing: the soul's sense of being rejected and left desolate by God. But the poems also indicate a remarkable intensity of self-knowledge and self-encounter."[9] Moreover, their poetic form expresses "that spirit of faith of which the Scripture says, 'Because I believed, I spoke out'" (2 Cor. 4:13).

The speakers in these poems, despite their recognition of God's love and ultimate submission to His will, are not particularly comforted, nor is their pain lessened. "Always in Herbert and Hopkins the worst evil is not affliction but desolation and spiritual barrenness. They can bear God's storms but not his absence and their infertility."[10] Yet by recording their complaints, Herbert and Hopkins assign value to suffering and profundity to God's will, upon which, to the Reformers as well as the Jesuits, everything depends. Indeed, Hebrews 12:6 serves as the biblical analogue for the (w)reckoning experience depicted in these works: "My sons, do not disdain the discipline of the Lord nor lose heart when he reproves you; For whom the Lord loves, he disciplines; he scourges every son he receives."

Herbert's "story," as it is recorded in *The Temple* and *The Country Parson*, is a setting down of "the spiritual conflicts that have passed betwixt God and my Soul before I could subject mine to the will of Jesus my Master, in whose service I have now found perfect freedom." This story witnessed many revisions and much reflection as Herbert pondered his ecclesiastical vocation in light of the will of God.[11] The cross that Herbert bears in serving his God is clearly articulated in his poem "The Cross" which, in an explicit colloquy, reveals the depth of the conflict and "wrestling" he undergoes.[12] Three critics in particular—James Olney, Amy M. Charles, and French critic A.J. Festugière, O.P.—suggest possible causes of the conflict that underlie "The Cross." Olney believes that "some thought Herbert was foolish to

---

[9] Bergonzi 133.

[10] Olney, *George Herbert and Gerard Manley Hopkins* 61.

[11] Wall 14.

[12] Indeed, the sub-title to Herbert's *The Temple*—"Sacred Poems and Private Ejaculations," defined by fellow Cambridge minister Thomas Fuller as "short prayers darted up to God on emergent occasions"—underscores the Christian theme of colloquy in Herbert's works and confirms the immanence of God in his life.

retire from the courtly world as he did to Bemerton. His first editor, Barnabas Oley, says, 'And for our Author (*The sweet singer of the Temple*) though he was one of the most prudent and accomplish'd men of his time, I have heard sober men censure him as a man that did not manage his brave parts to his best advantage and preferment, but lost himself *in an Humble way*.'"[13]

Amy M. Charles contends that "The Cross" "almost certainly refers to Herbert's visit to the church at Leighton Bromswold for his induction in 1626," and that, although "few of [Herbert's] poems can be dated exactly or read for direct biographical statement...it is almost impossible to overlook Herbert's remarks about himself and his family and about a particular church, especially in the first two stanzas of 'The Cross.'"[14] Among the three churches that Herbert undertook to restore, this "splendid stone church of Leighton Bromswold" was the only cruciform church "that Herbert immediately decided to rebuild, with the help of his family."[15] Indeed, the account listing the names of benefactors indicates that Herbert clearly planned to undertake this re-building. Charles finds evidence in Izaak Walton's biography of Herbert to suggest that the year 1626 was also the year when Herbert's weakness in body and dejection in spirit was probably attributed to his "supposed Consumption."[16] The third stanza of "The Cross" wherein Herbert speaks of his agues or melancholia stresses the paradoxical nature of his "abilities"—talents or "skills" as he refers to them in "Justice (I)"— that have provided him the opportunity of singing and praising God, but which have also undermined his ability to perform his ministerial duties. Herbert's fear of sickness is also illustrated in a letter he sent to his mother, Lady Danvers, in 1622: "I alwaies fear'd sickness more then death, because sickness hath made me unable to perform those Offices for which I came into the world, and must yet be kept in it."[17]

Festugière aligns Herbert's spirit with that of Abraham. "And so God removed Herbert from his old life. But in this place, Herbert was not able to complete his task. God led Herbert to 'some place' where

---

[13] Olney, *George Herbert and Gerard Manley Hopkins* 121, n.1.
[14] Amy Charles, *A Life of George Herbert* (New York: Cornell University Press, 1977) 127.
[15] Charles 128.
[16] Charles 128.
[17] Charles 129.

he was to serve Him. Herbert moved all his possessions and his entire family. And then when, after much wrestling, this goal was attained [of being uprooted], God did 'take away/My power to serve thee.'"[18] Unlike the Church at Bemerton which Herbert paid for out of his own means, Herbert's vow to "Re-build that Church" at Leighton Bromswold was not fulfilled during his lifetime, a circumstance that, no doubt, contributed to his discouragement as his "hopes" became his "torture" ("The Cross," ll.23,27).[19]

Dejection and melancholia also accompanied Hopkins in his spiritual journey. From December 1882, until his death in Dublin of typhoid in 1889, Hopkins was the victim of recurring depression which seems to have been brought on, at least in part, by the burdens of teaching and examining students at Stonyhurst and Dublin. He was barely forty years old, but the image of Hopkins presented by himself and others is of a man suffering chronically from eyestrain, headaches, anemia, and depression. Hopkins went to Ireland in February 1884, as Professor of Greek at the John Henry Newman Catholic University in Dublin (also known as University College).[20] During his last years of teaching in Dublin (1884–89) the depression and pain increased. It is this depression of the Dublin years—a continuation of his earlier Stonyhurst condition—that is recorded in his Terrible Sonnets.[21] "The opening words of these sonnets tell a plain story, the biographical location of which is some four or so years before the poet's death. Simply as poetry the sonnets give us something of the depth and force of the great soliloquies of *Macbeth*."[22]

In a letter of September 1, 1885, the year in which Hopkins's "terrible" sonnets were probably composed, the "Star of Balliol," as Jewett referred to him twenty years before, told Robert Bridges:

---

[18] A.J. Festugière, O.P., *George Herbert: Poète, Saint, Anglican (1593-1633)* (Paris: Librairie Philosophique J. Vrin, 1971) 292. (my translation)

[19] Charles 129.

[20] McChesney 155.

[21] Joseph J. Feeney, S.J., "Hopkins as Teacher: The English Years." In *Gerard Manley Hopkins: New Essays on His Life, Writing, and Place in English Literature*. ed. Michael E. Allsopp and Michael W. Sundermeier (New York: Edwin Mellen Press, 1989) 219.

[22] Francis Noël Lees, *Gerard Manley Hopkins* (New York and London: Columbia University Press, 1966) 40.

...if I could but get on, if I could but produce work I should not mind its being buried, silenced, and going no further; but it kills me to be time's eunuch and never to beget. After all I do not despair, things must change, anything may be; only there is no great appearance of it.... [S]oon I am afraid I shall be ground down to a state like this last spring's and summer's, when my spirits were so crushed that madness seemed to be making approaches—and nobody was to blame, except myself partly for not managing myself better and contriving a change.[23]

Ignatius's word "desolation" as he defines it in his "Rules for the Discernment of Spirits" is given an accurate rendering in Hopkins's sonnets of desolation: "darkness of soul, turmoil of spirit...restlessness rising from many disturbances and temptations which lead to want of faith, hope, and love. The soul is wholly slothful, tepid, sad, and separated, as it were, from its Creator and Lord."[24] The sonnet "To seem the stranger" (1885–86) is a condensed summary of these circumstances, and an account of the cost of Hopkins's discipleship. Its direct and honest language and explicit theme render it as the "center of the 'terrible' sequence."[25]

The biblical allusion with which "To seem the stranger" concludes and on which "The Cross" focuses is Christ's parable of the man who set out to build a tower. He laid the foundation, but depleted funds caused him to be mocked by everyone who saw the failed enterprise: "That man began to build what he could not finish" (Luke 14:28–30). The context of the Lucan passage is Christ's invitation to His followers to "calculate the outlay" of Christian discipleship by renouncing familial and material ties and, indeed, one's "very self," an auditing that must be undertaken frequently by anyone who takes up the cross to follow Christ. A "lonely began," the concluding phrase which Hopkins uses to describe himself in "To seem the stranger," is not the same as a "beginner"; Hopkins was not at the elementary stage of Christian discipleship when he wrote this "dark" sonnet "To seem the stranger." He continues to "calculate the outlay" many times, as these sonnets of desolation reveal. Peter Milward, however, cautions that "these 'dark' sonnets are for the most part concentrated, or 'huddle in a main,' in one year and one portion of that year, the late spring and early summer

---

[23] Abbott, *The Letters of Gerard Manley Hopkins to Robert Bridges* 222.
[24] Puhl 142.
[25] Schneider 190.

of 1885. After that there are indeed intermittent spells of darkness, but never again anything so intense."[26]

Herbert's discouragement in "The Cross" is heightened by the realization that all of his abilities are confounded (l.10). Not only is he unable to rebuild the physical "design" of this Church, but the inner "wrestling" and "combat" have left him only with groans that "confound" harmony and poetic talent. There is no consolation in this experience. As Robert B. Shaw remarks, the poetic and the ministerial vocations are not dissimilar: "Poetry and the priesthood harmonize precisely in their being sacramental activities, each a means of realizing the presence of God and imparting that presence to others."[27] When one activity is "thrown down" ("The Cross," 1.22), the other suffers also, until the poet's words become Christ's words—"*Thy will be done*"—and both Christ and Herbert submit to the Logos and to the mystery of the crucifixion. By the final stanza, Herbert acknowledges "These contrarieties [that] crush" him, and engrafts his will onto that of Christ's, whose words become "my words, *Thy will be done*." In the closing three lines, "the whole edifice of self-will collapses."[28] When Helen Vendler writes that the last lines of "The Cross" "come suddenly, almost too suddenly to erase the earlier bitterness," she overlooks the supremacy of Scripture in Herbert's life.[29] The four words spoken by Christ—"Thy will be done"—balance the preceding stanzas of complaint. Herbert's physical and spiritual weakness are spurred to action when he contemplates the cross and its power to save him through the same "contradictions" that "sting" him and "throw [him] down."

The Christian theme of colloquy is clearly redefined in "The Cross" where Herbert "presents a human being speaking God's Word and bringing it to life by living it."[30] In reciting an inventory of pain and portraying in parallel clauses the symptoms of this pain—"One ague dwelleth in my bones,/Another in my soul" (ll. 13-14)—Herbert labors in God's presence to overcome both isolation and *acedia*. He is convinced that God is listening, and so his colloquy is directed at a God who allows His followers to "imp" their wings on His ("Easter

[26] Milward and Schoder, *Landscape and Inscape* 84-85.
[27] Shaw 95.
[28] Martz 135.
[29] Vendler 267.
[30] Bloch 44.

Wings," 1.19). Herbert realizes that only when his voice is joined with Christ's voice will he be able to love and praise.

Joseph Summers posits that Herbert's conception of God as artist—"As Creatures, he must needs love them; for no perfect Artist ever yet hated his own work" (*A Priest to the Temple*)—offers a most convincing argument against despair and serves as one of the most significant principles that undergirds both *The Country Parson* and *The Temple*. "Herbert rings all the traditional changes on 'stone'.... The hardness of the stone was generally recognized; it was the employment of that hardness in the construction of a true temple which appealed to Herbert's imagination."[31]

By surrendering his own "designs" in imitation of the Son, the speaker takes refuge in the Father's "design" and imposes a cruciform value on all things. However, with the passage of time, this conflict recurs, as subsequent poems in "The Church" verify. "In such dramatic surges and withdrawals of assurance lies one of the defining features of Herbert's poetic practice."[32] A reading of "The Cross" and other Herbertian poems as spiritual autobiography is further justified when the "contrarieties" and "harmony" are viewed as "cross actions" that restore the poet's self-definition and poetic ability. Indeed, the words "'cross actions' enable the speaker and the reader to visualize the relationship between the speaker's conflict and Christ's suffering, because 'cross actions' are those actions pertaining to the cross of Christ."[33] Though "The Cross" is centered on a symbol established by tradition, it conveys personal experience and becomes an emphatic witness of "my [Herbert's] words." "In Herbert's characteristic practice, even when the end of a poem is an absolute definition, it must form its contraction out of superfluities which invite, challenge attention, apply pressure, and yield but do not defect or abscond. 'The Cross' moves with full and passionate immediacy, both flowing and ebbing, before it is brought to a final diminution, an accepted point balancing all the extensive personal discoveries."[34]

---

[31] Summers, "Herbert's Form." *PMLA* 66 (1951): 1068-69.

[32] Stewart, *George Herbert* 98-99.

[33] Ronald G. Shafer, *The Poetry of George Herbert and the Epistles of St. Paul: A Study in Thematic and Imagistic Similarities* diss., Duquesne University, 1975, 123.

[34] Arnold Stein, *George Herbert's Lyrics* (Baltimore: The Johns Hopkins Press, 1968) 153.

Herbert's poems represent a developing spiritual maturity as the poet depicts the fluctuations between sorrow and joy, doubt and assurance that occur in the life of the Christian disciple. The fact that Herbert fails to restore the temple at Leighton Bromswold is concurrent with his own belief that the soul—the real Temple of God—is being created at each moment. Like language and poetry, the soul must constantly be renewed and refashioned in order to sustain its creative individuality.

The impulse that motivates Herbert to "Re-build that Church" at Leighton Bromswold parallels Hopkins's longing to "re-build" or convert the Church of England. Herbert experiences failure in his inability to rebuild the Church, an unfinished task which he always regretted. Similarly, Hopkins's inability to complete his "task," as he viewed it, of "wooing" his beloved England to Catholicism, causes him to feel removed and estranged from his family, friends, and community, and renders him "a lonely began." In a letter of July 3, 1886, to Canon Dixon, Hopkins writes of his intense desire to imitate "Christ our Lord," Whose life bears a striking parallel to the life of the speaker in the "terrible" sonnets:

> [Christ's] career was cut short, and whereas he would have wished to succeed by success—for it is insane to lay yourself out for failure...nevertheless he was doomed to succeed by failure; his plans were baffled, his hopes dashed, and his work was done by being broken off undone. However much he understood all this he found it an intolerable grief to submit to it. He left the example: it is very strengthening, but except in that sense it is not consoling.[35]

Hopkins learns that, in the total inscape of the life of the Christian disciple, success and failure are relational.

The sequence of these "dark" sonnets is uncertain, but they were all probably written in 1885-86. One of them, as Hopkins states in a letter of May 1885 to Robert Bridges, was "written in blood," and another four, as he states in a letter of September 1, 1885, also to Bridges, came "like inspirations unbidden and against my will."[36] In these sonnets of desolation, Hopkins approaches the central questions of the spiritual life: aridity, moral servitude, the bitterness of pride,

---

[35] Abbott, *The Correspondence of Gerard Manley Hopkins and Richard Watson Dixon* 137-38.
[36] Abbott, *The Letters of Gerard Manley Hopkins to Robert Bridges* 219, 221.

and the co-existence of sin and grace in the soul. Here he wrestles with the ultimate struggle between his vocations as priest and poet. For Hopkins, "the God who is, is terrible."[37] Although they may have been "written in blood," the "terrible" sonnets were channelled with the same perfect metrical precision as his earlier works. "Their greatness is realized not only in their technical achievement but in what they reveal, so powerfully, about the spiritual life."[38] These poems face despair but never succumb to it; there is a saving energy in them that is not seen in the outcries of *fin de siècle* despair emerging in the literary culture of the time.[39]

Hopkins's intention to follow Christ cost dearly; it is summarized economically by the three "removes" in "To seem the stranger." The first remove, signified in stanza one, is Hopkins's conversion to the minority religion of Catholicism, a decision that termed him forever "the stranger" to his own Anglican family, in the way Christ had predicted (Matt. 10:34–7). Christ's message of spreading "not peace, but division" is clearly demonstrated by Hopkins's placement of the virgule in line 4: "my peace/my parting" to symbolize the "sword and strife" caused by his removal from the Anglican to the Catholic Church. In a letter to Newman of October 15, 1866, Hopkins described his family's reaction to the news of his conversion as "terrible."[40] Part of his father's distress at his son's conversion was due to the estrangements which a convert to Catholicism experienced. "His father had written, 'by study hard WITHIN THE CHURCH YARD/IS FOUND THE PHILOSOPHER'S STONE.' Ironically, it was by following this advice that father and son became estranged."[41] John Robinson suggests that "the stroke which makes 'peace' and 'parting' interchangeable is Hopkins's means of showing, even when surrounded by people, the essential isolation of the self whose idealism makes such aloneness an inevitable consequence."[42] The poem is a hieroglyph of the biblical analogue where God's word is presented as being "living and effective, sharper than any two-edged sword. It penetrates and divides soul and

---

[37] Margaret Ellsberg, *Created to Praise: The Language of Gerard Manley Hopkins* (New York and Oxford: Oxford University Press, 1987) 27.

[38] Ellsberg 12.

[39] Bergonzi 133.

[40] Abbott, *Further Letters of Gerard Manley Hopkins* 29.

[41] Bump, *Gerard Manley Hopkins* 61.

[42] Robinson 145.

spirit, joints and marrow. All lies bare and exposed to the eyes of him to whom we must render an account" (Heb. 4:12).

The second remove, described in stanza two, is the result of two factors: Hopkins's decision to become a Jesuit, which caused an eight-year estrangement from Robert Bridges, and the curious and difficult poetic style in his verses and rhythm, which Bridges labeled odd and obscure. His creative attempts in *The Wreck* and *The Loss of the Eurydice* to "woo" to the true Faith his country of England, from which he derived his poetic inspiration, was rejected by publishers. While others defended England's honor, Hopkins was extremely conscious of being "idle," and so symbolized the further rejection brought on by his "creating thought" (1.6) by using the last letter—"Y"—at the end of "wéar" to signify his solitary and wearisome state. This "creating thought" was furthered by Hopkins's "obstinate love of Scotist doctrine," which "got him into difficulties" and caused his views to be distrusted by the Jesuit superiors.[43] W.H. Gardner suggests that the splitting of "wéar-Y" imitates the speaker's weariness in getting the word out and also emphasizes his drawn-out spiritual agony.[44] Moreover, this word-break signifies the quality of the colloquy between Hopkins and Christ. Unlike Herbert's "The Cross," Christ is not mentioned in "To seem the stranger"; however, the tone of this poem, as well as of the entire sonnet group, is Christocentric in its chronicling of the devastating breakdown of all coherences in Hopkins's life.[45]

The third remove, stated in stanza three, was to Ireland which, since 1860, had been a separate Jesuit Province.[46] Hopkins's use of repetition ("now") reinforces the drawn-out spiritual agony of stanza 2: "I am in Ireland now; now I am at a third" (1.9). As the only member of the English community in Ireland, Hopkins was regarded as "the stranger" who, like the captive Jews in Babylon, questions how he and his soul will "sing the song of the Lord in a foreign land" (Ps. 137:44). Though capable of giving and getting "kind love" (1.11), Hopkins labored scrupulously over his work in Ireland—the examining of students in classics—a task which seemed to him of little use, for he believed that the university was accomplishing scarcely anything of

---

[43] Schneider 189.
[44] Gardner 344.
[45] Mariani, *A Commentary on the Complete Poems of Gerard Manley Hopkins* 218.
[46] MacKenzie 180.

what Newman had hoped originally.[47] Moreover, Hopkins was torn
by the duty with which his superiors charged him and his own loyalty
to England. "In his dilemma, the more fully he did what he knew to be
his duty [stated in lines 7 and 8 as being 'idle' with regard to the politi-
cal situation], the more he contributed to the aid of England's enemies
in Ireland, a situation to him nearly intolerable."[48] In a letter of
March 2, 1885, Hopkins wrote to his mother: "the grief of mind I go
through over politics, over what I read and hear and see in Ireland
about Ireland and England, is such that I can neither express it nor bear
to speak of it."[49] His witnessing of shocking moral imperfections in
the Catholic clergy and reports of cowardice and panic among the
English troops at Majuba, a national disgrace he could not bear to think
of, contributed to the "baffling ban" (l.12) of his dark desolation.[50]

"To seem the stranger" is a synopsis of Hopkins's "terrible" son-
nets in its treatment of the critical conflict of England, Ireland, and the
Catholic Church as reflected in Hopkins's own pain of torn loyalties
and helplessness, and the related frustration of his creative powers by
internal and external forces. Its rather plain style reveals a soul at odds
with his lot in life, and a desire to acquire one word of comfort to
thwart "hell's spell" (l.13). A series of "clipped agonies and heavy
pauses interrupt the lines without destroying the verse-feeling," thereby
reinforcing the state of isolation and sterility.[51] But he hears nothing
to dispel the "baffling ban" of being the stranger—he must "hoard" it
"unheard"—and his experience of "the dark night of the soul" contin-
ues. His writing, like that of the psalmist, is the sole means of convey-
ing his thoughts, which he must now "hoard" or store within his heart,
yet the poem hints at his literary sterility, of which he complains in his
Letters. "Both the poet and his poem find themselves, finally, back
where they began. His years of service as a Jesuit do not seem to have
borne fruit, and so he is caught in a self-imprisoned past action: 'a
lonely began.'"[52]

Furthermore, Hopkins is distraught by the face of England in the
industrial nineteenth century. As his "bright" poems of creation and

---

[47] Schneider 188.
[48] Schneider 188.
[49] Abbott, *Further Letters of Gerard Manley Hopkins* 170.
[50] Schneider 188.
[51] Jim Hunter, *Gerard Manley Hopkins* (London: Evans Brothers Ltd., 1966) 122.
[52] Cotter 225.

nature analyzed in Chapter Two clearly demonstrate, he wants all of life to be arranged in a spiritual order and the peak of that order to be religious. "Instead, he sees the face of nature being corrupted and destroyed and no possibility of effective criticism: spiritual criticism would be simply disregarded as irrelevant."[53]

Yet, ironically, it is in the foreign country of Ireland, among strangers, where Hopkins writes his finest and most profound verses of resignation to the will of God. "They were wrung from him amid the prostrating anguish of ill-health, uncongenial surroundings, the tedium of heavy routine-duties, the depression of mental fatigue, and the sterility and impotence which constituted his spiritual aridity when he felt that his God had withdrawn His Love."[54]

An interrelated study of Herbert's "The Cross" and Hopkins's "To seem the stranger" as spiritual autobiography confirms the brokenness and loss incumbent on the Christian disciple in order that he or she may "experience the surpassing knowledge of my Lord Jesus Christ" (Phil. 3:8). Moreover, a super-imposing of the Ignatian contemplative tradition on these poems invites the reader to "a kind of psycho-immersion into the self to find Jesus abiding and then the plunging of that Jesus-self into the world of natural being to see the transcendent Christ."[55]

Crucial to a more complete understanding of "contemplation" in the Ignatian tradition is a consideration of the multivalent significances of the word. The word "contemplation" derives from the Latin *contemplari*, to observe carefully. Interestingly, the Latin word itself comes from two words: *com*, an intensive, and *templum*, the open space marked out by augurs in the Near East to observe the stars and thus discern the fate of things. (Roman augurs who wanted to determine the will of the gods also opened a space, usually in birds' entrails, and looked carefully to determine the meaning of the signs in that open space.) Furthermore, the root *temp* means to stretch or to extend (usually considered as providing the basis for the Latin *tempus, temporis* or time) and thus is also at the root of the word "temptation."[56] When the Christian disciple intends to do God's will, to be an epiphany of

---

[53] Olney, *George Herbert and Gerard Manley Hopkins* 172.
[54] Pick 143-44.
[55] Downes, "Beatific Landscapes in Hopkins" 141.
[56] *Oxford English Dictionary*, 2d ed., s.v. "contemplate, contemplation, temple."

God's time in the world, he or she inevitably encounters the spaces and places of temptations. Contemplation frequently precludes temptation. The temptation of Christ in the desert provides the biblical analogue for this understanding of the cycle of contemplation and temptation (Matt. 4:1—11). Jesus, after His baptism in the Jordan, went out to the wilderness—a place where He was without His strengths, a space where He encountered His fears—to discern God's will. There He was tempted as He attempted to spend time with God. The three temptations of Jesus, similar to the three "removes" of Hopkins, urge Him to remove Himself from quotidian things and to avoid the pain accompanying the cost of discipleship: to become, in fact, less than Who He is. By rejecting the temptations that remove Him from His Heavenly Father, Jesus incarnates total freedom and humanity and thus embodies the word "contemplation."

The same rejection or "removes" that carry Hopkins's pleading to the "unheard" ears of God also plead to "silent ears" in Herbert's poem "Denial." Herbert steadily sought the "unbroken consciousness of the presence of God; what troubled him was the brittleness, the uneven texture of the experience of [this] consciousness."[57] Herbert's contemporaries would have recognized the image of God's "silent ears" as an emblem of spiritual dryness. Moreover, the patterned disorder of the stanzas underscores Herbert's painful struggle with spiritual conflict. The narrative includes reactions to the ordeal and reflections on it; it concludes with a prayer. As Mario A. DiCesare posits, the poem is an outline of the Ignatian meditative pattern as it sequences an imaged place in stanzas 12, reflection in stanzas 34, and prayer in stanzas 56. Scenes, focused images, and *sententiae* are generated by the three faculties: memory, understanding, and will.[58] The imperfect harmony between the soul and God is symbolized by the unrhymed final line of each stanza until the last stanza, where the prayer for healing and harmony "mend[s] my rhyme" (1.30). The heart, "untuned, unstrung," and broken by grief and desolation, hopes to attain to union with God. Thus, the poem itself emphasizes the sacramental nature of poetry as an outward sign that signifies far more than the prosaic func-

---

[57] White 187.
[58] Mario A. DiCesare, "God's Silence: On Herbert's 'Deniall.'" *George Herbert Journal*, 10 (1986-87), 91.

tioning of the words.[59] Separation from God is compared with the nipping of the blossom, the "breaking" of a bow, the heart, music, rhyme, and a stanzaic pattern. Joseph Summers's contention that Herbert's poems are hieroglyphs is verified in "Denial" where Herbert presents, as does Hopkins in his "dark" sonnets, a visual embodiment for the theme of brokenness and spiritual desolation in the shape and structure of the poem itself. The speakers' prayers in these poems assume that such harmony and mending are possible, since the speakers believe that the Divine Auditor is attentive to the lives of His followers. The content of their poetic narratives reveals struggle, and the form conveys this struggle: the search for the Divine Love in the experience of suffering, and a language that can embody, describe, and define the experience of God.

The "denial" to which the title of Herbert's poem refers is based on the Christian call to humility and self-diminution. "'Deniall' is only a particular instance of what seems to be a general rule in *The Temple*: that union with God only comes through self-awareness contrived and then mastered. The theme of the poem is that only by overcoming self-consciousness does poetry become perfect."[60] Just as in "The Cross" Herbert uses parallel clauses to record his sufferings, in "Denial" he enumerates the corporal parts of grief—heart, knees, tongue, and soul—and so echoes the psalmist's and Job's complaints by cataloguing his woes and by charging God with damages to his poetry as well. "In very few places is the need for the divine presence felt and divine silence regretted as in 'Denial.' Here the creature prays to the Creator on

> Both knees...crying night and day,
> *Come, come, my God, Oh Come,*
> But no hearing
>
>   (ll.13—15).

Like the cry of the disconsolate Job in the trial of his faith, Herbert's cry is unheeded. He feels forsaken, with no reassuring trace of God's

---

[59] Miller 141.
[60] Miller 131.

presence."[61] In this poem especially, Herbert's images create the picture of a man with soul and body literally distracted and dissolved.[62]

The act of turning to God in pain gives the complaint its legitimacy and presupposes a belief in a God who listens.[63] By himself, the poet cannot mend his rhyme. But by achieving union with God, both the poet and God join in the creation of the poem. The faith of the speaker makes him whole, as it did the people who begged Christ for a cure. The speaker and the poem move from fear to "unstrung" discontent. Herbert ultimately overcomes denial by engaging in a colloquy with the Divine Auditor Who, Herbert hopes, will grant his request.

Herbert feels the contradictions of Christ's Passion turned toward himself and so laments day and night in order to engage the "silent ears" of God and to welcome Him into his heart and his verse by a process of spiritual awakening that consists of self-denial, imitation of Christ, and faith in Christ's love for His disciples. Likewise, Hopkins recounts the bitter blow or "fell" of the experience of "the dark night of the soul" in another "terrible" sonnet titled "I wake and feel" (1885), the title and initial lines of which recall the opening of Dante's *Divine Comedy*: "In the middle of the journey of my life I awoke to find myself in a dark wood where the straight way was lost."[64]

The spiritual awakening that Hopkins recounts in "I wake and feel" is achieved in three ways. First, the word "fell," which expresses the past tense of the verb "fall," signifies, as does the word "began" in the sonnet "To seem the stranger," both the literal action of the night and the spiritual fall of humanity. Second, the theme of colloquy is evidenced in the usage of the personal pronouns "we," "you," "I," "dearest him," and suggests a dialogue addressed, not only to the speaker and his heart, but also to the speaker and the "dearest him that lives alas! away" (1.8). "Hopkins' belief that poetic diction should be 'current language heightened' is refined by the practice of Ignatian colloquy. The Jesuit tradition strengthened the Victorian dramatic monologue and gave it a definite tradition."[65] F.R. Leavis's claim that the ruling spirit in this poem is the "living idiom" and the "speaking

---

[61] Mathai 147-48.

[62] Seelig 26.

[63] Bloch 266.

[64] John D. Sinclair, tr., *The Divine Comedy of Dante Alighieri, I: Inferno* (New York: Oxford University Press, 1939) 23.

[65] Bender 158.

voice" of Hopkins himself confirms the spiritually autobiographical nature of this sonnet.[66]

Third, Hopkins uses diction that "holds the hearer in the attitude of a correspondent."[67] The separation of Hopkins between himself and the "dearest him"—God—is likened to the abandonment a lover experiences when the beloved fails to respond to his or her letters. Just as the letter is the sole mode of communication for people separated by long distance, a dialogue with the Logos or Word of God, as well as the writing of the words of the "terrible" sonnets, are the sole means by which Hopkins conveys his "lament" and the "curse" of loss and brokenness. "Hopkins' habit of concreteness is still at work as he turns his communication with God into a literal correspondence, but as in other sonnets of desolation, the answer is unforthcoming."[68] Hopkins attempts this daring act of communicating with God on the basis of his understanding of the Logos, the Word made Flesh. Commenting on the Fundamentum of Ignatius's *Exercises*, Hopkins writes:

> God's utterance of himself in himself is God the Word, outside himself is this world. This world then is word, expression, news of God. Therefore its end, its purpose, its purport, its meaning, is God and its life or work must be to name and praise him.[69]

The word is valued because, as in *The Wreck*, it signifies "him that present and past,/Heaven and earth are word of, worded by" (II.29.229—30).

The various connotations of the Logos—human proclamation, Scripture, Christ—exist for both Herbert and Hopkins and are instrumental in forming the resolution of their speakers: that of surrender to the will of God. Both writers address a God Who is present in His absence and concealment. Such questioning or seeming "denial" of God's presence is no indication that Herbert or Hopkins waver in their faith or that their faith is inadequate for their life experience; rather, it illustrates how closely faith and experience coexist in the souls of the two ministers and poets. Indeed, the works considered in this chapter

---

[66] F.R. Leavis, *New Bearings in English Poetry: A Study of the Contemporary Situation* (London: Chatto and Windus, 1950) 188.

[67] Bender 158.

[68] Motto 113-14.

[69] James Leggio, "Hopkins and Alchemy." *Renascence* 29, 1977 (Winter) 2: 124.

and in Chapter Five depict the intense groanings which St. Paul described in his second letter to the Corinthians as the yearning

> to have our heavenly habitation envelop us.... While we live in our present tent we groan; we are weighed down because we do not wish to be stripped naked but rather to have the heavenly dwelling envelop us, so that what is mortal may be absorbed by life
>
> (2 Cor. 5:2,4).

In Hopkins's sonnet "I wake and feel," the speaker's "cries countless" fall like "dead letters" on the ears of "dearest him." The letters are termed "dead," not only because the One to whom they are addressed does not respond, but, more fundamentally, because the address itself seems to be wrong. In the experience of "the dark night," the victim can neither write properly nor even direct his prayers in the proper manner, and so the letter itself, like the writer, undertakes an indefinite journey.[70]

But God is not dead; He "lives alas! away." Hopkins's faith in God, like that of Herbert's, allows for questioning the reasons behind his time of trials and desolation, and demands a theodicy of God's actions. Hopkins says, "God's most deep decree/Bitter would have me taste" (ll.910) and thus mirrors St. Paul's statement: "How deep are the riches and the wisdom and the knowledge of God! How inscrutable his judgments, how unsearchable his ways!" (Rom. 11:33). Yet this "most deep decree" is "bitter" to the taste of Hopkins, as the scroll of the Word of God devoured by the exiled John, author of the Book of Revelation, was initially "as sweet as honey" but later became bitter in his mouth and stomach (Rev. 10:8-10). Instead of being nourished by the Bread of Life, the priest Hopkins experiences "heartburn" and severe internal disorders that accompany the state of his spiritual life. Hopkins's whole being was sick and enervated at these times. "The body cannot rest when it is in pain," he wrote on retreat in Ireland on January 1, 1888, "nor the mind be at peace as long as something bitter distills in it and it aches."[71] He is nauseated by a "dull dough" that has become soured by "selfyeast." The theme of nutriment is frustrated.

---

[70] MacKenzie 182.
[71] Devlin 262.

Here Hopkins recalls the parable where the Kingdom of Heaven is likened to a handful of yeast which is kneaded into dough and which ultimately rises to provide nourishment and sustenance (Matt. 13:33). However, Hopkins reverses the creative culinary talent of the housewife in the parable by admitting that his adherence to his own selfish will, rather than to God's will, causes a bitterness or a "sweating" to occur that obliterates the divine plan, furthers the primordial "curse" by separating him from the Author of life, and prohibits his rising to new life. Hopkins realizes that the "scourge" is not given by God, but by the self who, in turning in upon itself, sours and rots. "But, though he was enormously bothered by these personal and psychological perplexities, he had long since set his intellectual and metaphysical house in order. When he doubted himself the most he never doubted the rightness of his choice. [In his *Sermons and Devotional Writings*] he states: 'I do not waver in my allegiance, I never have since my conversion to the Church.' Hopkins' faith was eventually firm and his poems are serene in their assurance of a providential order."[72]

So God provides a "fell" or pelt—what St. Augustine terms the skins with which God clothes fallen humanity—and, although this skin might weigh heavily on him (the darkness is, indeed, "felt"), it also serves as a protective clothing and shield.[73] Herbert's apocalyptic cry in "Denial" of "*Come, come, my God, Oh come*" is met in Hopkins's "I wake and feel" by the biblical reminder that "In the Lord's eyes, one day is as a thousand...[and that] the Lord does not delay in keeping his promise—though some consider it 'delay'" (2 Pet. 3:89). Like Herbert, Hopkins underscores the Christian theme of theodicy by attributing all to God's just decree which seems to the Christian disciple, as it did to Job and other biblical personages, incomprehensible.

In the final tercet of "I wake and feel," Hopkins mentions the "lost" souls in hell who have no hope. Indeed, the medieval morality plays, *The Harrowing of Hell*, as well as *The Inferno*, are recalled here as Hopkins thinks of his own physical and spiritual torments. In *The Inferno*, the damned are continually referred to as "the lost," "the sorrowful," those who have abandoned all hope, even the hope of death. The crucial end-of-poem emphatic "worse" in "I wake and feel" recalls Satan's terrible condition in Book Four of *Paradise Lost*:

[72] Olney, *George Herbert and Gerard Manley Hopkins* 38.
[73] MacKenzie 181-82.

Now conscience wakes despair
That slumberd, wakes the bitter memorie
Of what he was, what is, and what must be
Worse; of worse deeds worse sufferings must ensue

(IV.23—26).[74]

Unlike Satan, the speaker in "I wake and feel" answers pride and self-will with his own emptiness and desolation in his failure to meet the Lord whom he knows "lives" but Who remains "alas! away." Although the speaker has inherited the sinful and fallen nature from Adam, he is hopeful that a comforting message of grace will arrive from "dearest him" to illumine the "black hours" and relieve his soul, albeit in the distant future. Unlike the lost souls, Hopkins still addresses God in his prayers and still tries to purge himself of his sins so as to acquire union with his Creator, for Whom darkness is not dark.

Although the pain of the lost souls in hell is "worse" than his, Hopkins's theories of individuation and inscape, proposed so eloquently in his creation poems and his earlier works, are given a dark side in this sonnet. Yet the last stanza also suggests that there is always something "worse" than being one's morbid self, in being one's own "blight" ("Spring and Fall," 1.14), and that is being trapped, as was Satan, in one's own self, therefore being damned to hell and total alienation from God, a state which he addresses in "No worst."[75] Hopkins concludes this sonnet that critics view as the introduction to the "dark" sonnets, having completed what he calls, in a letter to Bridges, "the longest sonnet ever made and no doubt the longest making."[76]

"Purgation for Hopkins, then, consists, not of fire, but of the stress and strain of removal from God," a punishment that renders great mental anguish, as he states in his Sermons.[77] Although this may appear to be of little consolation to the soul in spiritual desolation, its effects are enormous and cause Hopkins to resist the horror which fills his being. This stress is regarded by Hopkins as a mystery. Consequently, it is assumed by the reader and is felt as stress along every

---

[74] Shawcross, *The Complete Poetry of John Milton*.

[75] W. Johnson, *Gerard Manley Hopkins: The Poet as Victorian* 28.

[76] Milward and Schoder, *Landscape and Inscape* 89.

[77] Harris 110.

nerve and fiber.[78] "Selfyeast of spirit a dull dough sours." Stephen
Spender believes that Hopkins's despair was too self-deprecatory, for
it is this spiritual yeast which "ferments in other poets" and renders
Hopkins a seminal influence on English literature.[79]

"With witness I speak this" (l.5). No stronger proof for a reading
of this poem as spiritual autobiography exists than Hopkins's own
assertion of this Johannine allusion. Like St. John, the beloved apostle,
Hopkins is beloved by the "dearest him" Who created him, flesh and
spirit, from His own Mystical Body. "Hopkins insists, as he does in
The Wreck, that what he is saying is autobiographical and true. But
what happened on one particular night happened, with varying degrees
of intensity, over a much longer period," as the other "terrible" son-
nets demonstrate.[80]

The "witness" of the Christian themes of theodicy and colloquy is
further authenticated in Herbert's poem "Complaining," where the
speaker asks directly, "Art thou all justice, Lord?" (l.11) and proceeds
with a series of rhetorical questions to sound the Job-like and Davidic
plaints as he questions the justice of God's harsh dealings with him.
"This renewed attention [of the speaker to God] becomes translated
into a linguistic form—'calling' to God—and into a ready fiction that
God, Who always listens, must nonetheless be made to hear. Thus, the
narrower sense of invocation contains the germ of the broader mean-
ing—of linguistically expressed attention to God, the source of all be-
ing."[81] Herbert's colloquy with God centers on his "right," as Rich-
ard Strier regards it, "to complain of affliction. This commitment of
calling upon God and 'groaning' to Him was one of the duties as well
as one of the prerogatives of the Christian."[82]

The word "dust," which occurs quite frequently in the Scriptures,
is also used recurrently by Herbert in *The Temple*. In his poem "Deni-

---

[78] I take exception to Yvor Winters and other critics who view "I wake and feel" as
emotional self-indulgence and as the most depressing of the "terrible" sonnets in inter-
preting the last two words—"but worse"—as Hopkins's self-loathing and bitterness.
Rather, I render significant spiritual growth to these final words, which serve as a posi-
tive assertion of Hopkins's determination to oppose the "curse" of self-indulgence and
acedia.

[79] Ruth M. Stauffer, "Note on the Genesis of Hopkins' Sonnets of 1885." *Renascence*
22, 1969 (Fall); 43.

[80] Mariani, *A Commentary on the Complete Poems of Gerard Manley Hopkins* 220.

[81] Sherwood 12.

[82] Strier 178-79.

al," Herbert questions God's lack of response: "Oh that thou shouldst give dust a tongue/To cry to thee,/And then not hear it crying!" (ll.16–18). In the first stanza of "Complaining," Herbert reconstructs the story of Creation when he claims to be "Thy clay that weeps, thy dust that calls" (l.5). Further scruptural analogues reinforce the parallels that Herbert draws between biblical personages and himself. Both the Davidic psalmist and Job recall the Mnemosynaic qualities of God. The psalmist writes: "For he knows how we are formed; he remembers that we are dust" (Ps. 103:14). Job, in demanding justice, says, "Oh, remember that you fashioned me from clay! Will you then bring me down to dust again?" (Job 10:9). The afflicted psalmist, bargaining for his life, cries to the Lord: "What gain would there be from my life blood, from my going down into the grave? Would dust give you thanks or proclaim your faithfulness?" (Ps. 30:10). In the boldness of the speakers' addresses to God, the immanence of God is felt as the pathetic nature of mortality emerges in the pleading of guilt and the begging for mercy. When analyzed as spiritual autobiography, the reader sees that the particular Herbert poems considered in this chapter record the spiritual journey which Herbert undertakes before he "find[s] relief" ("Complaining," 1.20). This "relief" is found as he "climb[s]" the three stages of Christian mysticism: the purgation by the "wrathful power" (1.16) that causes weeping and crying (1.14); the illumination that the speaker is "but...a silly fly" (1.8) and God is the source of "gracious power" (1.18); and union with the Father and ultimate freedom.

This Christian "prerogative" or "right" to complain of affliction is voiced with even more vehemence in Hopkins's matching poem "No worst" (1884–85), where the speaker, feeling trapped in a wretched life, desperately wishes for a respite from his pain and grief. Such critics as Gardner, Milward, and MacKenzie, among others, recall the allusions in this "terrible" sonnet to Aeschylus's *Prometheus Bound*, which Hopkins translated into verse; to Shakespeare's *King Lear* where Edgar, his optimism shattered as he views his blind father, arrives at a conclusion similar to that of Hopkins's: "Who is't can say 'I am at the worst'?/I am worse then e'er I was.../And worse I may be yet" (IV.i.25–8); and to Milton's *Paradise Lost* where Moloch addresses his fellow-sufferers in hell: "What can be worse/Than to dwell here?" and Belial retorts, "Is this then worst,/Thus sitting, thus consulting, thus in arms?" (II.85–86; 163–73). Hopkins deepens and universalizes the experience of "the dark night of the soul" by identifying with these prototypes whose sufferings rose to a level or "pitch of grief" that seems to exceed the normal. The significance for Hopkins of the stories of the suffering protagonists alluded to is that all were illuminated by their suffering: all achieved some measure of self-knowledge and knowledge of God. "Through a tense but creative juxtaposition of his own state and the mythic imagination of the past, both secular and biblical, Hopkins also was able to come to increased knowledge and peace, although the peace was more like an armed truce: 'all/Life death does end and each day dies with sleep.' In the depths of desolation, the conflict of despair and imagination results in a creative tension of self-knowledge and beauty."[83]

Hopkins looks in vain for comfort, first to the Holy Ghost or "Comforter," then to Mary, the mother of Jesus Christ. But the poet finds no relief from his agony. Patricia A. Wolfe's comparison of the emotional climate of this sonnet to the agony of Christ in the Garden of Gethsemane is noteworthy and accurate. "In effect, the poet is suggesting to his readers, 'My soul is sad, even unto death. Wait here and watch'" (Mark 14:34).[84] Hopkins's identification of the "pitch" with Christ's Passion, so dominant in *The Wreck*, is underscored in these "dark" sonnets as well. Hopkins maintained that, in the passion of Jesus, God entered into the innermost recesses of human affliction and death to make of them a sacred place for encountering His grace and salvation.

The inversions, repetitions, interruptions of word order, compressed diction, and lack of adjectives suggest the emotional constriction of the speaker and his overwhelming spiritual ordeal. "In Hopkins they serve to call the maximum attention to each word."[85] A passage from his Retreat Notes made at St. Stanislaus College, Tullabeg, on January 1, 1888, confirms a reading of "No worst" as spiritual autobiography. "All my undertakings miscarry: I am like a straining eunuch. I wish then for death: yet if I died now I should die imperfect, no master of myself, and that is the worst failure of all. O my God, look down on me."[86] Hopkins's fear that he is not imitating the life of

---

[83] Howard Fulweiler, *Letters from the Darkling Plain: Language and the Grounds of Knowledge in the Poetry of Arnold and Hopkins* (Missouri: University of Missouri Press, 1972) 158-59.

[84] Wolfe 93.

[85] Leavis, *New Bearings in English Poetry* 189.

[86] Devlin 262.

Christ, His Master, escalates into a "high degree of sensitivity, [for] he has now been placed on a higher level of suffering than his previously experienced grief. Christ's grace has pitched the poet into a new sphere of human activity."[87] Hopkins's suffering, then, is expressed through phrases like "pitched past pitch of grief" that recall the scriptural passages where God pitches His tent and dwells with His people, where angels visit Abraham at his tent with the message that he will become a father—in short, "pitched" assumes positive connotations in conveying the paradox of the harmonious stress of Hopkins's call: to be a eunuch for the sake of the Kingdom. "Hopkins, like a violin string, is strung tighter to play at the higher, more piercing and metallic tone of grief. 'Pitch' for Hopkins is the distinctive self, and in man this pitch is the most distinctive, most highly strung or stressed of everything in the world."[88] Hopkins himself confirms while on a retreat at Liverpool on August 20, 1880: "I find myself both as a man and as myself something more determined and distinctive, at pitch, more distinctive and higher pitched than anything else I see."[89]

Yet the straining and stress of his call to imitate Christ more profoundly is further accentuated by the repetition and alliteration in line nine of "No worst" where the "mind, mind has mountains." His "mind" recalls both his majestic nature and his inadequate state of being. He wills through his mental faculties to imitate Christ, but he fails. Therefore, the "mountains" of his mind are both appealing and repelling. Another section of his spiritual notebook serves as an additional commentary: "the keener the consciousness the greater the pain," and "both these show that the higher the nature the greater the penalty."[90] In the concluding sestet, Hopkins asks, as did Christ, to have this sacrificial cup of emotional and spiritual turmoil taken away from him through the comfort of sleep or death. But the request seems to be unheard by the Divine Auditor, and Hopkins continues to confront his own worst enemy: *acedia* or "wórld-sorrow" (1.6), rooted in his willful pride and determination to imitate Christ. As the "dark" sonnet "I wake and feel" demonstrates, Hopkins aligns his torments with those of the Hell in which he so strongly believes. In his "Medita-

[87] Wolfe 94.
[88] Mariani, *A Commentary on the Complete Poems of Gerard Manley Hopkins* 224.
[89] Devlin 122.
[90] Devlin 138.

tion on Hell," he considers how "we are our own tormentors, for every sin we then shall have remorse and with remorse torment."[91] However, the fact that all life is consumed by the sleep of death is a consolation which the abandoned souls in hell, alluded to in the sestet of "I wake and feel," do not receive. In his "Meditation on Hell," Hopkins echoes Christ's words: "'Their worm,' our Lord says, 'does not die and their fire is never quenched.'"[92]

David A. Downes renders a precise analysis of "No worst" when he states that its subject is "the toppling of the towering 'I' in us to the dark defeats of nonbeing. The poet grimly states that strange and odd condition of self thrown back on itself, discovering the defect of finitude, where the 'I' breaks off into nothing at all."[93] The speaker returns to the "dust," evident in Herbert's poem "Complaining," as he realizes that "all/Life death does end and each day dies with sleep" (ll.13–14). Like St. Paul, Hopkins finds comfort only after his own burden of weakness and despair. The following Pauline passage demonstrates the consoling work of God in the apostle's life and witnesses to a comfort that is found only when the Christian disciple learns to rely on God:

> We do not wish to leave you in the dark about the trouble we had in Asia; we were crushed beyond our strength, even to the point of despairing of life. We were left to feel like men condemned to death so that we might trust, not in ourselves, but in God who raises from the dead. He rescued us from that danger of death and will continue to do so. We have put our hope in him who will never cease to deliver us
>
> (2 Cor. 1:8–10).

Paul knew that life for the follower of Christ is not always lived on the mountains of consolation. Just as there is no winner without competition, no victor without a war, no wages without work, Paul knew that for the Christian disciple, there is no crown of glory without a cross of suffering. The God of consolation sends the Comforter to console, encourage, and support those who have experienced the kind of sorrow that transforms hearts and fulfills the aim of Ignatian spirituality: interior renewal.

---

[91] Devlin 241.
[92] Devlin 242.
[93] Downes, "Beatific Landscapes in Hopkins" 196.

Paul admits that, "in order that I might not become conceited I was given a thorn in the flesh, an angel of Satan to beat me and keep me from getting proud" (2 Cor. 12:7-8). The three poems of Herbert and the three poems of Hopkins considered in this chapter are literary and spiritual articulations that parallel Paul's three utterances in which "I begged the Lord that this [thorn in the flesh] might leave me." Like St. Paul, Herbert and Hopkins learn that "weakness, mistreatment, distress, persecutions, powerlessness, and difficulties for the sake of Christ" (2 Cor. 12:10) yield a harvest of grace and perfection in the Divine Image. This Comforter strengthens and walks alongside His disciples, not to reinforce their selfish interests, but to strengthen and comfort them in the ways of God. The "many dwelling places" that are in the "Father's house" (John 14:2) testify to the diverse and unfathomable nature of a Divine Auditor Whose plans and will often lead His faithful followers into spiritual bankruptcy, but Who always rescues them from the corruption and decay of their own self-will and "selfyeast."

Jerome Bump evaluates Hopkins as a twentieth-century poet by referring to "No worst" as "a paradigm of all of modern humanism in that it expresses the syndrome of ennui much as Petrarch did at the start of the Renaissance: a sorrow, caused not by a single blow of fortune but by a plenitude of causes, leading to despair and finally to a longing for death."[94] Bump credits the ambiguity and uncertainty of the experience underlying the sonnet to "Hopkins's maturity as a poet and to the modernity of the poem."[95] Yet as W.H. Gardner states, Hopkins's "faith gave him powers of recovery which many of his most sensitive modern readers would lack."[96] Indeed, the benefits accorded modern literature by its precursor, Gerard Manley Hopkins, find a germane affirmation in a further study by W.H. Gardner of the "priest-poet conflict" in Hopkins:

> ...whether the cry of anguish in the later sonnets was due to mutilation or to probation, the gain to poetry, on the whole, seems to me to outweigh the loss.

---

[94] Bump, *Gerard Manley Hopkins* 171.
[95] Bump, *Gerard Manley Hopkins* 172.
[96] Gardner 332.

Had Hopkins been physically stronger, less devout, less sensitive, less neurotic, we should have had more poems but not the ones we now treasure.[97]

Hopkins's goal is to attain the Kingdom of God, and to this end he writes the "terrible" sonnets. Time's eunuch, a lonely began, a man close to despair, knowing himself to be gall, heartburn, a man pitched past pitch of grief—these descriptions mark a Christian disciple who begs God to give an explanation of his suffering. But theodicy is not defined, and in this struggle lies the realization that Christ did not come to bring peace, but a sword. The call to Christian discipleship caused Hopkins to lose his life and to find it in conforming himself to the suffering, death, and resurrection of his Master. Indeed, the very criticism that Yvor Winters, Elisabeth Schneider, and Donald McChesney advance—that "No worst" is the least successful, the most violent and hopeless of the "terrible" sonnets—authenticates a study of the sonnets in the classical descent and ascent of the Ignatian tradition. The sonnets depict Ignatius's description of the soul: "I call desolation...darkness of soul, turmoil of spirit...restlessness rising from many disturbances and temptations which lead to want of faith, want of hope, want of love. The soul is wholly slothful, tepid, sad, and separated, as it were, from its Creator and Lord."[98] David A. Downes analyzes Hopkins's "terrible" sonnets as poems of the elective, rather than the affective, will, and, therefore, as the most Ignatian poems he wrote. "Their very subject matter is the religio-psychological process achieving a final and ultimate election of Christ as King of the soul."[99]

Hopkins does not look to the completion of his verse by God in the same manner as does Herbert—indeed, the unfinished temple is quite evident in this selection of Hopkins's works—but he does create an individual poetic style which is an intricate texture of biblical, patristic, and scholastic sources rendered in personal, experiential terms. The "terrible" sonnets are, indeed, the record of a soul "pitched past pitch of grief." The result is an original and effective account of spiritual autobiography and the cost of following the "dear Lord" and Master of life. God, though seemingly absent in Hopkins's experience of "the dark night of the soul," is present in these "dark" sonnets. As Louis

---

[97] John D. Boyd, S.J., "'I Say More': Sacrament and Hopkins's Imaginative Realism." *Renascence* 42, 1989-90 (Fall-Winter); 63.

[98] Puhl 142.

[99] Downes, "Beatific Landscapes" 194.

Rader posits, "whatever the extent and cause of the personal affliction described in the sonnets, it is evident that Hopkins' artistic talent and enthusiasm did not wane. Indeed, he was right that he may have hit another excellence."[100]

The central aspect of Herbert's resolution is also the need to imitate Christ and to accept the paradoxical nature of faith. Christ Himself demonstrated a life of paradoxes, many of which Herbert chooses as his themes. As Christ's disciple, Herbert has experiences that parallel Christ's: both share times of intense loneliness, abandonment, and futility. Herbert's resolve to conform himself to Christ—to enact, in fact, St. Thomas à Kempis's *imitatio Christi*—causes him to wrestle with the faith of a Christian disciple and thereby overcome his spiritual desolation. Likewise, Christ's resolve to do the Father's will reverses all His agonies and seeming defeats. When Herbert's prayers appear to go unheard and the presence of God seems to be withdrawn, he reminds himself that he is enduring what Christ Himself endured. This willing subjection to the divine plan makes Christ "a fellow-sufferer rather than a judge or a remote deity" to whom sighs and groans go unheeded.[101] Like Christ, Herbert learns that spiritual maturity can accept both consolation and desolation as character-forming gifts from the Creator. "Through a style that transmits a sense of process rather than a set of conclusions, Herbert invites the reader to share the experiences captured in the poems."[102] He is very honest about the difficulty of being a Christian disciple, and his works depict his willingness to pay the price. "To acknowledge that the faith is difficult is not the same as rejecting it. His attitude is characteristic of a century when it had seemingly become necessary to justify God's ways to men."[103] Herbert's private devotion is given a universal dimension befitting his title-page epigraph from Psalm 29:[9]: "In his Temple doth every man speak of his honor."

Spiritual conflict, then, for Herbert and Hopkins is purgative in its leading the soul to the value of suffering; illuminative in its forcing the

---

[100] Louis Rader, "Hopkins' Dark Sonnets: Another New Expression." *Victorian Poetry*, 5 (1967), 20.

[101] Vendler 238.

[102] Marion Meilaender, "Speakers and Hearers in *The Temple*." *George Herbert Journal* 5 (1981-82): 43.

[103] Joost Daalder, "Herbert's 'Poetic Theory.'" *George Herbert Journal* 9 (1985): 33.

soul to depend solely on God, not on itself; and unitive in its fostering in the soul an ultimate trust in God and a dispassionate merging of the immanent and the transcendent. Christ is a dominant Reality for both Herbert and Hopkins, watching over and partaking in their struggles. His presence gladdens them; His seeming absence frightens and torments them. But even this seeming absence is an element of their spiritual autobiography that both authors accent equally in their poems, prose, and "burning witness" to life.

Chapter Five

The Soul's (W)Rest: God's Pay and Reprieve

> All my attendants are at strife,
>   Quitting their place
>   Unto my face:
> Nothing performs the task of life:
>   The elements are let loose to fight,
>   And while I live, try out their right.
>
> [Herbert, "Affliction (IV)"]

THE MINISTERIAL COLLAR YOKES TOGETHER the poetic and ecclesiastical vocations of Herbert and Hopkins as both authors maintain their "witness" to a God Whose benevolence and love eventually overshadow and console their displacement and desolation. Select poems and prose of these two devotional writers continue to reveal the cyclical operation of the Ignatian principles of desolation and consolation as well as the three Christian themes and stages of mysticism. The coexistence of the ministerial and poetic vocations comprises the essential nature and inscape of Herbert and Hopkins, as the following select poems of Herbert and "terrible" sonnets of Hopkins demonstrate: Herbert's "The Collar" and Hopkins's "(Carrion Comfort)"; Herbert's "Affliction (IV)" and Hopkins's "Patience, hard thing"; Herbert's "Justice (I)" and Hopkins's "My own heart."

One of the advantages of reading the works of Herbert and Hopkins as spiritual autobiography is the discovery of the underside of their faith: the difficulty and struggle of the writers in holding on to what they most deeply believe. Particularly in these poems, Herbert and Hopkins report a trial by faith that is resolved favorably, though at the cost of severe personal sacrifice. The reader admires the two priests and poets who articulate their spiritual struggles vividly and honestly.

Herbert's "The Collar" is one of the most famous dramatizations of rebellion and disorder in *The Temple*. Like most of the selections considered in Chapter Four and this chapter, "(Carrion Comfort)" is "an Augustinian restaging of the primal act of disobedience. Man turns to the world and away from God, opposing his will to God's and allowing bad love (that which is characteristic of Augustine's earthly city) to take the place in him of good."[1] "(Carrion Comfort)," the title which was provided by Bridges, is perhaps unsurpassed as a representation of Hopkins's spiritual bewilderment and futility. "The Collar" and "(Carrion Comfort)" allude to the experience of Jacob, who wrestled all night with an angel in human form. "This encounter, which has become a type of struggle during spiritual trial, took place at a turning point in Jacob's life."[2] "Jacob was left there alone" (Gen. 32:25). These words have a plaintive ring about them. In order to appease his brother Esau whom he had defrauded of his birthright, Jacob sent on ahead his wife, children, and flocks, together with lavish presents for Esau. Little did he dream that this hour of solitude—of being alone with God—would be filled with blessing. To signify the change in the relationship between God and Jacob, God changed Jacob's name to Israel, a leader who now had power with God and his people, since he "contended with divine and human beings and prevailed" (Gen. 32:29). "Though the speaker's temptation in '(Carrion Comfort)' to eat carrion plays upon the biblical dietary restriction that the Jacob story illustrates, the quest for the divine name is the dominant theme."[3] In "The Collar" and "(Carrion Comfort)," Herbert and Hopkins use the experience of Jacob to typify their own spiritual experience. The difference is that the antagonist for Herbert and Hopkins is not an angel but Christ, as the terms surrounding the allusion signify: "My Lord," "terrible," "lionlimbed," "winnower," "King," "hero," "God."

In both poems, the speakers engage in a colloquy with a God from Whom some measure of theodicy—some explanation for the seeming injustice and endless "dark night" experienced by the speakers—is demanded. Question marks dominate the stanzas of both poems as Herbert and Hopkins continue their search for answers to the questions implicit in spiritual autobiography: "Who am I in the eyes of God?" and "Who is this God who insists on a wrestling match before He sets His servants free?"

"The Collar" recalls a past experience in language that is immediately retrospective and narrative: "I struck the board, and cried, No

---

[1] William H. Halewood, *The Poetry of Grace: Reformation Themes and Structures in English Seventeenth-Century Poetry* (New Haven and London: Yale University Press, 1972) 128.

[2] J. Angela Carson, "The Metaphor of Struggle in '(Carrion Comfort).'" *Philological Quarterly* 49 (1970), 548.

[3] Leggio 125.

more" (1.1). The speaker's "rational contention is that the discipline to which he has subjected himself should lead to some fulfilling end. That does not happen here. He has only losses to recount, only the chronicle of an unproductive future in prospect."[4] For a time, the speaker rejects the discipline inherent in his ministerial responsibilities. He chooses no longer to be "in suit" (1.6). The spiritual dress for which he was fitted for his duties, like the new Aaron, is replaced by clothing that would "serve his need" (1.31) instead of God's design.

"The Collar" addresses the necessity of the Christian disciple to answer the calling for which he has been fitted with special gifts. In "The Parson's Surveys," Herbert acknowledges:

> All are either to have a Calling, or prepare for it: He that hath or can have yet no employment, if he truly, and seriously prepare for it, he is safe and within bounds. Wherefore all are either presently to enter into a Calling, if they be fit for it, and it for them; or else to examine with care, and advice, what they are fittest for, and to prepare for that with all diligence.[5]

Episcopalian clergy of the seventeenth century wore special collars which distinguished them from the laymen. "Perhaps the fractiousness dramatized in this poem is that of the clergyman irked by the disciplines of his office" and his perception of his vocation as that of a master-servant relationship.[6] Here the speaker experiences the spiritual life only in terms of duties, obligations, and Old Testament legal servitude. Interrupting these rebellious thoughts comes the Lord's call "*Child*" reminiscent of two biblical analogues: Samuel's willingness to listen to the Lord speak, since he is the Lord's servant (1 Sam. 3:10), and St. Paul's assurance that he is not a bond-slave to God, but a son, an heir to the promises and the Kingdom of God (Gal. 4:3-7; Rom. 8:14-17). Helen Veith believes that there is no better gloss on "The Collar" than Luther's statement: "When the word of God comes, it runs contrary to our thought and desire," a belief confirmed equally by Samuel, Paul, Herbert, and Hopkins.[7]

Marchette Chute attributes "The Collar" to Herbert's frustration that "All the worlds of love and courtliness and learning were open to him, [only] to be bound by so tight [the] tether" of his ministerial

---

[4] Mathai 154.
[5] Wall 101.
[6] Rickey 100.
[7] Veith 221.

vocation.[8] When "The Collar" is read as spiritual autobiography, the dimensions of homophonous punning of the title are enlarged to include God as the Caller to the beloved, and the "choleric" personality—"fierce and wild" (1.33)—of the speaker who sports a clerical "collar" as the sign of his ministerial office.

The Oxford English Dictionary lists the following meaning of "collar" from the sport of wrestling: "a manoeuver in which the opponent is tackled by the neck," a meaning that entered the language in the sixteenth century.[9] The speaker in "The Collar" is contained swiftly and decisively by his Divine Adversary's manoeuver. Hopkins, who has gained among twentieth-century critics a substantial reputation as an acute literary critic himself, refines the wrestling image in "(Carrion Comfort)" to supplement this definition with the established motifs that inform Herbert's "The Collar."[10]

In "(Carrion Comfort)" (1885), the same portrayal of a personal God Who calls to His creatures and expects a response to this call is indicated. "(Carrion Comfort)," unlike Herbert's poems, does not contain an overt reference to God speaking, but the implication is stated, parenthetically at first, then more declaratively in the last line when the speaker is illumined to regard himself as a "wretch" who "lay wrestling with/(my God!) my God." In her comparative study of "The Collar" and "(Carrion Comfort)," Mary Ann Rygiel points out that Hopkins's "last line is the analogue to Herbert's last four lines, when the poet has a moment of recognition which both strengthens and chastens."[11] In "The Collar" and "(Carrion Comfort)," the speakers move from the initial horror of their own humanity to humble submission to the God of the "wrestlers" Jacob and Job. This God demands a (w)rest from His creatures: a wrestling or a struggle—a desolation through purgation and illumination—until they attain to consolation and union with God. But as these poems demonstrate, although the immediate struggle with God is over, the loneliness and separation from God continue.

---

[8] Marchette Chute, *Two Gentle Men: The Lives of George Herbert and Robert Herrick* (New York: E.P. Dutton and Co., 1959) 110.

[9] *Oxford English Dictionary*, 2d ed., s.v. "collar."

[10] Mary Ann Rygiel, "Herbert and Hopkins: Two Meditative Poets." *Hopkins Quarterly*, 1983; 10(2), 48.

[11] Rygiel 45.

However, the immanence of this God is striking. Because God speaks, He is presented, not as a passive object of contemplation, but as an active God Who engages in a personal relationship with Herbert. "At every word" (1.34) there is the one word "*Child*" (1.35) that God utters. Although at the outset the speaker clearly takes the initiative, he eventually understands that this God is in control and that his own place in the scheme of things is *sub specie æternitatis*. "The Collar" parallels the cyclical pattern of the Scriptures: that of the rebellious lover and his return to the resting place of God. "In the biblical view of history we find the paradigms that govern the movement of so many of Herbert's poems: man sins and repents; God admonishes him and bids him welcome. The happy endings of Herbert's poems, then, are not really as 'easy' as some readers might suppose. They are absorbed into the larger cyclical patterns of the volume, momentary intuitions of blessedness in a chronicle that is also filled with despondency and bitterness of spirit."[12] Sharon Seelig underscores this belief by stating that, while the titles of such Herbert poems as "Life," "Death," "Man," "Peace," "Sin," and "Affliction" may seem to ask and resolve easy questions, they "should not be mistaken for the poet's own. To induce the obvious responses to which we may be prompted may be part of Herbert's plan, for when 'Life' turns out to be about death, and 'Mortification' shows us life in death, we find that we have been outwitted by simple little poems that begin in man's world and lead to God's."[13] Like the Scriptures, Herbert's poems bear "witness" and testimony to God's saving grace, and to the speaker's desire to know God with a longing that rivals the mystics' search.

Itrat Husain explains "The Collar" as Herbert's "awakening of the self into the 'Purgative Way.'"[14] He underscores the complexity of Herbert's character posited by Tuve: Herbert's desire for both the Church life of the spirit, and the Court life of "pleasure, learning, and wit."[15] There is something profoundly honest and courageous in Herbert's expression of his rebellion as the occasion of his illumination, given the fact that the seventeenth century frequently sought to restrain and steady the expression of passions and emotions. The vicissitudes of the human spirit and the imagination often frightened and discour-

---

[12] Bloch 167–68.
[13] Seelig 10.
[14] Husain 140.
[15] Husain 140.

aged such expression. Yet Herbert "hurls" his feelings of estrangement and doubt into the face of God with the honesty and confidence of the mystics themselves as he demands to be known.[16] In spite of the speaker's vehemence and apparent freedom, his rebellion has plunged him into a proverbial dead end, thus demonstrating the logic of its own folly. Arnold Stein's study of the style and form of Herbert's verse suggests that "in 'The Collar' the voice calling '*Child*' (an ultimate expression, silent until the end) abruptly collects [the speaker's] apparently runaway freedom of self-expression, restricting a personal fluency which is not limited to the 'right' feelings."[17] Concord results, paradoxically, from increasing disorder on both the spiritual and poetic planes.

The unevenness of the lines and the bewildering rhyme scheme reinforce the strain and violent disorder experienced by the speaker. Joseph Summers terms this poem "a formalized picture of chaos," and "one of Herbert's most deliberate ventures in 'hieroglyphic' form."[18] He explains: "Until the final four lines, the poem dramatizes expertly and convincingly the revolt of the heart, and its imitation of colloquial speech almost convinces us of the justice of the cause."[19] But the successful resolution of the poem, as well as of the speaker's spiritual life, is contingent upon an ordered principle of existence "in a vulnerable present where images cannot be secured."[20]

Despite the turmoil, disorder, and confusion experienced by the speaker and the reader, "[f]rom the viewpoint of eternity, the irresistible power of grace and human experience are all made to correspond to the preordained and infallible plan of God. The form of 'The Collar' images precisely the world view of reformed spirituality."[21] When it seeks to be autonomous, to be its own master, the soul is in disharmony. Integrity comes only when "*Child*" recognizes "*My Lord*" and surrenders to the will of God. "Thus Herbert's poems dramatize one of the most important requirements of the religious temper, which is that God should be other than oneself. This is a necessary implication

---

[16] White 184–85.
[17] Stein 153.
[18] Summers, *George Herbert* 90.
[19] Summers, *George Herbert* 92.
[20] Harman 88.
[21] Veith 109.

of Christian doctrine."[22] The speaker rededicates his life to the service of religion and to the spiritual benefits of the "board" and the temple. Metathesis depicts the speaker's transformation from rebellion—"I will abroad" (l.2)—to acceptance of Christian discipleship—"I will aboard." The spontaneity of the "one calling, '*Child*'" (l.35) is matched by the readiness of the speaker who, purged, is now willing to return to "*My Lord*" (l.36). "The relations between man and God are more than reconfirmed; they are renewed. The reality of God's love has broken through the pretenses, and the debater gives up his clever line of retreat."[23]

The process by which Hopkins surrenders to the will of God in his ministerial and poetic vocations leads him through a consideration of "carrion comfort" or despair whereby all effort toward union with God is abandoned, to the realization that the incarnate God is immanent and immediate in his life. In "(Carrion Comfort)," Hopkins views suffering as a purifying process. His Retreat Notes of January 1, 1888 compare his ministerial responsibilities to a collar in a manner reminiscent of Herbert:

> [My] life is determined by the Incarnation down to most of the details of the day.... The Incarnation was for my salvation and that of the world: the work goes on in a great system and machinery which even drags me on with the collar round my neck though I could and do neglect my duty in it. But I say to myself that I am only too willing to do God's work and help on the knowledge of the Incarnation.[24]

In "(Carrion Comfort)," the "bones and veins" that God has bound in him (*The Wreck* I.1.5), together with the fibers of his spiritual being "laced with fire of stress" (*The Wreck* I.2.16), have become slack as he feels his energy leaving him. But Hopkins refuses to cease all effort. He takes a definite stand—"I can" ["(Carrion Comfort)," l.3]—an act of volition that allows him to "not choose not to be" (l.4). "This repetition of 'not' at the beginning of the poem emphasizes the determination to withstand the almost overwhelming pull of despair. The pauses and staccato nervousness of the fourth line show the frantic search for the way out of the experience of this dark night of the soul. The con-

---

[22] A.D. Nuttall, *Overheard by God: Fiction and Prayer in Herbert, Milton, Dante and St. John* (London and New York: Methuen and Co. Ltd., 1980) 3.

[23] Stein 124-25.

[24] Devlin 263.

cept of 'the dark night' is reinforced by the exhausted, elliptical 'wish day come.'"[25] As Patricia A. Wolfe points out, "ironically, in not choosing not to be, he is pitting himself against the Almighty, for it is not man's place to choose to be. Not choosing not to be is an ungodly answer: it is rooted in human pride rather than Christ-like humility; and because the poet suggests this as a possible way of asserting himself, he encounters a divine enemy."[26] By reverting to the negative—"not choose not to be"—Hopkins applies the *via negativa* method that Herbert uses in "The Quiddity" in order to attain to union with God.

St. Ignatius, in his *Rules for the Discernment of Spirits*, advises the exercitant to see all things in God, to regard everything as a gift from God, an opportunity to serve Him. "In this sense, 'Despair' and the possibility of repelling it can be understood as a gift from God. And so, at one and the same time, Hopkins is wrestling with 'Despair' and with God."[27] In "(Carrion Comfort)," the speaker, like that in Herbert's "The Collar," rejects a taste, but the taste he rejects is the meat of despair which would furnish a feast that would only "untwist—slack they may be—these last strands of man/In me" (ll.2–3).

Hopkins intends to wrestle with "carrion comfort" by engaging in a colloquy with Christ, Who is as present to Hopkins during this "darkness" as He was to the nun in *The Wreck*, in "the unshapeable shock night" (*The Wreck* II.29.227). Initially, however, Hopkins views Christ as a "terrible" lion with "darksome devouring eyes" whose meaning is difficult to determine, and wonders why this lion scans his "bruisèd bones" ["(Carrion Comfort)," ll.5–7]. In her article "The Metaphor of Struggle in '(Carrion Comfort),'" J. Angela Carson cites Old Testament passages from the Douay-Rheims Version (New York 1899) where the epithet of "thou terrible" (l.5) is used to refer to God. "He is called 'a great God, mighty and terrible' (Deut. 7:21; 10:17); the God of heaven is 'strong and terrible' (2 Es. 1:15; 4:14); and the 'Lord is high, terrible, and a great king' (Ps. 46:3). Even his name is 'holy and terrible' (Ps. 110:9; 93:3); and of the place where Jacob had the vision of the ladder reaching to heaven he said, 'Indeed the Lord

[25] Ann Louise Hentz, "Language in Hopkins' '(Carrion Comfort).'" *Victorian Poetry*, 9 (1971), 344.
[26] Wolfe 91–92.
[27] Malcolm H. Villarubia, S.J., "Two Wills Unwound in the 'Terrible' Sonnets." *Renascence* 1975 (Winter); 27 (2), 73–74.

is in this place and I knew it not. And trembling he said: How terrible is this place! This is no other but the house of God and the gate of heaven'" (Gen. 28:1-7).[28] Labelling as "terrible" the six sonnets which Hopkins wrote "in blood" underscores and dignifies the growth and development that shaped these inspired writings into works of spiritual autobiography.

The speaker in "(Carrion Comfort)" asks, "Why wouldst thou rude on me?" (1.5), in search of an answer that will justify God's ways to him. The Christian theme of theodicy is satisfied when Hopkins and the reader realize that "thou terrible" is "the Lion of the tribe of Judah, the Root of David" (Rev. 5:5). This image, with its Christocentric focus, combines the note of royalty with that of power and anticipates the images of Christ which follow. The Lion rocks the speaker with his "wring-earth right foot" (1.6) in order to conquer Hopkins's inclination to *acedia*, which is lamented also in "No worst." Similarly, Job's address to God reveals how God "hunts me like a lion; repeatedly you show your wondrous power to me" (Job 10:16). Continuing the biblical metaphor, Hopkins experiences Christ—as Job felt God (Job 38:1)—in the strong gusts of whirlwind.

Frequently in the Old Testament, the storm serves as a backdrop for the appearances of the Lord; in *The Wreck* and "(Carrion Comfort)," the Lord's immanence and transcendence occur in "turns of tempest" ["(Carrion Comfort)," 1.8]. "The 'turns of tempest' not only lifts the fanning above the agricultural level and intensifies the violence, but also shows the tormented being twisted around and buffeted from all sides at once, as well as describing the turmoil within the speaker's soul."[29] All of these disparate images of God's hand and feet are unified by the central metaphor of God's anthropomorphism. The *agon* is evident here as the speaker, with "bruisèd bones," is scanned "With darksome devouring eyes" (1.7) and yet is, once again in Job-like fashion (Job 9:17), "frantic to avoid thee and flee" (1.8). Perhaps Herbert best expresses the dialectical and spiritual stress of Hopkins in his concluding line of "The Pulley": "If goodness lead him not, yet weariness/May toss him to my breast." Both writers cling to the hope that consolation is forthcoming.

In the sestet of "(Carrion Comfort)," Hopkins posits a theodicy that summarizes the purpose of his sufferings in the kissing of "the

---

[28] Carson 549.
[29] Hentz 345.

rod" (1.10). Since the word "rod" may also be given the Old English spelling of "rood," it becomes evident that the very instrument which the speaker had previously accused God of using to "rude on me" (1.5) now becomes the means of the speaker's salvation.[30] This becomes the act of saying "yes" at "lightning and lashed rod" (*The Wreck* I.2.9-10), which recalls the question: "Why do men then now not reck his rod?" ("God's Grandeur," 1.4). What Hopkins "kissed" was not merely the "rod" or cross of Christ crucified, but more so the "hand" of God, an act that arouses joy, laughter, and cheer in his heart. But even after Hopkins kisses the rod, the wrestling continues for "That night, that year/Of now done darkness" (ll.13-14). In stanza 2 of *The Wreck*, this divine rod is vividly described as a sweeping and hurling movement that "trod/Hard down with a horror of height." In "(Carrion Comfort)," the rod is described as a "héaven-handling" that "flúng me, fóot tród" (1.12). The cyclical nature of consolation and desolation continues to inform the Christian's life of faith. The dull repetition of the heavy monosyllabic line emphasizes the monotony of a life lived without God and without hope in this world: the weary succession of days reminiscent of Macbeth's soliloquy, "Tomorrow and tomorrow and tomorrow creeps in this petty pace...To the last syllable of recorded time" (*Macbeth*, V.v.19-21).[31]

The concluding quatrain begins with a rhetorical question—"Cheer whóm through?" (1.12)—and proceeds to enact the wrestling match between Hopkins and his "hero" Christ in much the same way that Jacob, struggling all night with the angel of the Lord at Bethel (Gen. 32:23-32), emerges, maimed but victorious. The speaker's tone changes, however, from that of pride in his own audacity at wrestling with no less an adversary than God to humble adoration before "my God" (1.14). "The bracketed 'my God!' before the final 'my God' is seriously witty, in the seventeenth-century manner: Hopkins shows how unthinkable it now seems that he should have fought against God, of all people."[32] The concept of Christ as the hero-king is Ignatian and is found

---

[30] Ann Louis Hentz's article "Language in Hopkins' '(Carrion Comfort)'" is an excellent source for the Anglo-Saxon echoes in this poem: the use of alliteration; the archaic form of the adverb "rude" reinforcing a meaning of "violently" rather than "impolitely," thereby suggesting the primitive, natural, and elemental qualities of God's action; and Anglo-Saxon compound words such as "wring-world right foot."

[31] G.B. Harrison, ed., *Shakespeare: Major Plays and Sonnets* (New York: Harcourt, Brace and Co., 1948).

[32] Hunter 95.

in the chapter titled "The Kingdom of Christ" in the *Spiritual Exercises*. The exercitant is urged to become a subject of Christ, Who is described as generous and noble-minded and Whose service demands that His followers share the hardships of His campaign. "Whoever wishes to join me in this enterprise must be willing to labor with me, that by following me in suffering, he may follow me in glory."[33] Evidently, before Hopkins's struggle began, he had pledged his submission and had been sustained by God in the conflict in which God engaged him.

Religious wrestling underscores the paradox that the Christian disciple, in finally bending to God's will, further defines himself or herself and is victorious. In kissing the rod, Hopkins realizes, as does Herbert in "The Collar," that his freedom is to be found in becoming God's servant or "Child." "For Hopkins, the world is dappled, even when he celebrates what he sees as the brightest moment in its history, the Incarnation of Christ.... Man's dark element is not wholly forgotten."[34]

In both "The Collar" and "(Carrion Comfort)," the poets indicate the length of the period of spiritual desolation. Herbert questions: "Is the year only lost to me?" ("The Collar," l.13). Hopkins suggests that the event that triggered "(Carrion Comfort)" lasted "That night, that year" (l.13). Perhaps Hopkins alludes here to the event in "I wake and feel" that was of interminable duration: "when I say/Hours I mean years, mean life" ("I wake and feel," ll.5-6). In "The Collar," one action, one speech, and, finally, one act of submission, all three concretely depicted, represent the culmination of a more generalized spiritual dissatisfaction of one poetic year. As Amy Charles points out, perhaps this year—1630—is when Herbert was removed from the courtly and literary circles to which he was accustomed and relocated to the Bemerton parsonage. "Here...he would come to know that the scholar and the orator must dwindle to a country parson."[35] Likewise, in "(Carrion Comfort)," Hopkins expresses the conflict between his poetry and ministerial vocation. He first presents a speech and an action (ll.1-8) which temporally occur once, but he then depicts in the sestet other "toil" and "coil" which subsequently take place throughout a year of inner turmoil.[36] Mary Ann Rygiel's theory that each poet's

[33] Puhl 44.
[34] W. Johnson, *Gerard Manley Hopkins: The Poet as Victorian* 146-47.
[35] Charles 138.
[36] Rygiel 46.

reference to a year-long period of disturbance may be intended as a reference to the liturgical calendar which begins in a spirit of hope with Advent and proceeds to the sufferings of Lent and Christ's Passion reinforces the Ignatian meditative cyclical pattern of consolation and desolation and mirrors the life of faith. For both Herbert and Hopkins, particular nights and events are subordinated to a timeless unity in which their souls seek oneness with God.[37]

Biographically, the year 1884–85 was a year of darkness and stress for Hopkins. But even previous to this year, Hopkins records in his Journal of September 18, 1873:

> I had a nightmare that night. I thought something or someone leapt onto me and held me quite fast: this I think woke me, so that after this I shall have had the use of reason.... I had lost all muscular stress elsewhere but not sensitive, feeling where each limb lay and thinking that I could recover myself if I could move my finger, I said, and then the arm and so the whole body. The feeling is terrible: the body no longer swayed as a piece by the nervous and muscular instress seems to fall in and hang like a dead weight on the chest. I cried on the holy name and by degrees recovered myself as I thought to do.[38]

Hindsight, reflection, and examination of conscience illumine Hopkins's sufferings and account for the time shifts from the present tense in the octet of "(Carrion Comfort)" to the past tense in the sestet in a manner comparable to that of Herbert's in "The Collar." Where Herbert's poem begins in the past tense and shifts to the present tense, Hopkins's "(Carrion Comfort)" does the reverse, perhaps because the possible occasion of Hopkins's struggle—his choice of vocation—is "now done" (1.14), yet its effects remain. "Although the successive questions in this sonnet appear increasingly retrograde, searching the past, its motion becomes, as the growing urgency and velocity of its questioning suggest, progressive" and posits an affirmative response to Hopkins's desolation.[39]

W.A.M. Peters, S.J., says in a tribute to Hopkins anticipating the centenary of Hopkins's death that "Any man who in darkness lies wrestling with (his God!) his God is not even to be pitied; compassion

---

[37] Philip Page, "Unity and Subordination in '(Carrion Comfort).'" *Victorian Poetry*, 14 (1976), 29.
[38] House 238.
[39] Motto 112.

is not the true reaction."[40] If the expletive "(my God!) my God" is paralleled with Jesus's cry to His Father during His crucifixion—"'Eloi, Eloi lama sabachthani' which means, 'My God, my God, why have you forsaken me?'" (Mark 15:34)—the affinity of Hopkins with Christ is apparent. By His *kenosis* or self-emptying, Jesus surrendered to death. So must the Christian disciple. So must Hopkins. Hopkins found that in his sufferings God was fanning and winnowing him in order that "my chaff might fly; my grain lie, sheer and clear" (1.9). "For a person to be 'sheer' is to be exempt, clear, acquitted from guilt or crime, as well as being bright and pure."[41]

In surrendering to God's will, and in detaching himself from his own intellectual and creative powers, Hopkins destroys the "Lucifer of the self" and is filled with a peace and joy that no suffering or failure can destroy.[42] The parenthetical expletive—"(my God!)"—demonstrates the sudden union between God and the speaker in a way that parallels St. Thomas the Apostle's "My Lord and my God!" Here Hopkins "expresses and induces the ecstatic surprise which governs the entire poem."[43] The second "my God" is Hopkins's resignation and submission to this Deity with Whom the speaker has wrestled. The final line suggests that the speaker is no longer blinded by darkness. He finally submits to the "lapped strength" and "joy" that fortify him against the initial temptation to feast on the carrion comfort of despair, and realizes that, throughout the wrestling, his basic loyalties have remained steadfast. Hopkins's submission to the will of God and his acceptance of his own crucifixion is analogous to that of the tall nun in *The Wreck*: "The cross to her she calls Christ to her, christens her wild-worst Best" (II.24.192).

Herbert's thorny experience is contradistinctive to the "grain" of Hopkins's experience. Herbert looks back on his year of sighs and tears and sees "no harvest but a thorn" ("The Collar," 1.7), former "wine" now dried by his sighs, and "corn" now drowned by his tears (ll.10–12). But Hopkins, who looks back on his year of wrestling with God, refuses to "feast" on "Despair" ("[Carrion Comfort],"l. 1) and regards himself as grain, "sheer and clear" (1.9). Both Herbert and Hopkins underscore the theme of nutriment by the biblically based

---

[40] Peters, *Gerard Manley Hopkins: A Tribute* 80.
[41] Carson 553.
[42] Downes, "Beatific Landscapes in Hopkins" 196.
[43] Page 32.

image of harvest. The winnowing process, suggestive of the process of purification, along with the fasting, the night, and the suffering of this "soldier of Christ," reinforce the ascetical nature of these "terrible" sonnets.

"Our hearts will not rest, O God, until they rest in Thee" is the prayer of Hopkins as well as of St. Augustine. The "terrible" sonnets embody the Pauline paradox of finding the strength of God in acknowledging one's own weakness. Hopkins learns that his source of courage and spiritual consolation is twofold: the recognition of God as his adversary, and his "kiss[ing] of the rod."[44] Thus, in "(Carrion Comfort)," "the pattern of desolation followed by consolation and illumination crystallizes."[45]

The co-existence of this seemingly contrary and contradictory spirit in the soul's pattern of consolation-desolation is further authenticated in Herbert's "Affliction (IV)" where the speaker describes himself in the oxymoronic phrase a "wonder tortured" (l.5), a poor creature "in the space/Betwixt this world and that of grace" (ll.4–6). Seelig views the Herbertian series of five "Affliction" poems as "a spiritual autobiography in miniature" which redefine the meaning of affliction and parallel the abject state of the speaker in "Affliction (IV)" with "the dark night of the soul" of St. John of the Cross.[46] Confirming the *schola cordis* tradition, "Affliction (IV)" begins with a broken heart: "Broken in pieces all asunder" (l.1). The speaker's thoughts are contained within "a case of knives" (l.7), where their capacity to wound the heart and prick the soul gains momentum. Recalling "Bitter-sweet" and Psalm 51:19, where the Davidic psalmist speaks of his "broken and contrite heart," "Affliction (IV)" addresses the fluctuations that the Christian disciple undergoes between the affliction of sin and the joy of redemption, both of which take place within the heart.[47] "Herbert's often harrowing tension arises from his art of epitome, of cramming—literally, metaphorically, and religiously—so much in so small a space, so as to induce in the reader the kinæsthetic sensation of strain."[48]

---

[44] Rygiel 46.
[45] Mariani, *A Commentary on the Complete Poems of Gerard Manley Hopkins* 229.
[46] Seelig 31.
[47] Frank L. Huntley, "George Herbert and the Image of Violent Containment." *George Herbert Journal*, 8 (1984), 23–24.
[48] Huntley 27.

Hopkins's matching poem, his sonnet of desolation titled "Patience, hard thing" (1885-86), underscores the universality of the *schola cordis* tradition by its use of the first-person plural pronoun to convey a similar brokenness of spirit: "We hear our hearts grate on themselves: it kills/To bruise them dearer" (ll.9-10). The grating of the heart on itself portrayed by Hopkins and the heart broken in pieces personified by Herbert depict the heart as an image of contained violence that awaits the patient bending of God to its "ruins of wrecked past purpose" ("Patience, hard thing," ll.10,7), and the dissolution of the knot by the God Who alone provides "relief" in the rebuilding of the heart ["Affliction (IV)," ll.22, 28-29].

As in "The Collar" and many other Herbertian poems, much of the artistry in "Affliction (IV)" lies in Herbert's coordination of the imagery of battle and that of the broken vessel. He relies on the figures of the human being as a broken vessel, persecuted by his or her enemies, thereby echoing Psalm 31—"I am forgotten like the unremembered dead; I am like a dish that is broken" (Ps. 31:13)—and Job's plaints.[49] One reason that Herbert's religion appears so humane, in a century when religion was frequently associated with fear and gloom, is that his God is a God of the living. Because he learned from experience to find life "at hand"—in "Vanity (I)" he chides "Poor man, thou searchest round/To find out death, but missest life at hand" (ll.27-28)—these homely metaphors possess a freshness and vitality.[50]

Rosemond Tuve and Chana Bloch are credited with "opening" the images of containment proffered by Herbert. Tuve views Herbert's poems, particularly those with a predominance of household imagery, as efforts "to make the ineffable more nearly tangible."[51] While Bloch refutes Tuve's belief that the homely and husbandry imagery in religious poetry of the period does not offer "the least offence to decorum," she does agree with Tuve's statement that what is needed is "new knowledge about the exact connotations of particular words to

---

[49] Amy M. Charles notes on p. 121 of *A Life of George Herbert* that, as canon of Lincoln Cathedral and prebendary of Leighton Ecclesia, Herbert recited Psalms 31 and 32 privately each day. This may explain his frequent allusion to their lines and tropes. But even such faithful service to God does not exempt the Christian disciple from the purgative "case of knives" ["Affliction (IV)," l.7].

[50] L.C. Knights, *Explorations: Essays in Criticism Mainly on the Literature of the Seventeenth Century* (New York: New York University Press, 1964) 145.

[51] Rosemond Tuve, *Elizabethan and Metaphysical Imagery: Renaissance Poetic and Twentieth-Century Critics* (Chicago: University of Chicago Press, rpt. 1961) 217.

Elizabethans and Jacobeans."[52] Both Tuve and Bloch view Herbert's *Temple* poems as extensions of the Pauline metaphor of the Living Temple—the household of God—and the imagery therein as presenting a picture of the world that the simple and poor person can readily comprehend. "These images explore with endless fascination, at the level of everyday life, one of the controlling ideas of *The Temple*: God dwelling in man and man in God."[53] Furthermore, Bloch views the images as "free inventions in the biblical mode, exploring the vein of Jesus's 'salt of the earth,' 'moth and rust,' two Sparrowes solde for a farthing.'"[54] The "wat'ring pots [that] give flowers their lives" ["Affliction (IV), 1.10] suggest, metaphorically, the need of the speaker for "the purgative influence of water to destroy [his] sin." Moreover, the speaker "needs water to replenish his life and make him grow toward Christ—the source of light and life."[55] By the end of this poem—and the series of "Affliction" poems—the speaker envisions his regeneration.

"The devotional poet is called to express prayerfully how the human being, an essentially linguistic creature, becomes built as a fit and living temple of God."[56] Yet, paradoxically, any belief in the sole power of the individual to construct the building must also be broken as part of the process of rebuilding God's Temple in the human heart. Herbert engages in a perpetual struggle after inward peace in an unceasing effort to bend a proud and passionate nature into conformity with a strict conception of the religious life. In keeping with the *schola cordis* tradition, the battle is continually re-fought and re-won.

The original title in the Williams Manuscript of "Affliction (IV)" was "Tentation" or "Temptation." F.E. Hutchinson believes that "the Williams Manuscript represents an earlier stage in Herbert's work."[57] Eight of the poems in the Williams Manuscript were retitled by the time they were copied at Little Gidding, for the purpose of infusing additional meaning.[58] While no definite reason can be cited for the

---

[52] Bloch 224–25.

[53] Bloch 220.

[54] Bloch 221.

[55] Nancy Allen-Stainton, *Spiritual Autobiography in the Poetry of George Herbert and Gerard Manley Hopkins*. Master's Thesis, Duquesne University, 1982, 64.

[56] Sherwood 99.

[57] Vendler 281, n.1.

[58] Rickey 116–17.

change, Herbert's aligning of the words "temptation" and "affliction"
confirms an analysis of this poem in the Ignatian meditative pattern and
underscores the close affinity between contemplation and temptation.
The dark temptation for the speaker is to accept grief and despair.
Instead, he cries out against them, as did Christ in the Garden of Geth-
semane—"Oh help, my God!" ["Affliction (IV)," 1.19]—and realizes
that he needs God's daily support for his "relief" (ll. 27–28).

Furthermore, as Mary Ellen Rickey postulates, perhaps a change
from the original title suggests an association between "the mode of
temptation treated here, that of one's own rebellious thoughts, with
those of the other Affliction poems—illness in 'Affliction (I),' aware-
ness of one's own unworthiness in 'Affliction (II),' grief which shows
man his affinity to Christ in 'Affliction (III),' and the vicissitudes of all
men after Adam which, properly undergone, make him stronger than
the first man in 'Affliction (V)'—and so makes the group a five-part
complement commenting on human calamity."[59] Joseph Summers
attributes the "Affliction" poems to "a developing spiritual maturity in
the attitudes which they express."[60] The image of the
"cinquefoil"—the marks or "cipher[s] of suffering Christ" employed so
successfully by Hopkins in *The Wreck* (II.22.175,170)—is enriched in
the Herbertian "Affliction" poems as the speaker, overcome by grief,
becomes pierced and purged, as were Christ and the nun in *The Wreck*,
by the "elements [that] are let loose to fight" ["Affliction (IV)," 1.17]
within his soul.

The torturing becomes the means by which the speaker is rebuilt
and fitted for "heav'n, and much more thee" (1.3). The image of
"building" is contrasted with "broken pieces" at the outset of the po-
em. Chana Bloch's refuting of lines 29 and 30—"building me,/Till I
reach heav'n"—as allusions to the Tower of Babel is well-founded in
her view of the speaker as a broken, not an arrogant, man "who,
through faith, has become a tower. The following poem in *The Temple*,
'Man,' calls that tower a 'stately habitation' (1.2) for God the builder
to dwell in."[61]

Far from being an idle or arid waste, affliction serves a purpose:
that of purifying the soul by dissolving violently the "attendants"
["Affliction (IV)," 1.13] that fail the speaker in the accomplishment of

[59] Rickey 117.
[60] Summers, *George Herbert* 87.
[61] Bloch 276.

his "task of life" (1.16), namely, union with his Creator. The speaker
is assured that God will build and restore his soul to Himself. Purga-
tion and illumination occur with God's scattering "by his light/All the
rebellions of the night" (ll.23-24) initiated by the experience of "the
dark night of the soul" where "the elements are let loose to fight"
(1.17) within this Christian disciple. Like Job, who was more blessed
at the end of his life than at the beginning, the speaker, by engaging in
a colloquy and a wrestling with God, learns that the one who has sur-
vived afflictions emerges stronger than the one who is not hunted by
the Lord (1.2). He confirms his readiness "to be rebuilt by God's pow-
ers into a new vessel worthy of heaven."[62]

Thus, Herbert's theology and poetry, when analyzed as spiritual
autobiography, strongly confirm that the pain of trying to love God has
its compensations and consolation. Like Hopkins, Herbert knew his
deepest and most consistent desire was to live a life in union with God
and His will. The fulfilled self preserves its individuality or instress
even when it is "indistinguishable from God" and when it unites with
God through "states of reciprocity and identity."[63] However, the reali-
ty of momentary existence and spiritual difficulties recurs, which is
why a chronological reading of any *Temple* poems, especially the
"Affliction" poems, masks the characteristic problems of the spiritual
life.

Amid afflictions and seeming despair, the Christian disciple fre-
quently prays for patience, a virtue that becomes the subject of Hop-
kins's "terrible" sonnet "Patience, hard thing." In this poem and in
"My own heart," Hopkins begins the upswing movement to recovery
and consolation. He discovers that without war and wounds he will
attain neither the virtue of patience nor the resolution of his spiritual
conflict. This virtue is not something he will receive passively; he must
actively "pray" and "bid for" (ll.1-2) it with the currency of the spiri-
tual conflict he has been experiencing. Hopkins, continuing the auction-
eering diction of the opening lines, will bid the dear price necessary to
buy patience: war, wounds, weary times, tasks.[64]

Patience was "a virtue that Hopkins needed often," says Robert
Boyle, S.J., gathering successive passages from Hopkins's letters and

---

[62] Rickey 69.
[63] Vendler 152, 251.
[64] Mariani, *A Commentary on the Complete Poems of Gerard Manley Hopkins*
235-36.

poems.[65] "Patience," writes Boyle, "is rooted in pain and endurance; it stays with the suffering heart, wrecked so often in its past high endeavors, and masks the scars."[66] In the last lines of the poem, Hopkins develops St. Paul's list of the fruits of the Spirit where peace is followed by patience and kindness (Gal.5: 22–23). A gloss on the derivation of the word "patience" from the Latin *patior*—I suffer—admits of the suffering of afflictions and pain with a calm spirit. "That is the true theological virtue of patience; when a man asks for this, he is by corollary inviting 'afflictions, pain, toil'—he may well be said to be asking for a continuance of the conflicts in which he is already being buffeted," namely, "war" and the "wounds" that follow.[67]

The patient person, like Christ, bears all things and is still kind. Whoever asks for patience also asks to suffer, to obey Christ, even to death. "In an order [the Jesuits] which was organized 'to fight and not to heed the wounds,' it was given to Hopkins to fight only interior battles, an infinitely harder 'war.'"[68]

The Spiritual Exercises instructs the exercitant on the correspondence between patience and the classical descent and ascent of the movements in the soul:

> When one is in desolation, he should strive to persevere in patience. This reacts against the vexations that have overtaken him. Let him consider, too, that consolation will soon return, and in the meantime, he must diligently use the means against desolation...insist more upon prayer, upon meditation, and on much examination of ourselves. We can make an effort in a suitable way to do some penance.[69]

Nearly six years earlier, Hopkins, in his curtal sonnet "Peace," complained that his prayer for peace had brought him only a substitute: "Patience exquisite" ("Peace," 1.8). "But Hopkins had struggled too hard with himself in the interim to use any such delicate epithet now. Patience is now in the 'terrible' sonnet that 'hard thing'; in place of the cooing of the wood dove, we now 'hear our hearts grate on themselves.'"[70] In the curtal poem, Patience given to the soul is expected

---

[65] Robert Boyle, S.J., *Metaphor in Hopkins* (North Carolina: University of North Carolina Press, 1961) 116–17.

[66] Boyle 114.

[67] MacKenzie 184.

[68] McChesney 161.

[69] Puhl 143.

[70] Mariani, *A Commentary on the Complete Poems of Gerard Manley Hopkins* 234.

to grow up into Peace; in the "dark" sonnet, Patience connotes war, yet allows peaceful healing.[71] More than ever before, Hopkins now realizes that his present need is not just for Patience. In *The Wreck*, he had already recorded this experience of "Time's tasking" (II.27.211); now he is more firmly convinced of what his soul requires.

The plant imagery in the second quatrain of "Patience, hard thing" is reminiscent of the flowers and plants that dominate many Shakespearean soliloquies and dramas. "Rare patience" (1.5) requires a harsh soil in which to flourish, soil that "wants wounds; weary his times, his tasks" (1.3). Once patience takes hold, it makes failure endurable. However, once it becomes rooted "in these, and, these away" (1.5), it spreads like ivy over ruins, and "masks" or denies acknowledgements of "past purpose." It "basks/Purple eyes and seas of liquid leaves all day" (ll.6-8). Indeed, "purple eyes" is a soft and sensuous image, suggestive of Hopkins's attempt to treat himself more kindly. But the speaker is not deceived for long into believing that this calm surface contains no pain. As in the aforementioned "dark" sonnets, human hearts continue to "grate on themselves: it kills/To bruise them dearer" (ll.9-10). Yet the "rebellious wills" (1.10) seem to satisfy the Divine Gardener, "who more and more distills/Delicious kindness" (1.12) even before the Christian disciple submits to His authority. "It would seem, then, that the purpose whose ruins patience masks is equivalent to the end for which man was created—union with God. The purpose is ruined by man's pride in himself, for he is not satisfied to be a part of the divine vineyard; rather, he wants to be the master of it. As a result, he becomes merely a vine yielding sour grapes. Patience is needed, therefore, if man is ever to fulfill the purpose of his existence."[72]

Although this is another one of the "dark" sonnets in its search for the "dearest him that lives, alas! away," it represents a great advance upon the previous "terrible" sonnets in its assurance that "Patience fills/His crisp combs and...comes those ways we know" (ll.13-14). The "Delicious kindness" of line 13, in addition to the imagery of bees and honey that follow, recalls the psalmist who prays that the "kindness" of God comfort him and who is assured by the Lord's promises which are "sweeter than honey to my mouth" (Ps. 119:76, 103). The sacramental and incarnational natures of Hopkins's spirituality are evident

[71] Heuser, *The Shaping Vision of Gerard Manley Hopkins* 116, n.5.
[72] Wolfe 100.

in the concluding line where the "crisp combs" of the eucharistic wa-
fers and the beehive of the temple, along with "those ways," recall the
Emmaus experience where the disciples "recounted what happened on
the road and how they had come to know [Jesus] in the breaking of
bread" (Luke 24:35). Colloquy and nutriment shared with Jesus pro-
vide the Christian disciple with an understanding of the immanent ways
God deals with His people. Furthermore, the "crisp combs" suggest the
firmness of the disciplined will, acquired through the transforming
process of wars and wounds to healing and peace. Like the other "ter-
rible" sonnets, "Patience, hard thing" is dominated by the theme of
nutriment: the search for comfort one can taste. The speaker asks:
"Where is he who more and more distills/Delicious kindness?"
(ll.12–13).

   "What he needs above all is 'comfort,' a word that recurs in a
variety of ways in his poems of this period."[73] In this particular po-
em, comfort, for Hopkins, resides in the Most Precious Body and
Blood of Christ and the Resurrection. Tasting the sacramental bread
and wine becomes his ultimate goal as priest and poet. His Journal and
Retreat Notes express his hope that, at the Last Judgment, he will find
total incorporation of his self into the Body of Christ. Regarding the
Last Supper, Hopkins writes:

The Eucharistic Sacrifice was the great purpose of [Jesus'] life and his own chosen
redemption: perhaps he would have instituted it and into it have disappeared—as
at Emmaus.[74]

"God above all is patient; for Him, and therefore for the poet, it is the
end which matters, and there is the consolation."[75]
   The (w)reckoning experience undergone by the speaker results in
a theodicy that confirms the patience of God and the significant role of
patience in forming the Christian disciple into the image of God. This
poem, along with The Wreck, other "terrible" sonnets, and matching
poems of Herbert, reaffirms "the change which patience can effect in
the tempest-tossed shipwreck of the self."[76] The enigmatic and deso-
late nature of "dark heaven" depicted in "To seem the stranger" para-
doxically sheds light, comfort, and consolation in "Patience, hard

---

[73] Milward and Schoder, Landscape and Inscape 120.
[74] Devlin 162.
[75] Hunter 99.
[76] Mariani, A Commentary on the Complete Poems of Gerard Manley Hopkins 235.

thing." Hopkins learns that the only way to acquire patience which, like every other grace, is a gift from God, is to bend to "His crisp combs." The homophonous punning of "combs" as a verb underscores the humanity of Christ and His coming in times of war, weariness, and desolation as well as in the sensuousness of "Purple eyes and seas of liquid leaves." For Hopkins, this sonnet is more than a poetic exercise; it is a means of transforming himself into the likeness of his God. His dull "selfyeast" spirit learns to wait for God to move it upwards to an ascending level of love. One crucial battle is nearly over, but the war with the self continues: "Yet the rebellious wills/Of us wé do bid God bend to him even so" (ll.10–11).

Whereas the other sonnets of desolation employ the first-person-singular pronouns, "Patience, hard thing" uses the first-person-plural noun to signify Hopkins's objectivity in remedying the failure and disappointment common to the human race. The Christ Who is be-moaned by the speaker in previous sonnets as the One Who "lives alas! away" and Who "bides in bliss" is depicted here as "working every-where in the cosmos to bring creation to fulfillment."[77] The final defi-nition of "patience," therefore, is total incorporation into the Mystical Body of Jesus Who fills the universe with the nutriment—the "crisp combs"—of His love. Mysterious are the ways God comes into our lives; we and "those ways we know" ("Patience, hard thing," l.14) can only approximate God's patient knowledge and wisdom. The order of the "terrible" sonnets presented in Chapter Four and this chapter dem-onstrates Hopkins's gradual progression and acceptance of the limita-tions of his humanity and the fact that he struggles, not merely against something but, rather, for something: a reconciliation with the Spirit from Whom he came and toward Whom he is moving. Hopkins learns that "those ways we know" allow us to experience this reconciliation through the complex virtue of patience. "The acceptance and assump-tion of the victim of the sacrifice, as Hopkins writes, enables him to follow Christ and to receive from Him a special guidance, a more particular providence."[78]

"Patience, hard thing" and "My own heart" are rejoinders to po-ems which Hopkins wrote on the same sheet of paper: "To seem the stranger" and "I wake and feel." These four sonnets are attempts, not

[77] Cotter 229.
[78] Wolfe 101.

at understanding, but at resignation. The latter two establish a fixity ("my lot," "God's decree," "the curse") with which the former two seek ways of coming to terms (patience *can* come, Hopkins must "leave comfort root-room").[79]

The spirit of reconciliation that moves by "a special guidance, a more particular providence" into "the dark night" of Hopkins also impels Herbert to "skill" or justify God's ways to him and his "ways" to God. The unpredictable nature of God frustrates Herbert's attempts to define theodicy in a skillful or comprehensive manner and renders him, as it does Hopkins, "a lonely began." Yet in "Justice (I)," Herbert celebrates the incarnation and immanence of Christ as a general instance of grace and the redemptive process. "Herbert's Christ, like his conception of grace, gentles and liberalizes Reformation doctrine—especially as it is represented in Calvin—making both Christ and grace available to all."[80] The divine mercy of the Lord with Whom Herbert engages in a colloquy overshadows the wounds and killings He also inflicts on the soul. Herbert describes God's mercy, patience, and "*reprieve*" (l.5), as well as His bestowal of grace, in similar terms in "Prayer before Sermon" at the end of *The Country Parson*. This prosaic selection may be cited as a gloss on many *Temple* poems, but fits "Justice (I)," as well as the companion poems to Hopkins's "terrible" sonnets (especially "Patience, hard thing"), with special closeness:

> But thou Lord, art patience and pity, and sweetness, and love; therefore we sons of men are not consumed. Thou hast exalted thy mercy above all things; and hast made our salvation, not our punishment, thy glory: so that then where sin abounded, not death, but grace superabounded; accordingly, when we had sinned beyond any help in heaven or earth, then thou saidest, Lo, I come. He took flesh, he wept, he died.... Blessed Savior! many waters could not quench thy love! nor no pit overwhelm it. But though the streams of thy blood were current [contemporaneous with and flowing] through darkness, grave, and hell; yet by these thy conflicts, and seemingly hazards, didst thou arise triumphant, and therein mad'st us victorious.[81]

"In Reformation theology, as in Paul's epistles, both sin and grace are conceived of as forces independent of the individual personality, though not external to it."[82] The same warring within the members of the

[79] Robinson 144.
[80] Halewood 104.
[81] Wall 113.
[82] Strier 21.

body and mind that St. Paul describes in Romans 7:23 is given a dual poetic emphasis in Herbert's "Justice (I)" by the italicized apostrophe of the speaker to the Lord, and by the conjunction "*yet*" in the second hemistich. In the pairing of alternatives stated in each line, Herbert and the Christian disciple find the best-formulated definition of the three Christian themes and the three stages of mysticism. The acceptance that God's ways are not his ways—"I cannot skill of these thy ways" (l.1)—removes Herbert to a higher plane of "life and praise" (l.6) and to an acknowledgement that he not only fails to understand God's ways, but that he also lacks a proper understanding of "these my ways (l.12). In "Justice (I)," Herbert "ponders on the continual alternation between faith and doubt, between confidence in salvation and fear of reprobation, and decides that God has chosen this means to strengthen his faith and to keep it fervid and alive."[83] Herbert was accurate in saying to Nicholas Ferrar that he had finally found "perfect freedom in the service of Jesus [his] Master." Combat and competition with God were no longer, in the end, necessary to him.

A "picture of a spiritual conflict" is portrayed in these select poems that recount the dying and rising of the soul of this parson and poet. L.C. Knights views Herbert's poetry as "a way of working out his conflicts. But it does not, like some religious poetry, simply *express* conflict; it is consciously and steadily directed towards resolution and integration."[84] Knights agrees with F.E. Hutchinson, who describes Herbert's poems as "colloquies of the soul with God or self-communings which seek to bring order into that complex personality of his which he analyses so unsparingly."[85]

Like Paul's letter to the Romans, "Justice (I)" treats what another seventeenth-century English divine, Richard Sibbes, called "the mystery of sinfulnesse." "Justice (I)" is a poetic response to Sibbes's exhortation to his auditors that they labor "to have as deepe conceits in our understandings as we can of that mystery of sinfulnesse that is in us."[86] Troubled by the war that is waging within him—"*I would do well, yet sin the hand hath got*" ["Justice (I)," l.10]—Herbert looks to God but finds no reason to quarrel with Him, as he did in previous

---

[83] J.B. Leishman, *The Metaphysical Poets: Donne, Herbert, Vaughan, Traherne* (New York: Russell and Russell, Inc., 1963) 130.

[84] Knights 138.

[85] Knights 138.

[86] Strier 35–36.

poems analyzed in Chapter Four and the present chapter. He confesses that "when I mark my life and praise,/Thy justice me most fitly pays" (ll.6–7), and justifies his soul's wrestling with God as a prerequisite for his earning a resting place in the Temple. The subsequent words—"*mean*," "*stray*," "*would*," "*delay*"—suggest human failure. By substituting "my" for "thy" in the last line of the poem, Herbert acknowledges the incomprehensibility of God's ways and humankind's ways.

In *George Herbert's Lyrics*, Arnold Stein demonstrates how Herbert's spiritual and literary development conforms to the complex demands of discipline and form apparent in the style of "Justice (I)," which is "repetitive, interlocking, circular. Man's complete dependence and complete inability to understand are hammered out in purposive rhetoric and rhyme, original, brief, eloquent, yet without a striking word or phrase, subtle in conception and worked out with fine attention to detail and structure."[87] Herbert's style depicts the "dichotomy [that] exists within his self, which behaves paradoxically: one part of it says 'Yes,' but the other half moves in the negative direction."[88] Yet rather than condemn himself, Herbert appeals to the Lord to continue the process of spiritual regeneration and growth, and attempts a compassionate and kind move from his soul's "*delay*" (1.11), responses that parallel those of Hopkins in the final "terrible" sonnet to be analyzed, "My own heart."

"My own heart" (1885–86), the last of Hopkins's "dark" sonnets of 1885, measures the distance Hopkins has traveled in these "dark" sonnets from "God knows when to God knows what" (1.12): an acceptance of the incomprehensibility of God, and the poet's lack of skill in describing this Logos. Patricia A. Wolfe regards "My own heart" as a companion piece to "Patience, hard thing." "It is a recognition that man, though he can actively seek patience, cannot actively seek solace."[89] Although his "terrible" travels have taken him "Betweenpie mountains" of spiritual, emotional, and physical conflict, terror, and desolation, they have become for his soul "lights a lovely mile" (1.14). This poem demonstrates the coexistence of consolation and misery as Hopkins clarifies the terms of his inner struggle with greater equanimity than in the previous "terrible" sonnets. It expresses an attempt, as

---

[87] Stein 25–26.
[88] Mathai 142–43.
[89] Wolfe 101.

does "Patience, hard thing," to live with his problem patiently. In "My own heart," Hopkins takes this insight literally: he attempts to be more patient, kind, and charitable to himself, and to perform his duty to God by sorrowing for his past sins and imperfections.[90] "Hopkins was much chastened at this point, but he could recognize God once more in the beauty of the world."[91]

In spite of the first line—"My own heart let me more have pity on"—this sonnet, also written in the *schola cordis* tradition, rejects self-pity. By "reflexive reduplication of key words," enjambment, and a self-deprecatory tone, Hopkins depicts the "selfyeast of spirit" and the "dull dough" evident in "I wake and feel."[92] He does not want his "sad self" to "live this tormented mind/With this tormented mind tormenting yet" (ll.2-4). In some of the "terrible" sonnets, Hopkins sets himself up as his own judge; in others, especially "No worst" and "(Carrion Comfort)," he attributes his stress and afflictions to a Being Whom he addresses as "thou terrible." In "My own heart," however, Hopkins renders into poetic form a section of an essay titled "The Possibility of Separating Ethics from Political Science" (1867), written when Hopkins was an undergraduate at Balliol for his tutor Robert Williams: "But we also hear of a man's duties to himself...self-love becomes the reverse of selfishness and self-respect of self-conceit."[93]

During his novitiate training, Hopkins learned that self-scrutiny should not be merely self-torturing. Father D'Arcy attributes Hopkins's over-scrupulousness to the fact that Hopkins was a convert who brought with him "the atmosphere of rectitude which belongs so especially to the High Anglicans in Victorian times."[94]

The host of images in the octet—the tormented mind, a prison cell devoid of light, a thirst—argues and prepares for the part played by God's grace in healing his "Soul, self...poor Jackself" (l.9) in the sestet, "who has been dulled by the proverbial 'all work' and no joy. Nowhere else in the 'dark' sonnets is 'Soul' used. Therefore, it seems most likely that 'Soul' is in opposition with 'self.'"[95] The string of

---

[90] Mariani, *A Commentary on the Complete Poems of Gerard Manley Hopkins* 238. The word "pity" is derived from *pietas* or duty to God.
[91] Fulweiler 160.
[92] Schneider 195.
[93] House 124.
[94] Pick 112.
[95] Villarubia 79.

personal epithets confirms the divisions in the soul between its human and spiritual nature.[96]

Although Hopkins proceeds to describe his "cast[ing] for comfort" (l.5) as in "No worst"—"Comforter, where, where is your comforting?"—he realizes that such thoughts merely renew his self-torment, a condition that only makes him "jaded." "He therefore exhorts himself to 'let be'—leave things as they are; to 'call off' his thoughts, as a hunter might call off his pack of hounds, and to direct them 'Elsewhere.'"[97] Although he searches, as do the "blind/Eyes," and "thirst[s]" (l.6-8), he transforms self-pity into ironic detachment from the desired comfort. Paul Mariani believes that there is also a sardonic parallel here "between Actaeon turned into a hart and torn apart by his own hunting dogs and the poor, jaded Jackself of Hopkins being internally torn apart by his own tormenting thoughts."[98]

The "smile" or consolation of dark comes when it is least expected: at "unforseentimes" (l.13) and in God's own measure or "size" (l.11).[99] Hopkins compares God's smile to the sunshine that unpredictably breaks through the sky between darker masses of "Betweenpie mountains" (l.14). The "mountains" suggest flight and freedom, two elements which Hopkins uses to soar to a specific, directed end: union with God. "Flight in Hopkins enacts the directions of assent. The poem's image begins to soar into seemingly limitless space and time as it moves out and up toward an immortal future."[100] Moreover, the final tercet suggests the biblical analogue of Psalm 121: "I lift up my eyes toward the mountains; whence shall help come to me? My help is from the Lord, who made heaven and earth" (Ps. 121:1-2).

"Betweenpie," another one of Hopkins's own words, is based on his favorite word "pied," and suggests a momentary restoration of Hopkins's faith in the creative powers of his poetic and ministerial vocations. In the sestet, the speaker realizes that God's favor and kind-

[96] Downes, *The Great Sacrifice: Studies in Hopkins* (Lonham: University Press of America, Inc., 1983) 111.

[97] Milward, *A Commentary on the Sonnets of Gerard Manley Hopkins* (Chicago: Loyola University Press, 1969) 172.

[98] Mariani, *A Commentary on the Complete Poems of Gerard Manley Hopkins* 239.

[99] I suggest that Herbert's poem "The Size," especially stanza three, also serves as a matching poem to "My own heart" in its economical expression of this "terrible" sonnet. The concluding line of "The Size"—*"These seas are tears, and heav'n the haven"*—provides a gloss on the theodicy of "the dark night of the soul." Hopkins takes another title of a poem, "Heaven-Haven," from this line.

[100] Motto 119-20.

ness—His "smile"—is not "wrung" from Him by the self-pitying cries
of the speaker. Rather, it comes at unexpected times, "pied" or vari-
ous, and provides an interval of consolation that enlightens and eases
the journey of the Christian disciple as it did that of the two men on
the road to Emmaus who were comforted (etymologically, "strength-
ened") by the resurrected Christ. Thus, Hopkins completes the "dark"
sonnets with a vision of consolation. St. Ignatius says that one of the
purposes of spiritual desolation is "that we may interiorly feel that it
is not ours to get or keep...spiritual consolation, but that all is the gift
and grace of God our Lord." The *Imitation of Christ* also advises: "As
for comfort, leave them to God; let Him do therein as shall best please
Him."[101]

In a prophetic and fortuitous voice, Manley Hopkins addressed one
of his poems, "To a Beautiful Child" (1843), to Gerard, his first-born.
The poem, published only a year before the birth of Gerard, reads in
part: "thy sport is with the storm/To wrestle;—and thy piety to
stand/Musing on things create, and their Creator's hand!"[102] This
poem finds its fulfillment in *The Wreck* and the "terrible" sonnets,
Hopkins's account of his soul on its journey to the "Creator's hand."

The select works of Herbert and the six "terrible" sonnets of Hop-
kins considered in Chapters Four and Five are modern psychodramas
rooted in a mind and heart in anguish where the main actors are the
speakers Herbert and Hopkins. The two poets and ministers are similar
in their "underlying determination to plot the stresses of religious
conflicts as they are rather than as they should be."[103] Their verse
and prose also parallel the Ignatian method of meditation in their recall-
ing of the spiritual truth to be considered, their treatment of obstacles,
and their consideration of resolutions. Herbert and Hopkins realize that
Christian discipleship encompasses both light and dark, blessings and
despair, and is, therefore, "a thoroughly paradoxical whole, one that
is ultimately redemptive."[104]

Like other spiritual autobiographers, Herbert and Hopkins attempt
to justify their religious experiences by depicting their universal signifi-
cance. In treating the impact of Christ's Incarnation, Passion, and

---

[101] Pick 147.
[102] Bump, *Gerard Manley Hopkins* 8.
[103] A. Alvarez, *The School of Donne* (New York: Pantheon Books, 1961) 78.
[104] Seelig 33.

Resurrection on humankind, these writers also treat the consequences of these realities on the life of the Christian disciple who "says yes" to the experience of being humbled, crucified, and exalted with the Risen "Lord of life."

"One ague dwelleth in my bones,
Another in my soul (the memorie
What I would do for thee, if once my grones
Could be allow's for harmonie)...."

Chapter Six

Lenten Fast to Paschal Feast: "The Church's Mystical Repast"

Lord I have invited all,
      And I shall
Still invite, still call to thee:
For it seems but just and right
      In my sight,
Where is all, there all should be.
            (Herbert, "The Invitation")

HERBERT AND HOPKINS ACCORD such significance to the spiritual sustenance that nourishes their lives that the motifs of hunger, banqueting, and satiety underlie much of their verse and prose while redefining the three Christian themes and the three stages of mysticism. The care and dignity with which both parsons treat the sacramental elements mirror their respect and love for the Divine Presence and their desire to lead themselves and their congregations to the communion table where the Bread and Wine of everlasting life are consumed. Isaiah 55 and the Acts of the Apostles 2: 42–46 underscore the significance of food in the Israelite and Christian communities and serve as the biblical *loci* for the select poems and prose of Herbert and Hopkins in the present chapter that incorporate, most specifically, the theme of nutriment. The invitation to grace, as well as to bodily and spiritual growth, repair, and sustenance, is extended to the Christian disciple who thirsts and hungers for imperishable food.

    The direct references and allusions by Herbert and Hopkins to biblical themes lend crucial emphases to their matching poems of nutriment: Herbert's "The Invitation" and "Superliminary" and Hopkins's "New Readings"; Herbert's "The Banquet" and Hopkins's "Easter Communion"; Herbert's "The Bunch of Grapes" and Hopkins's "Barnfloor and Winepress"; Herbert's "The Holy Communion" and Hopkins's "The Half-way House"; Herbert's "Love (III)" and Hopkins's "The Bugler's First Communion." When read as a unit, each pair of poems is a study in the human experience of temptation, downfall, and regeneration. The events described in biblical typology are readily available to the speakers in the poems, while the "new reading" posited by Hopkins enriches the action and the voice of the speaker in the Christ-event. Consequently, these select poems of Herbert and Hopkins treat the immanence and transcendence of this event, the nourishment of the Christian disciple by the Logos of sacred Scripture as well as the Eucharist, and defend the position "that one's spiritual autobiography has been recounted in Scripture and already lived by so many others."[1] Both writers attend to the Johannine injunction: "You should not be working for perishable food but for food that remains unto life eternal, food which the Son of Man will give you" (John 6:27). Just as the Israelites looked to the manna to provide daily sustenance and life, Jesus exhorts the Christian disciple to look to Him, to digest His teachings as the source of wisdom, knowledge, and daily nourishment. The Christian disciple learns that faith in Jesus and submission to God's Word and work in him or her are vital to growth and regeneration. In order to achieve this end, he or she learns to assimilate the glorified flesh and blood of Jesus, as the poetic and ministerial vocations of Herbert and Hopkins authenticate.

The present chapter considers the select poems and prose of Herbert and Hopkins as reminders of how the glory and the Passion of Christ result from the purgative wound in His side, and of how the dualism which the speakers initially inhabit is unhealthy for the Christian disciple. The speakers' pilgrimages are ones of enlightenment. Their lives undergo various "readings" and interpretations as they enact the sacrificial and eucharistic counterparts of Christ's life.

Hopkins learned from Herbert the poetic use of the Christian traditions of iconography and typology. Herbert proved that it was possible to use a plain style and diction for spiritual ends; moreover, he wrote a poetry that, "though humble and devout, was also argumentative and dialectical. The lesson was not lost on Hopkins, whose temperament needed precisely this combination of qualities."[2] Although Hopkins had yet to be plunged into the experience of "the dark night of the soul," these early poems express a yearning to possess the transcendent God and to experience His sensuous, immanent love. As the records of their spiritual autobiographies unfold, Herbert and Hopkins learn that the *Imitation of Christ* provides direction for their souls in its statement: "When you are troubled and afflicted, then is the time to merit.

---

[1] Labriola, "Herbert, Crashaw, and the *Schola Cordis* Tradition" 22.
[2] Bergonzi 22.

You must pass through fire and water before you come to refreshment."[3]

Louis L. Martz confirms that, "through many different guises, the Communion imagery permeates Herbert's *Temple*, not only in poems explicitly devoted to praise of the sacrament, but also in dozens of brief references to the 'feast,' the 'board,' the 'meat,' the 'banquet,' the 'blood,' the Cross, the wounds."[4] Likewise, the poems of Hopkins's Oxford period reveal that he is already finding his own distinctive expression for his Christian insights. His works "are Christocentric in their use of eucharistic and penitential themes; they draw from traditional imagery to express his personal effort to make contact with Christ."[5]

C.A. Patrides terms the Eucharist "the marrow of Herbert's sensibility" and maintains that if the *Temple* is a structure, "it is a eucharistic one" in form and content: an act of thanksgiving.[6] Patrides makes a cogent distinction between communal sacramentalism and the act of worship in the Anglican Church by defining the former as "the essence of things, the very nature of nature, in that it reflects the activities of the divine architect-poet both during his initial act of creation and his subsequent preservation of the world. These diverse strands merge in Herbert's thought because they depend on a singular reality, the immanence of God in history through the sacrament of the Lord's Supper, the Eucharist."[7] Patrides continues that Herbert's poetry is "replete with words reminiscent in their literal dimension of Roman Catholic claims" and lists many of the words cited by Martz to prove this concept.[8] When analyzed as an interrelated unit, the select poems of Herbert and Hopkins in this chapter depict speakers who move from spiritual blindness to insight as they progress through the Church and the purgative rod of chastisement and illumination. The poems depict the advancement toward union with God which culminates in "Love (III)" and "The Bugler's First Communion" wherein the speakers ultimately attend the Great Feast that is promised to the Christian disciple who

---

[3] Albert J. Nevins, M.M., tr., *Imitation of Christ* by St. Thomas à Kempis. (Indiana: Our Sunday Visitor, Inc., 1973) 43.

[4] Martz 302.

[5] Cotter 7.

[6] Patrides, *The English Poems of George Herbert* 17.

[7] Patrides, *The English Poems of George Herbert* 18.

[8] Patrides, *The English Poems of George Herbert* 18.

persistently puts his "lips on pleas/[that] Would brandle adamantine heaven with ride and jar" ("The Bugler's First Communion," ll.45–46) until he attains "Love."

The incremental repetition of "Come ye hither all" at the outset of five of the six stanzas of Herbert's "The Invitation" clearly indicates the speaker's hope that the Christian disciple "draw near" to the altar or table to share "the church's mystical repast." As a Reformation theologian, Herbert accepts Communion as a feast and employs imagery to reinforce this principle. "He sees both baptism and the Lord's Supper as 'dispatches from [a] friend' ("The Holy Communion," l.24), as visible Words from God that he must attend to, direct communications of the Gospel of Christ, 'dispatches' that can be 'read' and interpreted endlessly."[9] In the Reformed churches, Communion was celebrated at a table as a re-enactment of the biblical feast of spiritual nourishment provided at the Last Supper.[10] "Herbert's frank avowal of Christ; his passionate yet restrained colloquies with God; his vigorous and subtle expression of doctrine; his significant quaintness and happy conceits—all these elements are found, in duly modified form, in the later Hopkins."[11]

In Chapter XXII of *The Country Parson*, titled "The Parson in Sacraments," Herbert avers to the Lord as "not only the feast, but the way to it."[12] The journey undertaken by the Christian pilgrim on his way to the banqueting table is preparatory and vital to the total enjoyment of Christ as the feast, as Hopkins's "New Readings" (1864) corroborates in its capitalizing of the word CHRIST and in its setting where the sower of the seed is juxtaposed with the "soldiers platting thorns around CHRIST'S Head" (l.4). "Grapes grew and drops of wine were shed" (l.5) by a Christ Who hazarded all to bring "Food for five thousand" (l.12) in a manner that was anything but "easeful" (l.15). Despite the "thorn" (l.7) and "flinty road" (l.9) befalling the corn seed, Christ gathered all together from His desert experiences to feed the multitude and to provide for them "Grains from His drooping Head" (l.13). Although the "drooping Head" has an ironic connotation, new wine and new life emerge from thistles, wastes of rock, and all seem-

---

[9] Veith 220.
[10] Veith 219.
[11] Patrides, *The English Poems of George Herbert* 28.
[12] Wall 85.

ingly barren and moribund forces. Herbert and Hopkins assure the
reader of "The Invitation" and "New Readings" that "Here is love,
which having breath/Ev'n in death,/After death can never die" ("The
Invitation," ll.28-30). Death, then, is heralded, not feared, in Her-
bert's and Hopkins's Christian view.

Even though Herbert was keenly aware of the need to develop an
inner life, he also "held to the ancient Christian view that personal and
private devotion was subordinate to the corporate worship life of God's
people gathered together in prayer and thanksgiving to hear God's
Word read and preached and to celebrate His bounteous goodness
through sacramental action."[13] Herbert's biographer Nicholas Ferrar
notes that "Though he abounded in private devotions, yet went he
every morning and evening with his family to the Church; and by his
example, exhortations, and encouragements drew the greater part of his
parishioners to accompany him daily in the public celebration of Divine
Service."[14] Herbert's verses are a continual exploration of the spiritu-
al life as it is subsumed under corporal worship. They derive meaning
from the significance he placed on the Bible, Book of Common Prayer,
the worship services, and the tenets of his Anglican faith. St. Paul's
injunction to the young bishop Timothy in Ephesus to "remain faithful
to what you have learned and believed" and to regard the sacred Scrip-
tures as "the source of the wisdom which through faith in Christ Jesus
leads to salvation" is witnessed in Herbert's use of Scripture in both his
ministerial and poetic vocations "for teaching—for reproof, correction,
and training in holiness" (2 Tim. 3:14-16).

An essay published by T.S. Eliot in 1928 on Lancelot Andrewes,
a contemporary of Herbert, describes the men of the Reformed Church
of England during the first half of the seventeenth century as exponents
of both "the old authority and the new culture."[15] Eliot applauds their
ability to question but also to affirm, to appreciate both the uniqueness
of the individual and the necessity of the corporate and the traditional,
and to confirm the need for both an inwardly and outwardly directed
Christian life.[16] The seventeenth century was characterized by what
Eliot describes as a "determination to stick to essentials, an awareness

---

[13] Wall 4.
[14] Wall 4.
[15] Wall xii.
[16] Wall xi.

of the needs of the time, a desire for clarity and precision on matters of importance, and an indifference to matters indifferent."[17] Herbert's capacity to conjoin seemingly disparate elements and to recognize their inner worth and uniqueness is undoubtedly what attracted Hopkins and amplified his theories of *haecceitas* or "thisness," inscape, and instress. Herbert's embracing of the contraries of human experience further attracted Hopkins in his own struggle to find a way of thinking, living, and praying his faith amid the complexities of his contemporary society.

The Temple is the sole foundation upon which Herbert situates his poems, leading the reader from "The Church Porch" to "The Church" in a series of literary colloquies with God which reveal a soul in dialogue with its Creator, questioning, resisting, and, finally, accepting the will "of Christ, my Master." Many of *The Temple* poems, including the six considered in this chapter, are "retrospective narratives told from the point of view of one who has already come through."[18] They "tend to move more and more into the present as they proceed—only to return suddenly, at the height of the 'action,' to an awareness of the original narrative perspective" and deepened self-consciousness on the part of the speaker.[19]

In "Superliminary," the transitional poem between "The Church Porch" and "The Church" poems, the speaker, in the first quatrain, invites the reader to "approach, and taste/The Church's mystical repast" (ll.3-4) and, in the second quatrain, admonishes the reader to "Avoid profaneness" (l.5), to "further go" (l.8) into the Temple only if holiness, purity, and wisdom (clarity of vision)—or the pursuit of these virtues—attend the life of the Christian disciple. The biblical analogue of this poem is also an invitation to God's salvific grace: "All you who are thirsty, come to the water!... Why spend your money for what is not bread; your wages for what fails to satisfy? Heed me, and you shall eat well, you shall delight in rich fare" (Is. 55:1-3). The appeal to enter the Church door and therein learn to live the mysteries of the banquet table is extended in Herbert's "The Invitation."

In "The Invitation," Herbert depicts both Christ and Aaron, the biblical prototype of the true priest. In the opening stanza, God is

---

[17] Wall xii.
[18] Strier 117.
[19] Strier 12.

anthropomorphized as being "prepar'd and drest" (1.4) for the feast, the Perfect Host Who has prepared His table for the communion banquet to which all are invited, particularly those "whose taste/Is [their] waste" (ll.1-2). The subsequent stanzas define the conflicts or *agon* experiences that have occasioned this invitation. The second stanza addresses those "whom wine/Doth define" (ll. 7-8), and concludes by instructing the reader to "drink this,/Which before ye drink is blood" (ll.11-12). Here Herbert attempts a description of the "blood" of Christ as a means of grace, a symbol of nourishment and Christ's presence, a difficult task, "seemingly experiencing, in the Lutheran manner, the Real Presence of Christ."[20] The witnessing of the transcendent in the ordinary is translated here as a gentle reminder to the "guests" and reader.

Herbert's technique of imagistic recurrence reinforces the "waste" and "weeping" of the opening stanzas by personifying "pain" in stanza three as being "arraign[ed]" (1.14). However, Herbert compresses its force by commanding the reader to "Taste and fear not: God is here/In this cheer,/And on sin doth cast the fright" (ll.16-18). The Christian paradox that sorrow is subsumed in joy is evident in the following stanza where Herbert alludes to the Flood and its ironic lesson that "Here is joy that drowneth quite/Your delight" (ll.22-23). Particular to the agricultural image of drowning is the claim that the occasionally deliberate flooding of fields and meadows is necessary for improved cultivation. In "The Invitation," the Christian theme of theodicy is embodied in a Shepherd Who seeks all who are destroyed by the perfidious joys of life, and Who sometimes sends waters of purification to cleanse the souls of His disciples.

The poem also addresses the temptation to neglect temporal happiness and joy and to yearn, instead, for a love which "After death can never die" (1. 30). The dove, signifying the temporal and one-sided love that "exalts you to the sky" (1. 27), rounds out a poem that treats earthly phenomena as the vessels or conduits that lead the soul to God. The concluding stanza might have been used as an epigraph for *The Temple* poems as the speaker undertakes his responsibility to enjoin all people to praise God.[21] The Lord and the speaker alternately extend

---

[20] Veith 215.
[21] Summers, *George Herbert* 108.

and accept the invitation: "Lord I have invited all,/And I shall/Still invite, still call to thee" (ll. 31–32).

Like Herbert, Hopkins has full intellectual control of his banqueting imagery. The metaphorical Herbertian "letter" on which the invitation to the Eucharistic banquet is issued is transliterated by Hopkins in "New Readings" (1864) into the thorns that surrounded the head of Christ. (The image of the "letter" is later recalled in Hopkins's "terrible" sonnet "I wake and feel" [1885]). Bernard Bergonzi describes "New Readings" as "an intelligent pastiche of Herbert," a criticism confirmed by Paul Mariani who comments that "New Readings" is a reworking of "Barnfloor and Winepress" and that it also "shows the influence of George Herbert in its metaphysical nature" by its parabolic method of conveying Scripture.[22] "Certainly [Hopkins's] interest in fruit, flower, and other natural objects (evident in diaries of the late sixties as well as poetry) both as phenomena to observe and as nature to be given 'readings' new or renewed suggests again and again a parallel with Herbert."[23] David A. Downes posits that "New Readings" is Hopkins's attempts to write a biblical poem in conscious imitation of Herbert.[24] The capitalization of CHRIST in "New Readings" enriches the charisma of the Anointed One as it draws attention to Christ's hegemony over "that legion of winged things" (1.14), ready at a "moment's notice" to provide a secure defense against the wrecking and wrenching experience of the Garden of Gethsemane (Matt. 26:53–54). Hopkins alludes to the Matthean parable of the sower and the seed (Matt. 13:4–7) and the Lucan story of Christ feeding the multitudes by the multiplication of the loaves and fish (Luke 9:12–17) to depict a Christ Who uses "wastes of rock" (1.11) from which no "corn" (1.8) would grow to provide "Food for five thousand" (1.12). Hopkins's invitation is written "On thistles that men look not grapes to gather" (1. 2), and is read by the Christian disciple whose only recourse is to a Christ Who "at all hazards fruit hath shewed" (1.10), Who prefers suffering to easy deliverance, and Whose bloodshed "from His drooping Head" (1.13) informs Christian discipleship. The "easeful wings" (1.15) of Hopkins's legions bear a striking resemblance to Herbert's metaphor of those "whose love/Is your dove" ("The Invitation,"

[22] Mariani, *A Commentary on the Complete Poems of Gerard Manley Hopkins* 10.
[23] W. Johnson, "Halfway to a New Land" 119.
[24] Downes, *The Great Sacrifice: Studies in Hopkins* 88.

ll.25–26) which "exalts you to the sky" (l.27), a love that is merely
ephemeral and ultimately powerless, in order to instill in the speaker
a dependence on God which Jesus also embraced in His temptations by
Satan in the desert.

In Hopkins's Sermon for Monday Evening, October 25, 1880, on
Divine Providence and the Guardian Angels, he writes that:

> if we were not forced from time to time to feel our need of God and our
> dependence on him, we should most of us cease to pray to him and to thank
> him.... God desires nothing so much as that his creatures should have re-
> course to him.... In the meantime God's providence is dark and we cannot
> hope to know the why and wherefore of all that is allowed to befall us.[25]

The "New Reading" to which Hopkins challenges the Christian disciple
is an interpretation of *agon* experiences as literal banquets whereby the
nourishment for our spiritual lives is provided, not on "easeful wings"
(l.16), but on paradoxical "thorns," "thistles," and "drops of wine"
along the "flinty road" where Christ eats and walks with His followers.

The flowing of Christ's unity of being into His followers is exem-
plified in Hopkins's principle of "inscape." "The term 'inscape' sug-
gests 'shape' and 'creation' so that Hopkins designates the 'scapes' of
the world as emblems of God's dynamic creativity.... It is a principle
of being which keeps a thing in existence." [26]In "New Readings," as
in the scriptural account of the three temptations of Christ, Christ
refuses to use a *scala* to escape heavenward from this earth; rather, He
willingly engages in the *kenosis* experience by becoming the capital
Logos Who renders meaning and significance to the human pilgrimage.

Herbert's and Hopkins's view of God as a generously benign Mas-
ter is witnessed in "The Invitation" and "New Readings" wherein the
speakers invite the reader to the banquet table in order to partake, not
only of the "thorns" and "thistles" of weakness, temptation, and down-
fall, but also of communion with the resurrected Lord. In "the Invita-
tion," Christ is omnipresent; indeed, Herbert uses the word "all" in the
final stanza to signify the inclusiveness of Christ's loving receptivity to
and forgiveness of sinners as well as the elect. Herbert, like the Lu-
therans, believes that Christ died for all people and that anyone can be
saved. "This last stanza, with its allusions to Luther's Christology,

[25] Devlin 90–92.
[26] Downes, *The Great Sacrifice: Studies in Hopkins* 28.

emphasizes the doctrine of the Real Presence that is suggested through-out the poem."[27] Here again is seen the parson's responsibility to call others to God. He "invites eaters and drinkers to excess—in language so tactful and witty that it barely registers disapproval."[28] In a cheer-ful tone, the parson recommends that the sinner substitute Christ's body and blood for less substantial food and drink. He addresses his people directly, calling them to serve God and to reject sin with its promise of temporal illusions. "The liturgical *'dignum et justum est'* ["For it seems but just and right," 1.34] gives the sinners a final redeemed and almost divine place at the banquet."[29]

Probably the most important point of connection between Herbert and Hopkins is that they were both dedicated to the imitation of Christ.[30] Clearly in "New Readings," the headship of Christ super-sedes a life of ease as the speaker reinterprets the life of Christ and, analogously, his own life. The speakers in "The Invitation" and "New Readings" struggle with the Logos and the world, yet the diction and imagery suggest that they are active participants in life and searchers of God in His creation.

Of particular significance to the Christian asceticism of the young Hopkins is a predisposition to physical suffering as a corollary to the imitation of Christ. "Penances, denials, chastenings—the harshness of the Lent spirit with its conviction that if something is enjoyed there is spiritual value or benefit in giving it up—are much in evidence in the early Hopkins."[31] A serious commitment to the Lenten self-chastise-ment with its resultant spiritual reward of Easter Communion leads Hopkins to develop the "physicality of his poetry."[32] His attempts to express the beauty of asceticism are evident in his sonnet "Easter Com-munion" (1865) in which the suppression of natural desires and "myrrhy-threaded golden folds of ease" (1.12) is undertaken in order that self-will may be replaced by an imitation of Christ.

However, Hopkins revolts against the principle of dualism with its antithetical view of matter and spirit; furthermore, it was this revolt that precipitated his reception into the Roman Catholic Church on

---

[27] Veith 217.
[28] Benet 184.
[29] Vendler 31.
[30] Bump, *Gerard Manley Hopkins* 192.
[31] Robinson 6.
[32] Kitchen 69.

October 21, 1866. His poetic images reinforce and reflect the Real Presence of Christ in the profane as well as in the sacred.

The profundity of Hopkins's asceticism is best demonstrated in his "word-music of 'Easter Communion.' Words whose meanings relate them to the pain of Lent are rhymed by short *e* assonance—'lenten,' 'breath-taking,' 'chequers,' 'ever-fretting,' 'punishment'—while words whose meanings are associated with the joy of Easter are rhymed by long *e* assonance—'feast,' 'Easter,' 'sweetness.' From the striking rhyme of 'fasted,' 'feast' in the first line, alliteration and assonance stress the connection between these apparently antithetical sensations."[33] The Catholic doctrine of transubstantiation (a dogma resulting from the Fourth Lateran Council of 1215) incarnated, translated, and redeemed for Hopkins whatever was base into the unity of being. "One of the attractions of the doctrine of the Real Presence for [him] was that it was the central instance of a metaphor participating in the reality it represents, the archetype for a sacramental poetry of nature."[34] The traditional decameter lines in "Easter Communion" underscore the rich poetic heritage that Hopkins inherits and invigorates by his own sprung rhythm and other creative poetic techniques and principles.

Hopkins's writing impels the reader to an attentiveness and vigilance that mirror the theme of this sonnet: a single-minded anticipation of the God Who "comes all sweetness to your Lenten lips" (l.2). The New Testament analogue of the wise and foolish virgins is recalled in "You vigil-keepers with low flames decreased" (l.8), as well as the Psalmic counterpart of being anointed with the "oil of gladness" (l.10) above other kings. The dignity of both speaker and God is evident as God's biblical promise of being with His people to "strengthen all the feeble knees" (l.14) concludes a sestet, the purpose of which is to manifest God's munificence, forgiveness, and healing to those imprisoned in their own fasts. "Breathe Easter now" (l.7) becomes imperative to the "Pure fasted faces" (l.1) of those holding in secret the "breath-taking whips" (l.3). The entire sonnet serves as a direct address to those Christian pilgrims whose feeble knees and tortured spirits will be the very instruments of their invitation to and feasting at the Easter Communion table.

---

[33] Bump, *Gerard Manley Hopkins* 57–58.
[34] Bump, *Gerard Manley Hopkins* 62.

The significance of analyzing these works as spiritual autobiography lies in the ironic vision that both writers demonstrate in addressing seemingly irreconcilable polarities. For example, the simultaneity of the dual nature of Christ—His divinity and humanity—is evident in Herbert's and Hopkins's works. The sensuous nature of the sacraments, especially Holy Communion, constitutes the core of Herbert's spiritual nutriment poems and forms the nexus of imagery by which he attempts a description of their mysterious nature.

"The Banquet," a nine-stanza "emblematic summary of all the themes of the Pascal triduum and the soul's union with these mysteries through the Eucharist," is Herbert's meditation on the Communion elements.[35] The bread and wine are the means by which the speaker engages in a direct, personal colloquy with Christ. He tastes and smells the elements by which Christ revealed Himself to His Apostles and finds in the elements the means of expiation for his sins by the total and unconditional love of the One Who has the power to raise him from the ground. The bruised and broken body of the speaker is renewed by the remembrance of Christ's bruised and broken body: "God, to show how far his love/Could improve,/Here, as broken, is presented" (ll.28–30). Herbert, like Hopkins, uses the poetry of the banquet of the senses, familiar from the Song of Songs, to transcribe his religious experience. Aware of Hopkins's favorable attitude toward Herbert, the reader is not surprised that Hopkins speaks of Herbert's poetry as "fragrant sweetness" and utilizes much of that sensuous imagery in his own works.[36] "There are, of course, connotations of sumptuousness and splendour in the word 'banquet' itself in its original meaning, though it must be borne in mind (as the N[ew] E[nglish] D[ictionary] shows) the word had acquired the sense of 'a light repast between meals' by Herbert's time."[37]

The stark imagery that reflects the asceticism of Hopkins in "Easter Communion" (Lent 1865) contrasts with the metaphors of melted sugar, sweetened wine, and the fragrance of "Flowers, and gums, and powders" ("The Banquet," l.16), images surpassed by "Only God, who

---

[35] Sister Rita Marie Yeasted, C.D.P., *George Herbert's Poetry and the "Schola Cordis"* Tradition, diss., Duquesne University, 1981, 183.

[36] Patrides, *George Herbert: The Critical Heritage* 50.

[37] E.B. Greenwood, "Herbert's 'Prayer (I).'" In *George Herbert and the Seventeenth-Century Religious Poets* by Mario A. DiCesare, ed. (New York: W.W. Norton and Co., Inc., 1978) 249.

gives perfumes,/Flesh assumes,/And with it perfumes my heart" (ll.22–24) in a description of Herbert's religious experience. Herbert's familiar and affectionate treatment of the Eucharist is contained in this "ditty" (1.50), regarded by Martz as another example of Herbert's use of sacred parody. The outcome reveals a rededication by the speaker to the service of religious love, "in terms that remind us of the various addresses to his voice and lute that have occurred earlier, and also of the common Elizabethan love of 'musical strife.'"[38] "As the language of the Anglican liturgy recalls ('Christ our Passover is sacrificed for us: therefore, let us keep the feast,') the symbols of the sacrifice and the banquet are typologically united; but whereas the altar emphasizes the earthly aspect of suffering, the banquet reflects the eternal triumph."[39] An intertextual study of "The Banquet" and "Easter Communion" permits a unification of seemingly divergent elements concurrent with the "church's mystical repast" while it enjoins the reader to consider the constitutive elements of the banquet itself, and to accord the emotional colloquy between the speaker and God the significance it demands.

These elements undergo a process of pressurization for Herbert and grafting for Hopkins as the reader becomes further grounded in biblical typology with Herbert's "The Bunch of Grapes" and Hopkins's matching poem "Barnfloor and Winepress" (1865). Indeed, Wilson F. Engel III finds parallels between Hopkins and "the seventeenth-century poets who were fascinated with the motif of Christ in the Wine-press."[40] The Exodus event with its liberation story of the Israelites is central to both poems. Like the Israelites, the Christian disciple also wanders in the desert wilderness of bondage and emotional scourgings, murmuring in temporary shelters and securities until he or she crosses over to the Promised Land where, like Noah, he or she plants a vineyard (Gen. 9:20), cuts down "a branch with a single cluster of grapes on it," and names the place *Eshcol* or "cluster" (Num. 13:23–24). The Christian disciple is transplanted from a place of spiritual enslavement and engrafted onto the true vineyard of "Noah's vine" (Ps. 80:8–12) and

[38] Martz 317.

[39] Seelig 42.

[40] Wilson F. Engel III, "Christ in the Winepress: Backgrounds of a Sacred Image." *George Herbert Journal*, 3 (1979–80) 45. Where Engel's study depicts how the winepress image is at the heart of Herbert's "The Agony," my discussion centers on winepress imagery and typology in "The Bunch of Grapes."

Christ Himself (John 15:1). "The speaker thus views his spiritual life, searches his heart, and perceives his changing relationship with God in relation to Old Testament history, Christ's Paschal experiences, and liturgical and sacramental symbolism."[41]

Both poems use rich biblical and sensuous imagery in recalling the locales—the Red Sea and the Barnfloor, respectively—and the process—Pressing and Winepress—accompanying the liberation and redemption events. Both poets use personal pronouns: "I," "my," and "thee" by Herbert and "we," "ye," "us," and "our" by Hopkins to emphasize the close personal bond and the sublime nature of the colloquy between the speakers and God.

"From Law (the Mosaic dispensation) to Love" could serve as the sub-title of this pair of companion poems that depicts the cycle of sin, repentance, and thankful remembrance of God's mercy and "ancient justice" ("The Bunch of Grapes," 1.14). "If the never-ending process of self-examination is what these poems record, it is also what they provoke" in the reader who discovers that apparent success and achievements, though temporary and incomplete, serve as the means by which God reveals Himself and carries out His loving plan of salvation.[42] "Herbert's spiritual progess is no doubt historical and autobiographical. 'Seven yeares' (1.4) has its symbolic and representative significance as well. Herbert writes in a tradition which reveals the close relation between an individual spiritual experience and a national or racial or community spiritual experience."[43] Thus, every approach to the banquet experience and to the altar provides a new occasion for self-examination on the part of both the speaker and the reader. There is, ultimately, one "story" in salvation history that "pens and sets us down" (1.11), and the reader uncovers this story in the nutriment poems of Herbert and Hopkins. Both poets perceive Old and New Testament events and personages as "God's vast typological plan of recapitulation and fulfillments" of His will.[44]

The story uncovered by the speaker in Herbert's "The Bunch of Grapes" is one that celebrates a God "Who of the Law's sour juice sweet wine did make," One Who was pleased and willing to be

[41] Labriola, "Herbert, Crashaw, and the *Schola Cordis* Tradition" 20.
[42] Fish, *The Living Temple* 125.
[43] Olney, *George Herbert and Gerard Manley Hopkins* 196.
[44] Lewalski 131.

"pressed for my sake" (ll.27-28). The speaker receives the Gospel ("Scripture-dew," 1.16), the free forgiveness of sins ("His ancient justice overflows our crimes," 1.14), and the assurance of God's incarnational and immanent presence ("God's works are wide"; But much more him I must adore," ll.13,26) as he undertakes the journey of the Christian disciple "by God's command" (l.8). The Eucharist manifests for Herbert, not merely the Incarnation, but more so the Atonement as sacramental images of the water, bread, grapes, and wine are transformed into the elements of the pilgrim's spiritual and physical sustenance and regeneration. God's willingness to be "pressed for my sake" (1.28) emphasizes God's freedom in embracing the speaker and assures the speaker of God's desire to engraft him onto His own "good store" (1.25). "[E]ach Christian" (1.10) is as central to God's beneficence as was the entire wandering Jewish community. The poem "provides an historic and religious validation of Herbert's concern with his own experience" and manifests God's vulnerability to His creatures.[45]

The bunch of grapes is a symbol of Christ and of the Christian's communion. The prospering of "Noah's vine," like the cluster of *Eshcol*, was a sign of God's blessings. It was a partial fulfillment of His exhortation to Adam and Eve to "Be fruitful and multiply" (Gen. 9:1-2). Yet, as at Eshcol, God's blessing under the Law could become humankind's occasion for the repetition of sin and punishment. Noah's misuse of the vine resulted in the curse on Ham. Likewise, the bunch of grapes furnishes the image of the speaker's lost joy, the image of blessings refused or perverted, and also, paradoxically, the image of the Christian disciple's new-found joy, ever present if he or she will cease murmuring.

From Old Testament times, meals and sacrifices were synonymous. Even when animal sacrifices played a less significant role in Judaism, sacred meals retained a sacrificial character. Jesus, being a Jew, embraced His religious heritage even as He transformed it. The Holy Communion is not only an ageless reminder of Christ's sacrifice that established His joyful covenant with His followers, but also a foreshadowing of the eschatological feast. "The vines also suggest the bountiful supply of Christ's blood for the salvation of all humankind, an outpour-

[45] Strier 156.

ing produced in the winepress of the cross. "[46] The blessing and adoration assumed by the speaker in the concluding stanza indicate that joy is no longer lost. Complete and lasting joy may not be fully realized until the Promised Land is reached, but God provides for His pilgrims a foretaste of it in the "cluster of Eshcol" and in His Son's communing with His disciples through His own Body and Blood "pressed for [our] sake" (1.28). Unlike Moses, who was denied entrance into the Promised Land, the Christian who feeds on "Law's sour juice" to make "sweet wine" (1.27) will acquire his inheritance and everlasting joy. In the process of complaining, the speaker ultimately realizes that his life does not parallel the rebellious and murmuring Israelites after all. He recognizes how much God has served him and, like St. Paul, acknowledges a personal sense of gratitude to this God "who loved me and gave himself for me" (Gal. 2:20). Moreover, he realizes that he is not destined to repeat the bondage of the past, but that he can move instead into the Promised Land of eternal fulfillment and lasting joy.

Herbert's typological poem "The Bunch of Grapes" "demonstrates how the Christian mind makes use of the past to understand the present, applying a 'doctrine' of history to the 'life' of the individual. Because he believes that the Bible is a record of man's spiritual development, Herbert is continually measuring himself against its scheme of events and promises in order to convey a sense of shared experience...and the mysterious way in which grace invades the human sphere." [47]Herbert clearly depicts here a reconciliation with God. Sin is followed by repentance, which gives way to the various ways of communing with God, and finally to love, which involves an emotional, joyful response to God based on the speaker's recognition of God's identity.[48]

The co-existence of sourness and sweetness reaffirms Herbert's reconciliation of the duality and cyclical recurrences inherent in the human experience: that of finding joy and consolation in adversity and desolation. Like many of Herbert's poems, "The Bunch of Grapes" "centers on the redemptive effect of Christ's spilled and shared blood,"

---

[46] Albert C. Labriola and John W. Smeltz, *The Bible of the Poor: A Facsimile and Edition of the British Library Blockbook C.9 d.2* (Pittsburgh: Duquesne University Press, 1990) 154.

[47] Bloch 127–28, 149.

[48] Veith 135.

and its import on the human heart.[49] Furthermore, it addresses the question of the reward to be found in God's service and the awe and joy discovered by the Christian disciple when he learns that God's gift of Himself to humankind is the supreme feast of the soul. "Through the educating process of the poem, this realization is both learned and felt, therefore, in the school of his own heart...so that the speaker can re-cover the joy and re-establish the loving relationship that he seems to have forsaken. After all, his awareness of some change in his relation-ship with the Lord prompted the meditation and self-examination that constitute the poem."[50] Indeed, Herbert learns that pardon is God's name, forgiveness His title. The theme of theodicy is examined by a speaker who learns that "justice is exacted in a gesture of consummate love and self-sacrifice" by a God Whose "ancient justice overflows our crimes" (l.14).[51]

Hopkins's evolving relationship with the Lord, inspired by Her-bert, prompts a matching poem, "Barnfloor and Winepress" (1865), that also combines scriptural and sensuous imagery. The poem express-es the sacrifice of Christ in conventional biblical and natural symbols of wheat and grapes. "It links the crucifixion to harvest, to grape-tread-ing and wheat-threshing" and thereby manifests Hopkins's strength and enthusiasm in his belief in the Real Presence.[52] This metaphysical religious poem was printed in autumn of 1865 in the *Union Review*, a High Church journal that promoted the unification of the Anglican, Catholic, and Eastern Orthodox communions.[53] The poem reveals how Hopkins extends the idea of the Mystical Body of Christ in the communion bread to the rest of nature. The wheat and grapes here are not only the raw elements for transubstantiation, but are active partici-pants in the Being of God. "One of the attractions of the doctrine of the Real Presence for Hopkins was that it was the central instance of a metaphor participating in the reality it represents, the archetype for a sacramental poetry of nature."[54] Like Herbert, Hopkins uses the New Testament image of the Mystical Body of Christ—"I am the vine, you are the branches" (John 15:5)—in the vine imagery of "Barnfloor

---

[49] Labriola, "Herbert, Crashaw, and the *Schola Cordis* Tradition" 13–14.
[50] Labriola, "Herbert, Crashaw, and the *Schola Cordis* Tradition" 20, 23.
[51] Labriola, "Herbert, Crashaw, and the *Schola Cordis* Tradition" 18.
[52] Kitchen 61.
[53] MacKenzie 22.
[54] Bump, *Gerard Manley Hopkins* 62.

and Winepress." The leitmotif in Hopkins's poems is his consistent "underthought" (his own term) of Christological metaphor to stress his relatedness to God, a principle he accentuates by the use of rhyming couplets throughout the poem.[55]

Further biblical typological allusions also enrich this poem. The epigraph cites the Second Book of Kings (6:24–30) wherein a king of Israel, during the siege and famine in Samaria, heard the weeping of a woman who cried out to him for help. He reproved her by saying, "The Lord help you! Where could I find help for you: from the threshing floor or the winepress?" (2 Kings 6:27). As he spoke further to her, she related the story of how another woman asked her to relinquish her son so he could become food for the famished victims of Samaria. The other woman promised that she would do, in turn, the same with her own son. The son of the woman beseeching the king was boiled and eaten, but when it was time for the other woman to hand over her son, she hid him. When the king heard the *planctus* of the woman relating this incident, he tore his garments and wore sackcloth next to his skin in atonement for the dishonesty and selfishness of the woman in his kingdom who refused to sacrifice her son as food for the people.

Similarly, the opening line of "Barnfloor and Winepress" is an address to those who "on sin's wages starvest," but who are "lifted from the roots" (1.4) and provided with "heavenly Bread" (1.8). The price of this Bread is costly, as was the price paid by the woman in 2 Kings when she sacrificed her son. Hopkins here also alludes to the birth of Christ in his use of such associative diction as "roof'd His head" and "At morn we found the heavenly Bread" (ll.7–8), images that recall the morning of Christ's nativity, here also suggesting the painful fashioning and lying of "Christ our Sacrifice" (1.10) "on a thousand altars" (1.9). In contrast to Herbert's method of indirection in describing the feast or banquet, Hopkins's method is direct and elemental in depicting "our altar-vessels stored/[With] the sweet Vintage of our Lord" (ll.19–20) and "our Savior's and our blood" (1.32) as the vital components of the "banquet food" (1.31).

Hopkins, like the woman in 2 Kings, is quite graphic in detailing the Lord's distress. The Matthean account of the Agony in the Garden, the Burial, and the Resurrection are compressed into stanzas two and

[55] Bump, *Gerard Manley Hopkins* 133.

three in a reminder to the reader that "We shout with them that tread the grapes" (l.12). "The cluster of grapes...anticipates Christ's crucifixion, a resemblance underscored in illuminated manuscripts that depict the savior in the winepress of the cross."[56] Christ, the fruit on the tree, is termed "Terrible" (l.15) by Hopkins, who subsequently wrote his own "terrible" sonnets in the midst of spiritual anguish and desolation. This affinity he experiences with Christ frequently informs and sustains his poetic range and Christian sensibilities.

Like the cedars of the forested Lebanon or the fruits of "Libanus" (l.28), the Christian disciple is planted so as never to fade by a Savior Who also "grafted [us] on His wood" (l.33) before His own Crucifixion at age thirty-three, a number coincident with the number of lines in this poem. The invitation to "come into the shade" (l.26) is extended, in spite of humankind's participation in "Calvary's distress" (l.17), to the weary who will "bear His leaf," (l.30) the yoke of Christian discipleship. Hopkins conveys the justified pride of the Christian disciple who considers such banquet food, as natural and ordinary as it may seem, to be the singular spiritual nourishment.

For Herbert, the reward of "coming into the shade" is "rest" which, in Deuteronomic history, symbolized the end of wandering, settlement in the Promised Land, and respite from war. Herbert frequently uses the word "rest" with its symbolic and biblical plurisignations. In "The Holy Communion," he pairs "rest" with "thy way" to read: "Making thy way my rest" (l.9). He seems to be drawn repeatedly "to the nodal point of history as it is recorded in Scripture, the juncture between Old and New, precisely because he encounters it time and again in his own experience. He finds in biblical history the paradigm of his spiritual struggles, his movement toward God and his miserable backsliding. Hence he is keenly aware 'not only of the pastness of the past,' in Eliot's phrase, 'but of its presence' as well."[57] The Old Dispensation had its value of richness, "fine array," and "wedge of gold," but in the New Dispensation and in the New Man that Herbert strives to become, God's presence far surpasses any material richness. What is crucial is that "To me dost now thyself convey" (l.4) and "Thou creep'st into my breast" (l.8) to provide "new nourishment and strength" (l.7) for the soul. Herbert uses the bread as a

[56] Labriola and Smeltz 154.
[57] Bloch 116–17.

means of grace, as "the way" (l.7)—Christ—enters the spiritual combat of sanctification.[58]

The Reformers considered it important that the congregation, even the most unlettered, understand the liturgy. Izaak Walton in the *Life of George Herbert* records how Herbert would take great pains to explain the liturgy to his congregation.[59] "The Holy Communion" proclaims Herbert's adherence to the simple rituals and observances of the worship of God. In his Commentary on "The Holy Communion," F.E. Hutchinson states that the first two lines of the poem provide "a contrast between the simple accessories of Anglican worship and the elaborate churches and vestments of the Roman Catholic rite." Moreover, he reminds us that the word "furniture" is used in the Book of Exodus (31:7-9) to designate the furnishings and utensils of the tabernacle.[60]

From the outset of this poem, the speaker participates once more in the Exodus event, with its theme of slavery and liberation and the theophany experience. The Old Testament figures have a primal innocence and a familiar relationship with God, as did Adam before the Fall, characteristics desired by Herbert, as the homely metaphor suggests: "He might to heav'n from Paradise go,/As from one room t'another" (ll.35-36). The tone is more intimate and subdued here than in other *Temple* poems, perhaps because this poem begins where many of Herbert's other poems end: with an emphasis on gratitude.[61] The speaker dismisses the cost of the lavish vestments and finery, which resemble the "beautiful Babylonian mantle" described in Joshua (7:21), retaining instead the priceless and kenotic body of Christ. He is not so concerned with sophistical reasoning, refutations, or theological insight but, rather, with partaking of the "nourishment and strength" ("The Holy Communion," l.7) that finds its way "into every part" (l.11) of his life, meeting and conquering "sin's force and art" (l.12).

The soul of the speaker is nourished by spiritual food, but Herbert's indirection is operative again in his withholding from the reader just how this nourishment is consumed and how his assurance concerning this event occurred. The speaker describes only the feelings of an unworthy soul who dismisses the theories of sophisticated theologians

[58] Veith 215.

[59] Charles E. Eliot, ed., *The Lives of John Donne and George Herbert* by Izaak Walton. (New York: P.F. Collier and Sons Corp., 1937) 400–06.

[60] Hutchinson 493, n.1 to "The H. Communion."

[61] Stewart, *George Herbert* 53.

concerning how that nourishment leaps over "the wall that parts/Our souls and fleshly hearts" (ll.14–15). "Only [God's] grace.../Knoweth the ready way,/And hath the privy key" (ll.19–21) of access to "the subtle rooms" (l.22) of the speaker's "fortified" soul, an embellishment of the battle imagery begun previously. Confirming the *schola cordis* tradition, the speaker can only experience the effects of God's presence at the door of his heart, but those effects are like long-awaited and welcome "dispatches" (l.24) or missives from a friend that help him triumph over "sin and shame" (l.18).

The second section of "The Holy Communion" poem (ll.25–40), titled in some editions "Prayer (II)," is a song composed by Herbert for his church services.[62] The quotations, meter, and *abab* rhyme scheme distinguish this section from the first twenty-four lines. "Herbert advised the Country Parson to inquire whether his parishioners were in the habit of 'singing of Psalms at their work, and on holy days' and wished to encourage the practice."[63] In this section, Herbert portrays the uplifted soul in harmony with its God, an action brought about by the reception of the sacrament, which the speaker can enjoy on select days "when I please,/And leave th'earth to their food" (ll.39–40).

Thus, Herbert's attempt to bring his own nature into intimate communion with God is depicted in a poem that combines poetic and musical craftsmanship in its treatment of the Eucharist as a subtly intense yet familiarly ordinary experience. His use of simple language and homely metaphors (key, rooms) confirms that nothing is mundane or unclean. At the same time, Herbert struggles with the ordinary tools of his art to establish and maintain his own "wedge of gold" (l.2) in a place within himself that is, ironically, apart from and yet connected to God.

The struggle to find a place or home wherein God may take up residence in the human heart is further arbitrated in Hopkins's matching poem "The Half-way House" (1865), an early autobiographical poem written during his period of resolution to enter the Catholic Church.[64] The title may have come from John Henry Cardinal Newman's statement in the *Apologia Pro Vita Sua* (1864) concerning New-

[62] Summers, *George Herbert* 157.

[63] Summers, *George Herbert* 157.

[64] W. Johnson, *Gerard Manley Hopkins: The Poet as Victorian* 25.

man's expressed belief, similar to that of Hopkins, that "Anglicanism is the half-way house between atheism and Roman Catholicism."[65] In a letter of June 1, 1864, which Hopkins wrote to his school friend Ernest H. Coleridge (grandson of Samuel Taylor Coleridge), he states:

> The great aid to belief and object of belief is the doctrine of the Real Presence in the Blessed Sacrament of the Altar. Religion without that is sombre, dangerous, illogical—with that it is—not to speak of its grand consistency and certainty—*loveable*. Hold that and you will gain all Catholic truth.[66]

Compromise seems impossible now to Hopkins: he can no longer rest in the "half-way house" of the national religion of Anglicanism. His conviction of the truth and viability of Catholicism ultimately leads to his reception into the Catholic Church by Newman on October 21, 1866.[67] His "national old Egyptian reed" (1.7) of Anglicanism gives way to the Good Shepherd's rod (Ps. 23:4) or rood (the Cross), words the Victorian philologists treated as being related.[68] The "Egyptian reed" alludes to Is. 36:5–6 in which Sennacherib, the King of Assyria, asks the Jewish king Hezekiah:

Do you think mere words substitute for strategy and might in war? On whom, then, do you rely, that you rebel against me? This Egypt, the staff on which you rely, is in fact a broken reed which pierces the hand of anyone who leans on it. That is what Pharaoh, king of Egypt, is to all who rely on him.

Hopkins's need to experience a "sensuous love of God, a felt sense of Divine presence," informs this poem.[69] The difficulty that he meets in perceiving this God as Love, his rejection of the established church of England which does not fulfill his spiritual needs, his desire to have Love "come down" to him, and his ultimate embracing of the Real Presence at Communion which consoles, cheers, and feeds him are "four rough ways" ("The Half-way House," 1.12) that Hopkins encounters in his journey to Christian discipleship.

Hopkins's entrance into the Jesuit community taught him that religious, in particular, are called to approach the sacraments, especially

[65] Phillips 321.
[66] Abbott, *Further Letters of Gerard Manley Hopkins* 17.
[67] Bump, *Gerard Manley Hopkins* 1.
[68] MacKenzie 25.
[69] Downes, *Gerard Manley Hopkins* 89.

the Eucharist, through the vows of chastity, poverty and obedience, and are nurtured in their vows by the Eucharist. The vows and sacraments, Hopkins learns, are concerned not so much with the material manifestations of God as with the revelatory power of His salvific love. His poems address this illumination. Hopkins's discovery of the immanence of God in the Host revolutionizes his poetic art and strengthens his belief in God's immanence until he subsequently finds Him also in nature, "under heaven" (l.15).[70]

"The Half-way House" opens with the speaker's misperception that God is "above" (l.5) and that there can be no colloquy between God and himself unless God will "come down to [him]" (l.6). The subsequent lines of the poem reinforce and reflect the "paradox" (l.13) of traditional incarnational theology. God is found in a man, Christ, Who is also termed Love. The closing couplet, reminiscent of Herbert, suggests Holy Communion as the physical form of knowing God. As Christ appeared corporeally to the disciples at Emmaus (Luke 24:13-35), so He appears to the Christian disciple in the sacrament of the Eucharist ("The Half-way House," ll.17-18). "Hopkins' sacramentalism was surely one of the strongest motivations for his conversion to Roman Catholicism. Ironically, it was this very sacramentalism that later caused him difficulty."[71] Where Protestant reforms increased the emphasis on individual responsibility toward the sacrament, locating greater significance in the hearts and consciences of the recipients, Catholic theology, from the time of the Church Fathers, repeatedly defines the sacrament of the Eucharist as the true body and blood of Christ. "As a Roman Catholic, Hopkins endorsed transubstantiation of the Eucharist—while the material accidents of bread and wine maintained their original appearance, their substances become wholly the body and blood of Christ."[72] "If there is any one doctrinal point which seems to have fired the intellect and imagination of Hopkins, it is precisely the doctrine of the Real Presence."[73]

The speaker in "The Half-way House" hungers for the divine food of the Real Presence, not for the mere symbolic presence espoused by Herbert and many prominent Anglicans. Unlike Herbert's nutriment

---

[70] Bump, *Gerard Manley Hopkins* 126.
[71] Fulweiler 100.
[72] Ellsberg 50–51.
[73] Mariani, *A Commentary on the Complete Poems of Gerard Manley Hopkins* 27.

poems, Hopkins's "The Half-way House" "looks beyond typology to
the Real Presence of Christ as a literal and daily feeding of faith not to
be 'interpreted' in a spiritual and Caroline sense, nor in Tennysonian-
Victorian symbols."[74]

Although Hopkins left the English church, he did not give up his
indebtedness to Herbert. He continued to be influenced by Herbert's
colloquies between the speaker and God, rhythms, repetition of sound
patterns, and alliteration.[75]

The welcome extended by Love to both Herbert and Hopkins at the
Communion table is related further in Herbert's "Love (III)," which
concludes "The Church" section of his *Temple* poems and, thereby,
Herbert's sequence on "the deeper mysteries of the creed and sacra-
ments."[76] In order to depict God's grace in the Christian life, Herbert
"does not leave grace disembodied in generalizations; he makes its
influence tangible by making Christ the speaker [so as] to suggest the
speaker's consciousness of inspired thoughts from God."[77] Although
"Love (III)" concludes "The Church," it treats the most important
subject of *The Temple*—the final acceptance of the love of God—in
terms of manners, with the usage of social graces and polite formulae.
The relationship of the poet to God is that of a guest to the Host. On
this metaphor the whole poem turns. "The poet, too, reacts as a guest,
according to the code: he is not clean enough to sit at table, being
'Guiltie of *dust* and sinne.' The essence of the poem is a kind of under-
stood tenderness...a combination of realism and personal tact that was
Herbert's special gift."[78] The sensuous imagery that embellishes these
poems reminds the reader of the earthly paradise which Milton de-
scribes in Book IV of *Paradise Lost* (132–65), a "delicious Paradise"
which was traditionally regarded as a "type" of the heavenly paradise.

"God's intervention in the speaker's life and the development of
their relationship have been in evidence" throughout this group of
poems.[79] In "The Invitation," the speaker bids: "Come ye hither
all...Bringing all your sins to sight:/Taste and fear not" for "Here is
love" (ll.1,15–16,28). In "The Banquet," the bruised and broken body

[74] W. Johnson, "Halfway to a New Land" 120–21.
[75] Summers, *George Herbert* 23.
[76] Fish, *The Living Temple* 110.
[77] Benet 194.
[78] Alvarez 88–89, 91.
[79] Benet 174.

of the speaker is restored by *anamnesis* or remembrance of Christ's own bruised and broken body: "God, to show how far his love/Could improve,/Here, as broken, is presented" (ll.28–30). "The Bunch of Grapes" serves as yet another reminder that "Ev'n God himself [was] pressed for my sake" (l.28) so that the Christian disciple might have "the fruit [of the grapes and wine] and more" (l.23). "The Holy Communion" poem cites two results of this communing of the soul with God—"nourishment and strength" (l.7)—and terms such interactions "Dispatches from [a] friend" (l.24).

"The whole of *The Temple* is remarkable for the unaffected ease of the speaker's discourse with God."[80] Not only is the discourse with God unaffected, but God's discourse with the soul of the speaker is just as familiar. At the outset of "Love (III)," "quick-ey'd Love" (l.3) draws near and, "sweetly questioning,/If I lack'd anything" (ll.5-6), speaks in language matching that of a shopkeeper or tavern worker who might ask an entering customer, "What do you lack?" (i.e., want). The fact that Herbert concludes *The Temple* with the intimate dialogue of "Love (III)" signifies the beauty and dignity he assigns to his religious and poetic vocations as the poem "moves from praise of God to self-denigration to a grateful acknowledgement of God's bounty and ends with the image of man, elevated by God's intimate regard, responding in love to God."[81]

"Love (III)" centers on the biblical passage that deals with the necessity of servants being prepared for the Master's return; such servants will be rewarded by the Master Who will "put on an apron, seat them at table, and proceed to wait on them" (Luke 12:37). The poem compresses the cycle of sinning, need for forgiveness, reconciliation, and restoration into God's saving Love. Herbert's economical diction and succinctness of religious expression caused Simone Weil to regard *The Temple* poems as "*une influence décisive*" in her life, and "Love (III)," in particular, as "*le plus beau poème du monde*," reciting it to herself in 1938 during periods of extreme physical pain. The poem served as a prayer and a mystical experience for her.[82]

"Love (III)" is a typical Herbertian poem in its echoes of the Psalms, parables, and Gospel narratives where the Christian disciple is

[80] Bloch 109.
[81] Bloch 295.
[82] Patrides, *George Herbert: The Critical Heritage* 35; Stein 196, n.29.

placed in God's scales of justice and is found lacking or wanting, due to the sinful nature he or she has inherited, but is also embraced in his or her imperfections and inadequacies. Herbert alludes to the Pauline doctrine of the magnanimity, mercy, justice, grace, and love that God bestows on His creatures to provide in "Love (III)" a synopsis of *The Temple* poems.

In "Love (III)," the speaker begins in a state of tension and unworthiness, with the soul personified as drawing back (1.1) from the welcome that Love extends. The speaker states simply and honestly that he is "unkind, ungrateful" (1.9) in his relationship with God, as well as "Guilty of dust and sin" (1.2). However, once again the cycle of religious awakening from the Old Dispensation to the New reminds the speaker that Love already "bore the blame" (1.15) and is now prepared to take the speaker's hand, smile (1.11), and seat him at the banquet table, an invitation which the speaker ultimately accepts: "So I did sit and eat" (1.18). Undoubtedly, God's unconditional love is victorious over the sinner's unworthiness and that Love is determined to win back the sinner from "his assertion of his private self."[83] The speaker responds to the invitation, but, in the typical Herbertian struggle between the Old Man and the New Man, the soul becomes the battleground and re-enactment of the *schola cordis* tradition. Douglas Bush points out that "[b]ountiful love on the one side, guilty reluctance on the other, are conveyed not only in words and implications but in quick and positive, hovering and broken rhythms" in this poem.[84]

The tendency of Herbert's verses to engage in the rhetoric of debate and gentle irony makes his poems, especially "Love (III)," comparable to "those contests of 'gentilesse' typical of medieval literature."[85] Before arriving at self-acceptance, the speaker submits to the humiliation of suffering, shame, and self-examination, and finally agrees to "serve," only to have Love make another demand: "You must sit down, says Love, and taste my meat" (1.17). Now the roles are reversed, and it is Love Who functions as the servant, as did Christ at the Last Supper, to remind the speaker that he can serve only if he allows himself to be served first by a patient and benevolent Master. The speaker's vocation of imitative service merely points to and glo-

[83] Vendler 54.
[84] Bush 62.
[85] Vendler 59.

rifies the Master of the temple. "The servant reminds us too of the dignity of all vocations in the eye of God, a favorite theme of the Reformers."[86] Now the speaker acquiesces to the supremacy of a Love Who "bore the blame" (1.15); he agrees to "sit and eat" (1.18) of the "marriage supper" of Revelation. Rather than focusing on the speaker's unfitness for the wedding feast, or the prodigal son's sinful and profligate living, Love ushers in the speaker with unconditional acceptance and boundless hospitality.

The Pauline assurance that nothing or no one "will separate us from the love of Christ" (Rom. 8:35) is also evident in this poem. Herbert conflates a pastiche of biblical and liturgical sources to fashion "a new parable, about an abashed, but loving man and a tactful, fine-grained, sweetly insistent God who wins him through love. In Herbert's parable Love issues the invitation; the guest, feeling unworthy, hangs back at the threshold; Love doesn't punish but gently persuades him; the guest offers to serve but instead is served by Love."[87] The conflict here resides in the speaker's capacity to receive Love; the perfect resolution is his acceptance of God's love. It is this "Love" that has the last word and terminal emphatic position in "The Church" poems. It beckons the Christian disciple to a heaven "in which a welcome, a smile, a colloquy, a taking by the hand, and a seat at a table stand for all the heart can wish."[88]

The desire of the heart for communion with God and the Christian community is underscored still further in Hopkins's "The Bugler's First Communion" (1879), one of Hopkins's mature poems. Hopkins's principle of individuation is operative here in the description of the unique qualities possessed by the bugler. The poem explicitly expresses the speaker's deep emotion when a young soldier partakes of the Body and Blood of Christ for the first time. Hopkins models his personal response to his parishioners on Christ Himself Who, while working and preaching in Palestine, "was thinking of us every moment of his life, of each of us separately," as Hopkins preached in a sermon to the people at St. Clement's chapel a few Sundays previous to the writing of this poem.[89]

---

[86] Bloch 227.
[87] Bloch 110.
[88] Vendler 276.
[89] MacKenzie 123.

Hopkins indicated in a note at the bottom of this poem, which he sent to Robert Bridges, that the bugler was stationed at Cowley Barracks, from which he was to sail to his assignment to Mooltan in Punjaub, Afghanistan, on September 30, 1879.[90] Hopkins met the young man during his weekly visitation to the army barracks. The bugler, after receiving religious instruction from Fr. Hopkins, asked Hopkins if he would give him his First Communion, and the young man went to Hopkins's parish, St. Aloysius, to receive It.[91] "Here he knelt then in regimental red" (l.9). Hopkins's ability to personalize the experience for the young man as well as for himself is evident in the simple and enthusiastic diction he uses to describe how he "Forth Christ from cupboard fetched, how fain I of feet/To his youngster take his treat!" (ll.10–11).

In addition to the immanence of Christ, Hopkins also acknowledges His transcendence in the consecrated wafer: "Low-latched in leaf-light housel his too huge godhead" (l.12) and prays that this host, which he terms in the primitive style of the Old English kenning "leaf-light," visit some spiritual gifts or graces on the first communicant: that It give him a heart to enable him to become "Christ's darling, dauntless" (l.14), a "Tongue true, vaunt-and tauntless" (l.15), and that It breathe in him the "bloom of a chastity in mansex fine" (l.16). Hopkins's belief in the power of the Eucharist to engraft Itself on the heart of this young man motivates his line—"Nothing else is like it, no, not all so strains/Us" (ll.29–30)—and assures the bugler, as it did many of Hopkins's parishioners, of the certainty of the "Realm both Christ is heir to and there reigns" (l.32). Hopkins gives the bugler "to the Lord of the Eucharist" (l.44), confident that God will take care of His "own Galahad" (l.40) throughout the "disaster" and "backwheels" that the youth will encounter on the journey "home" (ll.42–43).

Hopkins's characteristic visual and sensuous imagery patterns are evident in the stanzas that describe the paradoxical strenuousness (st.8) and satisfaction (st.6) of his pastoral responsibilities. The responsiveness he witnesses in the young soldiers makes him "tréad túfts of consolation/Dáys áfter" (ll.25–26) and renders his trips to the barracks where he teaches the Christian faith and administers the Eucharist a worthwhile, consoling, and religious experience. Hopkins describes the

---

[90] MacKenzie 123.
[91] Kitchen 193.

pliancy and flexibility of these youths in the alliterative phrase "limber liquid" (l.22). "The military homophone [of 'limber'] inevitably resonates in this setting: the limber of a field-gun enables its crew to move it rapidly into action."[92]

The fluidity and enthusiasm generated by these young soldiers are depicted in the type of stanza Hopkins assigns to this poem: a quatrain containing the technique of *overreaving* (*rove-over* or *run-over* rhymes), a practice of organizing a poem in sprung rhythm by stanzas rather than separate lines.[93] The scanning runs on without break to the end of the stanza, so that each stanza is one long line rhymed in passage rather than four lines with rhymes at the ends. This type of rhyme is thought to have derived from *odl udd* in Welsh; it places part of the rhyme at the end of a line, and the consonant to complete it at the beginning of the next.[94] Hopkins utilizes this technique in *The Wreck*, *The Loss of the Eurydice*, "Hurrahing in Harvest," and his translation of the "Corpus Christi" hymn of St. Thomas Aquinas titled *Sacris Solemniis*.[95] At the beginning of the "Author's Preface" to his poems, Hopkins defines running or "standard" rhythm, as he terms it, as follows:

Common English rhythm, called Running Rhythm, is measured by feet of either two or three syllables and (putting aside the imperfect feet at the beginning and end of lines and also some unusual measures in which feet seem to be paired together and double or composite feet to arise) never more nor less.[96]

In a partial draft of "The Bugler's First Communion," Hopkins marked "sprung rhythm, overrove; an outride between the 3rd and 4th foot of the 4th line in each stanza."[97] Examples occur in lines 3–4— "(*he*/Shares their best gifts *surely*)" —and in lines 11–12—"*treat*/Lowlatched in *leaf*-light."

The "sprung rhythm overrove" permits greater elasticity of expression for Hopkins, a characteristic that also suggests the bugler's acquired soldierly habit of accommodating himself to new places and

---

[92] MacKenzie 124.
[93] MacKenzie 236.
[94] MacKenzie 236–37.
[95] MacKenzie 237.
[96] Phillips 106.
[97] Phillips 362.

events while marching "abreast" (1.19) the "hell-rook ranks [that] sally to molest him" (1.18). The charisma and "bloom" (1.16) surrounding this young man is born of the "sweetest sendings" (1.13) of his "First Communion" (1.8) that render him "Christ's darling, dauntless" (1.14) in faith and courage and "tauntless" (1.15) in verbal and physical disputation and combat. Moreover, the bugler is strengthened and sealed by the "sacred ointment" (1.33) of the sacrament of Confirmation that relegates him to the "soldierly Christ's royal ration" (1.28). As in Herbert's poem "Love (III)," the speaker at the conclusion of "The Bugler's First Communion" agrees to be served by a Master Who rejoices in His royal heir and own "Galahad." Like the persistent widow in 2 Kings and the gospel narrative, the speaker puts his "lips on pleas [that] Would brandle adamantine heaven with ride and jar" (ll.45–46), assured that a soldierly "Forward-like" thrust to a "favourable heaven" (1.48) will conclude the journey. This journey seems, at times, to be channelled by a "divíne doom" (1.41), but it is led instead, as Herbert and Hopkins discover, by the "Lord of the Eucharist" (1.44) Who leaves no prayer "disregarded" (1.47) and Who draws His "self-wise self-will" (1.24) child to Him with chords of Love around the Eucharistic banquet table of eternal life.

The metaphysical works of Herbert and Hopkins depict a God Who furnishes His Christian disciples with a table in the wilderness and moves their hearts to cooperate with His invitation. Select verse and prose of these two writers describe a Eucharistic Feast, an eschatological banquet, that welcomes "all" to that Love Whose justice commends them to His "sight." Moreover, their works enrich both the devotional and intellectual sensibilities of the reader who analyzes them as spiritual autobiography: a record of the sacred journey from Lenten Fast to Paschal Feast.

Chapter Seven

The Unfinished Cornerstone

...birds build—but not I build; no, but strain,
Time's eunuch, and not breed one work that wakes.
Mine, O thou lord of life, send my roots rain.
(Hopkins, "Thou art indeed just, Lord")

SHORTLY AFTER HERBERT AND HOPKINS ENTER the temple of divine worship, they learn that the "building up" of their ministerial and poetic vocations hinges on their acceptance of Christ's invitation to "Come to Me, a living stone, rejected, but precious, nonetheless." This biblical analogue stipulates and underscores the organic and flexible nature of the spiritual life, and confirms an analysis of the poetry and prose of Herbert and Hopkins as spiritual autobiography. Select works of these two devotional writers, when read as spiritual autobiography, depict a self who is incomplete, and a genre that offers no finished products or patterns.

The genre of spiritual autobiography helps the writer as well as the reader to frame individual experiences and sharpen personal awareness while suggesting possibilities for self-disclosure and self-definition. Beyond an expression of factual truth, spiritual autobiography provides a unique depiction of daily life as it is experienced by the writers, and in this respect assumes its claim to authentic literary and spiritual interpretation. "Even if we can know nothing about ultimate human purpose and the end objectives of this mysterious process of life, we can derive gratification and hope from a conception of cosmic order where creative individuality adds forever to the growing richness of the world. There is nobility in our willingness to understand men [e.g., Herbert and Hopkins] on their own terms and to complicate our judgements by giving each man his due."[1] Any attempt to incorporate Herbert's *The Country Parson*, *The Temple*, or the *corpus* of Hopkins's works into an immovable structure desecrates the natural heart of the Christian disciple which both writers depict with fluidity and grace in their verse and prose.

---

[1] Weintraub, *The Value of the Individual: Self and Circumstance in Autobiography* 379.

This present chapter is a comparative analysis of Herbert's "The Church Militant" and "The Reprisal" with Hopkins's unfinished sonnets "The times are nightfall" and "To his Watch," the hymn "Thee, God, I come from," the lengthier but incomplete "On the Portrait of Two Beautiful Young People," the curtal sonnet "(Ashboughs)," and the sonnet "Thou art indeed just, Lord." These select works are literary monuments to the writers' attempts to integrate Christian discipleship with the unfinished nature of their poetic and ministerial vocations. The humility and integrity with which Herbert and Hopkins respond to and articulate their vocations augment their "witness" to Christian discipleship by suggesting an open-ended and corporate journey toward God. What John N. Wall, Jr., says of *The Country Parson* and *The Temple* is true also of Hopkins's works: both are "set forth to instigate change, yet [are] incomplete without the efforts of others to live out [their] precepts and add to [them]."[2] The response of the Christian disciple to select works of Herbert and Hopkins as spiritual autobiography leads him or her into the saving doors of the temple, "the ongoing life of the Church, within which God's Word is heard and responded to in prayer and praise."[3]

The physical temple signifies the vicissitudes, reversals, and reconstructions of the spiritual Temple, the Body of Christ. "The visible Church, that institution into which all English men in Herbert's day were required by law to be baptized, is at once the company of fallen men and women and the community of grace, the source of God's reconciling love.... For Herbert, the eschatological moment will entail the completion of God's reconciling work among all the faithful. In this heavenly work, man has a task in bringing about the full revelation of God's love for his creatures. It is to the furthering of that task that Herbert set himself in his poetic activities no less than in his priestly duties."[4] Herbert's verse, like the parish church or temple of worship, is an intricate, traditional structure, open for all to enter.

Like Herbert, Hopkins also views the temple or church as a web of significances. His writings, therefore, reflect values and meanings, not merely facts or events, and assign the final meaning of his poetic and ministerial vocations and the completion of his soul to the Logos:

---

[2] Wall 34.
[3] Wall 35.
[4] Wall 36-37.

God, lover of souls, swaying considerate scales,
Complete thy creature dear O where it fails,
  Being mighty a master, being a father and fond
        ("In the Valley of the Elwy," ll.12–14).

The scrupulous introspection and desolation that frequently accompany Hopkins are inextricable from the pursuit of lyric excellence and ministerial standards that comprise his greatest poetry. His life constructs and refashions his art; his art informs and distinguishes his life.

The frustration experienced by Herbert and Hopkins with language's inadequacy in conveying the nature of the Temple is aptly expressed by T.S. Eliot in "East Coker" where he refers to attempts to communicate on a verbal plane as

...a raid on the inarticulate
With shabby equipment always deteriorating
In the general mess of imprecision of feeling.[5]

Coincidentally, Eliot's visit in 1942 to a village in which Nicholas Ferrar established an Anglican religious community in 1625 prompted another poem in *Four Quartets* titled after this village in Huntingdonshire. "Little Gidding" provides a meditation on England's past and present, and the hope of redemption through purgation. The site itself—a chapel in the "midwinter spring"—impelled Eliot, as it did Ferrar and Herbert, to approach the temple by putting off

Sense and motion. You are not here to verify,
Instruct yourself, or inform curiosity
Or carry report. You are here to kneel
Where prayer has been valid. And prayer is more
Than an order of words, the conscious occupation
Of the praying mind, or the sound of the voice praying
                    (ll.45–50).[6]

Herbert's "The Church Militant," like Eliot's "Little Gidding," attempts to provide a narrative or *narratio* of salvation history. This chapter analyzes "The Church Militant" as the "unfinished

---

[5] *T.S. Eliot: The Complete Poems and Plays 1909-1950* (San Diego, New York, London: Harcourt Brace Jovanovich, rpt. 1980) 128.
[6] *T.S. Eliot: The Complete Poems and Plays 1909-1950* 139.

cornerstone" of *The Temple* despite, or perhaps because of, its incon-
clusive and seemingly austere tone.

The speaker in "The Church Militant" "adopts the public stance
and universal perspective of the church historian (a role the commenta-
tors often assigned to John of Patmos)" in a voice that seems far re-
moved "from the ultimate, personal voice speaking the lyrics of "'The
Church.'"[7] The tradition of the *narratio* is a long-established one,
originating with the *Demonstratio præficationis Apostolorum* of Iren-
aeus and Augustine's *De Catechizandis Rudibus*, a copy of which is
mentioned in Herbert's will as an item in his library. The *narratio*
begins with the creation of the world and climaxes with the birth of
Christ.[8] The point of this instruction of the catechumens was to pre-
pare them for total incorporation into the temple or church community
by teaching them the history of Creation, the history of the Fall, and
the promise of Redemption.[9] Thus, the candidate learned that the jour-
ney to Christian discipleship is arduous, that the Church and Sin travel
together, and that complete triumph and joy are found in the age to
come. Like the *narratio*, "The Church Militant" witnesses to the cycli-
cal nature of creation and redemption in the life of the individual. Yet
the speaker in "The Church Militant" is impelled to repeat the refrain
*"How dear to me, Oh God, thy counsels are! Who may with thee com-
pare?"* (a combination of Psalms 139:17 and 89:7) "in the face of the
overwhelming evidence for a quite different conclusion."[10] Herbert's
incorporation of this *narratio* to *The Temple* underscores his beliefs that
all Christian disciples must continue to build up their souls as fitting
temples for the Divine Architect, and that perfection will not be at-
tained in this earthly existence. "It is by refusing us that satisfaction [of
a definitive conclusion demanded by many Herbert critics], and by
referring us to a future moment it can neither present nor contain, that
the poem fulfills its function in the sequence."[11]

This devaluation of the present in favor of a future glory, while a
familiar theme of the seventeenth century, also underlies the works of
Hopkins and many twentieth-century religious writers. Building the
temple on Christ, the true Cornerstone, is paramount; a sure way for

[7] Lewalski 305.
[8] Fish, *The Living Temple* 145, 153.
[9] Fish, *The Living Temple* 147.
[10] Fish, *The Living Temple* 151.
[11] Fish, *The Living Temple* 157.

the writers to validate this doctrinal belief is to exalt Christ by relying
on Him to write the conclusion to their works, much as Hopkins does
in "The Valley of the Elwy." "To do otherwise, to catechize in a way
that would not make God prepossessed, would be to build the temple
on the rotten foundation of the self.... As a builder [the writer] must
never leave off hewing and polishing the living stones, but he, too, is
a living stone and is being fitted for his place in the Temple by an even
greater builder."[12] The structure of the literary works of Herbert and
Hopkins is left unfinished, in confident assurance that the true Logos
is already completing the work He has begun.

The Herbert's inclusion of "The Church Militant" argues in favor of
the unfinished nature of the Christian disciple; likewise, Hopkins's
works (particularly the "terrible" sonnets and select subsequent poems),
some of which have been analyzed in preceding chapters of this book,
support a structure that is psychically and religiously incomplete by
offering a speaker who engages in an explicit psychomachic struggle,
one that delineates the central Christian strain between self-debate,
ongoing sinfulness, and colloquy with God. Both Herbert and Hopkins
record the stress of religious strains and conflicts as they experience
them in their poetic and ministerial vocations. Hopkins's "terrible"
sonnets, in particular, reveal "the ongoing movement of the conscious-
ness of his own struggle with God's will, the bitterness of self-
determination, and the spiritual ideal of detachment by will. By the
time [he] writes 'Thou art indeed just, Lord,' he seems to have synthe-
sized his relationship with God and his own need to selve."[13] Howev-
er, the sonnet still contains the characteristic Hopkinsian technical
mastery—questions, nature imagery, the Christian themes of theodicy
and colloquy, and the Christian hope—that distinguishes his works.

The operative foundation for the temple alluded to by St. Paul is
the Christian disciple—"For the temple of God is holy, and you are
that temple" (1 Cor. 3:16)—a changeable creature whose evolution is
determined by the vagaries of human existence and established Chris-
tian doctrines. Gene Edward Veith, Jr., posits that the "structure of
The Temple is not really architectural, but it is somewhat spatial be-
cause the outside-inside-outside model portrays the Church as a whole,
a 'temple' both in the sense of the individual believer's being a temple

---

[12] Fish, *The Living Temple* 164, 165.
[13] Ellsberg 42.

of the indwelling God and in the sense of corporate, visible entity interacting with the world."[14] Since all the material in Herbert's *Temple* is intended as his "first fruits presented to God," the chronology of the poems, their placement, content, tone, even their emendations by Herbert merely serve to support the continuous strain of dissonance that mediates the life of the Christian disciple. The Ignatian themes of consolation-desolation, the three Christian themes of theodicy, colloquy, and nutriment, and the three stages of Christian perfection found in the purgative, illuminative, and unitive journey of the Christian disciple undergird select *Temple* poems when analyzed as spiritual autobiography and allow the reader to witness the unfinished nature of the speaker as well as of "The Church Porch," "The Church," and "The Church Militant." Positing a reading of *The Temple* as spiritual autobiography conjoins critical arguments that both support and challenge unification of the poems, since the genre of spiritual autobiography is, by its etymological and existential nature, the unfinished record of a writer's advancement to God, to be completed by the Logos at the end of time.

Although this book perceives numerical significance in the tripartite structure, it challenges claims by critics such as Joseph Hall and John David Walker who seek a direct correspondence between the three rooms of the temple and the three stages of Christian life, and between the proportions of the temple and those of the human body. Again, such attempts to "fit" the poetic *Temple* into a fixed hierarchical or ecclesiastical structure deny the incomprehensible nature of the soul of the Christian disciple in his or her journey to God, which is, I believe, the underlying theme of Herbert's literary *corpus*. Even though the parson Herbert is knowledgeable and respectful of the Anglican tradition and the nature of the temple, the poet Herbert readily models his poetic and ministerial vocations on the true householder—Christ—"who bringeth out of his treasure things new and old...and maketh the one serve the other," as he states in Chapter 23 of *The Country Parson*, titled "The Parson's Completeness."[15] The reader is also reminded of Herbert's admonition in "The Parson Preaching" that "none goes out of Church as he came in, but either better, or worse."[16] This state-

---

[14] Veith 229.
[15] Wall 88.
[16] Wall 62-63.

ment underscores the changeable nature of the Christian disciple who enters the physical temple, as well as of the reader whose analysis of *The Temple* as spiritual autobiography prompts self-examination and self-definition.

The tripartite structure of *The Temple* has been the subject of considerable debate. While some scholars believe that an organic relationship exists between "The Church Porch" and "The Church," they find difficulty in aligning the structural and thematic unity of these first two sections with the formal and stylistic aspects of "The Church Militant." In his edition of 1874, Alexander Grosart purposely moved "The Church Militant," together with the excluded Herbert poems and the Latin poetry, "so it will no longer contaminate *The Temple* with its proximity," thereby attempting to sever any "supposed" connections with *The Temple*.[17] Critics from G.H. Palmer (1905) to such recent critics as Lee Ann Johnson and Annabel M. Endicott view "The Church Militant" as an addendum to *The Temple*, a lengthy, five-part narrative, poetic structure that "reflects a divergence in style and treatment from the preceding poems."[18] Lee Ann Johnson's analysis of critics endorsing an organic unity to *The Temple* is particularly astute and comprehensive. She provides a synopsis of initial arguments that support a principle of organization by such critics as Joseph Summers, Louis L. Martz, John David Walker, Stanley Stewart, and Sara W. Hanley, and then refutes the premises on which their arguments are based.

Johnson proposes a convincing corollary by suggesting that careful attention be paid to the Hutchinson edition of Herbert's poems with regard to "The Church Militant":

A new section of the 1633 volume, as also of both manuscripts, is marked by the use of 'The Church Militant' as the page-heading for all that follows, as well as by FINIS after the preceding poem. In B there is a blank page between the sections, and in W five blank pages.[19]

She uses this evidence to support her view that, since the W manuscript is "the only surviving manuscript book of his poems which Herbert

---

[17] Miller 149.
[18] Lee Ann Johnson, "The Relationship of 'The Church Militant' to *The Temple*." *Studies in Philology* 67 (April 1971), 201.
[19] L.A. Johnson 205.

certainly handed," the poet must have "sanctioned the detachment" of "The Church Militant" from the other two sections.[20] She concludes that "the early manuscripts, and the inability of scholars to establish a link between 'The Church Militant' and the body of preceding poems offers further argument for consideration of the poem as a separate entity."[21]

While there is no denying the reasonableness of Johnson's arguments and her logical deductions from extant manuscripts and scholarly research, this study strongly argues for the placement of "The Church Militant" at the conclusion of *The Temple* as an appropriate and vital cornerstone to an analysis of Herbert's works as spiritual autobiography. The counter-arguments—namely, that the writing of "FINIS" after "The Church" poems, and the separating of "The Church Militant" from the two preceding sections by five blank pages—disregard the ongoing and cyclical nature of Christian discipleship. Furthermore, they fail to consider the organic nature of the physical temple of worship as well as of the spiritual Temple of the Christian disciple. Moreover, the word "militant" itself is derived from the Latin word *miles* or soldier, denoting a person in active and aggressive pursuit of a goal or standard. The Ignatian soldier and the Jesuitical contemplative tradition of Hopkins are recalled here in the verse and prose of Herbert who, like Hopkins, courts the high spiritual ideals of his Lord and Master.

To the argument that no conclusive evidence points to coherence among the three sections of *The Temple*, Chapter Four of *The Country Parson*, titled "The Parson's Knowledge," provides a prosaic account of Herbert's understanding of the Scriptures, Doctrine, and Truth, as well as a significant rationale for the ultimate placement of "The Church Militant." Herbert states:

> For all Truth being consonant to itself, and all being penn'd by one and the self-same Spirit, it cannot be, but that an industrious, and judicious comparing of place with place must be a singular help for the right understanding of the Scriptures. To this may be added the consideration of any text with the coherence thereof, touching what goes before, and what

---

[20] L.A. Johnson 205.
[21] L.A. Johnson 206.

follows after, as also the scope [main design, as opposed to specific words or passages] of the Holy Ghost.[22]

Here is clear evidence of the process of the mind and the pattern of coherence that order Herbert's life, a coherence based on spiritual inspiration and guidance more than on rational and logical analysis. Herbert continues by endorsing a variety of opinions on the Law and the Gospel as "diverse, not as repugnant: therefore the spirit of both is to be considered, and weighed."[23] This key passage alerts the critic and reader of Herbert to the rhythm and counsel that direct his writing, preaching, indeed, his essential being.

The tripartite structure of *The Temple* develops and guides the experience of the Christian disciple who participates in the life of the Church. "If we are constantly drawn toward participation in the life of the Church, so we are shown that the poetic achievement here makes sense only when seen in terms of God's ongoing authorship of his salvation history."[24] Herbert concludes his prefatory note to *The Country Parson*, titled "The Author to the Reader" (1632), thus:

> The Lord prosper the intention [to please God] to myself, and others, who may not despise my poor labors, but add to those points, which I have observed, until the Book grow to a complete Pastoral ['A Book relating to the cure of souls,' as Samuel Johnson defined the term].[25]

Again in his own words, Herbert supports a *Temple* structure that embraces the review of history that occurs in "The Church Militant," colored as it is by his "disgust with the worldliness and corruption of the Caroline court."[26] The crucial terminal placement of "The Church Militant" confirms Herbert's belief that "all possible art" builds up the Church and anticipates God's promise to complete the creation He has begun. "In 'The Church Militant,' the community of the faithful is seen as caught up in God's larger plan: that working out of his salvation which leads the Church onward toward 'time and place, where judg-

---

[22] Wall 58.

[23] Wall 59.

[24] Wall 45.

[25] Wall 54.

[26] Patrick Grant, *The Transformation of Sin: Studies in Donne, Herbert, Vaughan, and Traherne* (Montreal and London: McGill-Queen's University Press, 1974) 128.

ment shall appear'" (l. 277).[27] Thus, "The Church Militant," far from being regarded as "the holy of holies or highest step in an ascending scale" or, on the other hand, as "an earlier work included there for convenience," records the life of the Christian disciple and contextualizes it in the historical and ongoing life of the universal Church.[28]

James Joyce's technique of writing *Finnegans Wake* so that the onset of the work occurs on the last page underscores the cyclical pattern of fall and regeneration, and serves as a justification for a cyclical reading of *The Temple*. A reading of "The Church Militant" before "The Church Porch" or "The Church" provides an historical overview of the Christian disciple whose varied background informs and enriches the structure of the Church and *The Temple*. Thus, the meditative nature of *The Temple* poems evokes and disciplines the powers of the mind to a moment of illumination where the soul strives to achieve a unity of being.[29] With all its controversial interpretations and criticisms, "The Church Militant" becomes the "one work that wakes" critics and readers of Herbert to a distinct spiritual and literary perspective.

Malcolm Mackenzie Ross suggests that a deep concern for the welfare of England motivates the prophetic "Church Militant," and that the relative failure of the Church and the state within the limits of history stems from a sloth that "stilled the impulse of the gentry to action [so that] the drive of the age is no longer expressed in terms of a precarious but real alliance of the interests of land and money. Avarice destroys the old balance, and with it man's hope."[30] The "picture of the spiritual conflicts" that Herbert represents in "The Church Militant" exhibits the continuous combat that engages the souls of Christian

---

[27] Wall 47.

[28] Annabel Endicott, "The Structure of George Herbert's *Temple*: A Reconsideration." *University of Toronto Quarterly* 34 (1965), 234, 236.

[29] While I dispute Edmund Miller's remarks that "The Church Militant" is Herbert's "private truth," that it is "special, limited, because of its nature as a prophetic poem," that it is "an unnecessary sort of poem in the strictly religious sense: it provides a solution to a redefined problem," that it is "so really unimportant compared with the others," I do agree with his conclusion that "The question of the relationship of 'The Church Militant' to *The Temple* is not easily settled. We may at least suspect that Herbert did not mean it to be." Miller 152, 154.

[30] Malcolm Mackenzie Ross, *Poetry and Dogma: The Transfiguration of Eucharistic Symbols in Seventeenth-Century English Poetry* (New York: Octagon Books, 1969) 149.

disciples throughout history, a combat whose motivations are both pure and tainted. "In all, Herbert's goal was service to God, in spite of what might be advantageous to him in terms of secular or ecclesiastical advancement. [His] choice of a country parish declared his loyalty to Christ and his independence of the social and ecclesiastical value systems of the day.... The parish church in Bemerton was, after all, far from the centers of religious or political life in Stuart England. Herbert thus gained for himself an authority in speech that only personal integrity can provide."[31] The perspective with which Herbert views religion and politics is, therefore, clearer in scope and more inclusive in magnitude by virtue of its dissociation and detachment from external political or ecclesiastical disputations. Yet the fact that *The Temple* was read by those who "were probably not interested in poetry [since] some of them by that time [of publication] were in direct conflict with the Church that Herbert loved," as well as by King Charles who "studied the 'divine poems' the year before his execution," witnesses to the success of the book and the readers' appreciation of Herbert's addressing them "from a level of experience on which Christians knew no division."[32]

Herbert's characteristic "formula" of collapsing the two concepts of power and love is evident in the proem of "The Church Militant" which begins with "thy power" (1.3) and ends by praising "Not the decrees of power, but bands of love" (1.10).[33] "The opposites of 'power and love'—weakness on the one hand and malice or selfishness on the other—are the primary terms for characterizing man in the poetry of *The Temple*."[34] "The Church Militant," then, is a portrayal, not of triumph or rest, but of the struggle of the Christian disciple and a "reenactment of those conflicts within the soul of the reader.... Yet there is a very real possibility that we as readers may be no more perceptive than the *persona*, that we may fall into his errors, that we may take his views, which are no doubt often a reflection of Herbert's state of conflict."[35] *The Temple* reflects the significant relation between Herbert's pattern of verse and patterns of life, and sanctions the sacri-

---

[31] Wall 3.
[32] Chute 151.
[33] Strier 6.
[34] Strier 6.
[35] Seelig 11, 15.

ficial as well as the sacramental natures of his poetic and ministerial vocations.

Herbert's verse and prose function both as a model for and an indication of his spiritual life. As Sharon Seelig views it, *The Temple* "is not only a book made up of poems; it is in some sense a single poem.... Like his kinsman Sidney, Herbert wrote for fallen man.... The unity and the complexity of *The Temple* consists primarily in its presentation of a world in which the truth is perceivable but not always perceived, in which battles won in the first poem must be fought again even in the last, in which themes are constant but comprehension and treatment of them are not."[36]

Stanley Stewart supports a view of "The Church Militant" that subscribes to the Christian theme of theodicy. He believes that the refrain

> alludes to the idea of Providence [and that], as the history of the Church unfolds, the speaker reminds himself at intervals of the orderliness of God's plan in creation.... In this way the refrain does more than simply invoke a meditative tone; it places the past struggles of the soul in time (as pictured in 'The Church') in a wider and final perspective. [Like all *The Temple* poems] 'The Church Militant' emphasizes God's Providence as seen in His creation.... Just as the pain of human life was part of a larger design, the trials and tribulations of the Church must also be seen in perspective. Only a part of that perspective was available to man in time.... The speaker of 'The Church Militant,' who views creation in the fullness of time, is able to pronounce (after a short 'L'Envoy') a second, final, and soul-satisfying 'FINIS.' For now the whole of God's design lies open to his view.[37]

William H. Pahlka posits an interesting theory on the "gracelessness" of "The Church Militant" by suggesting that, whereas "Love (III)" at the conclusion of "The Church" serves as an invitation to "sit and eat" (l.18) of the Eucharistic banquet, "The Church Militant" reenacts this theme of nutriment, but moves

> from one kind of language to another, from simple doctrine to a doctrine in the form of a life. The language of ethical doctrine and the language of personal experience and transformation are no longer needed, because we have sacrificed our wills to God's service and become members of the Body of

---

[36] Seelig 17, 41, 42.
[37] Stewart, "Time and *The Temple*." <u>Studies in English Literature</u> 6 (1966), 108-10.

Christ. We enter into the language of history and prophecy as nameless and impersonal actors in the drama of unfolding time. The language may not be beautiful, but it does not need to be. Beauty has done its Augustinian work, attracting souls with the delights of material beauty. It was meant for use, not for enjoyment, and its use has been served. Delight is, as promised, turned into a sacrifice, and the poet, having resigned his own will with his sinful love of making words beautiful, presents the poem.[38]

The first part of "The Church Militant" (ll.9–100) depicts the progress of the church and religion. The second part (ll.101–258) deals with the progress of sin, with the characteristic Herbertian paradox that underlies *The Temple*: the fact that religion and sin co-exist and are simultaneously successful. The third and final part (ll.259–79) addresses the role of sin in the corporate history and religious life of the Church. "Despite the frustration that the success of religion is matched by the success of sin—culminating in the poem with sin triumphing as religion—the victory of religion is predestined and the tone remains celebratory. The vicissitudes of history are firmly under the control of God" as the beginning lines of the poem, the incremental refrain, and the continual account of history confirm.[39]

"The Church Militant" is a drama of *psychomachia* where the struggle between sanctification and sin is played out against the backdrop of salvation history. "'The Church' follows the process in an individual Christian life to its apocalyptic conclusion, but living Christians are part of 'The Church Militant,' and, as the term 'Militant' implies, are still participants in the warfare."[40] An analysis of "The Church Militant" as spiritual autobiography portrays Herbert's view of human history as a battle between sin and religion, and the *agon* of the Christian disciple as a result of the struggle between the power of sin and the power of grace. "This battle that the Church Militant is engaged in is not, however, limited to the Church, but it involves the life of 'Commonweals' (l.5) and empires (l.73 ff.), the progress of 'the Arts' (l.263 ff.), and such historical events as the colonization of America" (l.235 ff.).[41] Like the individual Christian, the Church also faces the ongoing struggle between sin and the indwelling Spirit of

[38] Pahlka 202.
[39] Veith 174.
[40] Veith 176.
[41] Veith 231-32.

God, to be concluded only at the end of time, "where judgment shall appear" (l.277). Unlike the Roman Catholic position espoused by Hopkins, which acknowledges both the visible and invisible church, the Protestant religion maintains that the institution of the Roman Catholic Church, with its unique doctrines and increasing power of the papacy, further removes the visible church from biblical and patristic truths. "This distinction allowed them [the Protestants] to profess faith in 'the Holy Catholic Church' of the Creeds, against which the gates of Hell cannot prevail (the invisible Church) while still condemning the Church of Rome."[42]

As Barbara Lewalski confirms, "The Church Militant" is a Herbertian Book of Revelation where Herbert renders "his own all-encompassing account of the providential course laid down for the visible Church throughout history."[43] While the reader is unfamiliar with this particular style in Herbert, the difference in tone, tempo, and speech reflects the variety, breadth, and scope of the author. For example, the end-stopped rhyming couplet, though written here before the Augustan Age, is used in "The Church Militant" for "neo-classical point. He also occasionally overrode the couplets for a freer, almost indolent effect of equal wit…. In Herbert's poems subject and image do not determine speech; they are transformed by it."[44] According to Joseph Summers, the nature of the genre—the extended narrative or description—accounts for the stylistic differences between "The Church Militant" and other *Temple* poems.[45]

An Herbertian controversy of a religio-political nature arises with the rhyming couplet in lines 235–36:

> Religion stands on tip-toe in our land,
> Ready to pass to the *American* strand.

Izaak Walton states that, when Nicholas Ferrar sent *The Temple* to be published, the Vice-Chancellor hesitated about licensing it because of these lines. But after Nicholas Ferrar insisted that the lines remain—he "would by no means allow the book to be printed, and want

---

[42] Veith 232.
[43] Lewalski 305.
[44] Summers, *George Herbert* 150, 152.
[45] Summers, *George Herbert* 217, n. 28.

them"—the Vice-Chancellor accepted the entire *Temple* for publication, stating:

> I knew Mr. Herbert well, and know that he had many heavenly speculations, and was a divine poet: but I hope the world will not take him to be an inspired prophet, and therefore I license the whole book.[46]

The Temple was published *in toto*, with the only addition being Ferrar's Preface. Yet, as John Nichol, the first professional academic to attend to Herbert, states in his Introduction to *The Poetical Works of George Herbert* (1863): "There is in the author and in his work catholicity enough to give his volume a universal interest, and make his prayer and praise a fit expression of Christian faith under all varieties of form."[47]

Stanley Fish attributes a further uniqueness of Herbert's addition of the *narratio* to "The Church Militant" "to the catechistical sequence. Only [Lancelot] Andrewes among the Reformation catechists I have read includes so much historical material, but his history comes in bits and pieces and does not take the form of a sustained chronicle."[48] Fish's concluding remarks on "The Church Militant" are themselves apocalyptic and merit serious consideration for both their scholarly insights and spiritual import. He reminds the reader that:

> the poem is still inconclusive, ill-proportioned, and anticlimactic, and it does not leave the reader with a satisfactory sense of closure. Nor is it meant to. The very idea of the Church Militant has at its heart the necessity of struggle and toil. Rest and closure are unavailable except in some premature and therefore dangerous assumption that God's building is already finished. It is a danger against which one must constantly be on guard.... Were we to leave the *Temple* with a sense of peace and security, then Herbert would have failed of his obligation as a teacher-catechist, which is to inure his reader-pupils to the patience that is the lot of those who labor in the service of God.... [O]thers misread 'The Church Militant' because they do not find in it what they want, the satisfaction of a resoundingly affirmative conclusion; but it is by refusing us that satisfaction, and by referring us to a future moment it can neither present nor contain, that the poem fulfills its function in the sequence. One might say, then, that both as a poem and as an experience, *The Temple*

[46] Izaak Walton, *The Lives of John Donne and George Herbert*, ed. Charles W. Eliot. (New York: P.F. Collier and Son Corp., 1937) 414-15.
[47] Patrides, *George Herbert: The Critical Heritage* 259, 260-61.
[48] Fish, *The Living Temple* 152-53.

is unfinished, and quite properly so.... Herbert would have us realize that the job can never be done, at least not by any human author.[49]

The sweeping view of salvation history in "The Church Militant" extends "both west and east" (1.274) and encompasses the powers of "Sin and Darkness" (1.272), as well as the "Church and Sun with all their power and skill" (1.273), drawing near "To time and place, where judgment shall appear" (1.277).

Likewise, the unfinished poems of Hopkins analyzed in this chapter center on the element of time and its power to restrict individual creativity and movement, and, ironically, to serve as the vehicle by which the Christian disciple attains to union with God. Two of Hopkins's unfinished sonnets—"To his Watch" and "The times are nightfall"? (both composed 1885–86)—center on the essential nature of time as it governs the life of the speaker. "That small commonweal" ("The times are nightfall," 1.11) includes the Herbert's term "Commonweals" from the proem of "The Church Militant" (1.5) with its political overtones, but with a "World within" ("The times are nightfall," 1.9) that is more unruly. Yet even amid the "distress" (1.4) and "wreck" (1.6) of this interior world, "Your will is law" (1.11). When "Your" is read as referring to God, as the tone of Herbert's "The Church Militant" suggests, time as *kairos* replaces *chronos*: God's omniscient view of time transcends both the exterior and interior "commonweal."

"The times are nightfall," like "The Church Militant," is somewhat uncharacteristic of its author. The paucity of imagery is replaced by a compressing of the metaphor of time and a plainness of diction that supplants the syntax and reflexive reduplication evident in the "terrible" sonnets and other verse by Hopkins. "To his Watch" alludes to the Metaphysical conception of time as *tempus fugit* and the limitations the speaker experiences within his "rock-a-heart" (1.1) that serves as both his "sweetest comfort's carol or worst woe's smart" (1.8). The cosmological vision of heaven and earth in both unfinished sonnets is interpreted by the will as a warning to root out personal sin in the tormented "heart" of the speaker. Lines from both sonnets—"There is your world within./There rid the dragons, root out there the sin" ("The times are nightfall," ll.9–10) and "we were framed to fail and die" ("To his Watch," 1.6)—depict the "commonweal" of a speaker, a heart

---

[49] Fish, *The Living Temple* 154-55, 156, 157, 161.

that was "once a world of art" ("To his Watch," 1.4). The need of Hopkins to "root out there the sin" is the subject of previous poems such as "The Candle Indoors" (1879) and "Spelt from Sibyl's Leaves" (1884), as well as of his "terrible" sonnets of 1885 and the poems of his final years.

When Herbert's "The Church Militant" and Hopkins's two unfinished sonnets are analyzed as an interrelated unit and treated as spiritual autobiography, the reader regards the Christian disciple as possessing a will, a mind, that as Hopkins says in his "dark" sonnet "No worst," "has mountains; cliffs of fall/Frightful, sheer, no-man-fathomed" (ll.9-10), and that now permits the temporal "ruins" that "waste" and "wither" him to "welcome death." Daniel A. Harris conjoins the tone of "The times are nightfall" and Herbert's "The Church Militant" by providing an expanded scope of Hopkins's view of time. He states that "the beginning of that larger sense of apostolic impotence in the face of imminent apocalypse has issue" in Hopkins's poem.[50]

In the watch of death, the Christian disciple aligns his spirit with Christ, Whose solitary and purgative watch at nightfall in the Garden of Gethsemane precluded His entrance into new life and union with the Father Who is timeless and boundless. John Pick captures Hopkins's spirit, as well as that of the Jesuitical tradition, when he justifies the "poignancy" penetrating lines 5-8 of the undated fragment "To his watch" in this manner:

> On the use man makes of his own powers and of created things depends his eternal status; his own weakness and the transiency of his years make the call of the future life overwhelmingly important. No wonder then that the spiritual takes precedence over all gifts and beauties in the priest-poet's [Hopkins's] admonitions and exhortations.[51]

Yet the sense of loss that accompanies this Christian perspective is the leitmotif of Hopkins's works. "As I. A. Richards was first to point out, Hopkins's poems are *about* loss—loss of humanity, loss of grace, loss of self, beauty, and life. And all loss happens in time, through time, because of time.... In the most excited exuberance of experience

---

[50] Harris 141.
[51] Pick 93.

and language, in the hurrahing of the happiest of poems, the need is sensed to seize the moment and stave off the loss that has to come."[52]

Hopkins's writings about time, like those of Herbert and the Metaphysicals, demonstrate this concern for personal and cosmic realities within a temporal perspective. He views with utmost gravity this task of "telling time" ("To his Watch," 1.5), and, thereby, "unfold[s] in fresh sensations what Eliot calls 'the intersection of the timeless moment.'"[53]

Some critics, among them Paul L. Mariani, correlate the times alluded to in these two unfinished sonnets with the political unrest in Ireland, and the laments in Hopkins's poems with the poet's uneasiness with the strife in the Irish commonweal, to which there was no final resolution.[54] Hopkins attributes his inability and unwillingness to effect a change in the socio-political "commonweal" to "the wreck" of his own poetic experience from which he tries (unsuccessfully, in his estimation) to "rescue" any "Work which to see scarce so much as begun" ("The times are nightfall," 1.7).

Hopkins's letter of October 13, 1886, to Robert Bridges (sent also to Coventry Patmore) expresses his dissatisfaction with the role of the ineffectual bystander, and his strong belief that art is largely political:

> Besides we are Englishmen. A great work by an Englishman is like a great battle won by England.... It will even be admired by and praised by and do good to those who hate England (as England is most perilously hated), who do not wish even to be benefited by her. It is then a patriotic duty.[55]

Yet the two sonnets "The times are nightfall" and "To his Watch" portray the writer's spiritual aridity and literary ineptitude.

Hopkins's essay on "The Origin of our Moral Ideas" serves as a prosaic counterpart to his unfinished works and informs the spirit that underlay his poetic and ministerial vocations:

> All thought is of course in a sense an effort at unity.... In art it is essential to recognise and strive to realise on a more or less wide basis this unity in some shape or other.... In art we strive to realise not only unity, permanence of

---

[52] Motto 122-23.
[53] Cotter 117.
[54] Mariani, *A Commentary on the Complete Poems of Gerard Manley Hopkins* 261.
[55] Abbott, *The Letters of Gerard Manley Hopkins to Robert Bridges* 231.

law, likeness, but also, with it, difference, variety, contrast: it is rhyme we like, not echo, and not unison but harmony.[56]

Hopkins realizes that true fulfillment will be achieved only when the New Jerusalem—God's dwelling—is reached in the fullness of time, when even the nutriment of the Eucharist and the "something that is greater than the temple" will give way to full and complete unity of all things in Christ (Rev. 21:2-3; 1 Eph. 10; Matt. 12:6). This is the inscape which he invites the Christian disciple and the reader to make.

While respectful of the approach taken by William Stallings Smith in his dissertation titled *The Poetry of Gerard Manley Hopkins: A Continuity of the Romantic Tradition*, I take exception to his aligning the spirit of permanence in Wordsworth with that in Hopkins. He states that "Hopkins's concept of poetry is compatible with Wordsworth's poetics, which views poetry as the 'spontaneous overflow of powerful feelings recollected in tranquility.'" Smith reiterates this belief later, explaining Hopkins's concept of instress as an experience that "pushes him one rung higher on the ladder of spiritual knowledge as he attempts a permanent reconciliation of the real and the ideal." In his conclusion, Smith views the "sonnets of desolation" as paradigms of "the Romantic fall-quest-realization structure, as the mind successfully reconciles the worlds of the real and the ideal."[57] Hopkins's Catholic persuasion, sacramental view of the universe, and understanding of particulars or *haecceitas* inspire verse, particularly the "terrible" sonnets, that are Christocentric, immediate, sometimes even disjointed, whereas much of the verse of Wordsworth and the Romantics is naturalistic, detailed, and discursive. Such attempts to term either Herbert or Hopkins as successful reconcilers of the breach between the real and the ideal, or as writers who return poetry to the central impulse of the Metaphysical or Romantic traditions, only legitimize T.S. Eliot's criticism of ineffective religious verse: "The capacity for writing poetry is rare; the capacity for religious emotion of the first intensity is rare.... People who write devotional verse [of a pious and insincere nature] are usually writing as they want to feel, rather than as they do feel."[58] The verse and prose of Herbert and Hopkins are honest depictions of

---

[56] House 83.

[57] William Stallings Smith, *The Poetry of Gerard Manley Hopkins: A Continuity of the Romantic Tradition*, diss., Duquesne University, 1985, 44, 78, 117.

[58] Weyand 60.

human experience and valid responses to daily life, very often at cross-purposes, only occasionally recollected in tranquility, rarely intended to portray a unity, permanence, or successful resolution to the complexity, intensity, and imaginative inspiration inherent in Christian faith and discipleship. Howard Fulweiler writes of the hope of ultimate reconciliation that underlies Hopkins's works as an interpretation that "does not resolve Hopkins' later conflict" but that does offer "the hope of a man who, [though] unable to resolve the conflict within himself, was unwilling to abandon the attempt."[59]

This book traces the struggle in Hopkins's poetry between the assertion of his will and the hegemony of God's will, and the attempt to achieve self-abnegation and humility. That it concludes with poems of Hopkins that are unfinished and incomplete is a testimony to the honesty and depth of Hopkins's struggle as a Christian disciple. His verse depict "ways in which with man's striving toward spiritual perfection the spiritual world crashes through his loneliness to engulf him in love. From an entry during his 1883 Beaumont retreat, we know that Hopkins understood the meaning of this growth: 'In meditating on the Crucifixion I saw how my asking to be raised to a higher degree of grace was asking also to be lifted on a higher cross.'"[60]

Hopkins's hymn "Thee, God, I come from," found along with a draft of the poem "To what serves Mortal Beauty?", may have been written during his retreat at Clongowes Wood College in mid-August 1885.[61] Hopkins's attribution of his poetic and ministerial vocations to the God from Whom he came and to Whom he returns—the "Judge that comes to deal our doom" (1.30)—parallels Herbert's relinquishing of his life to the same God described in "The Church Militant" as rendering "Judgment [that] may meet them both and search them round" (1.269). Fulfilling God's "purpose" furnishes the intent with which Hopkins directs his life. The second stanza of "Thee, God, I come from" redirects a statement from *The Wreck*—"For I greet him the days I meet him, and bless when I understand" (I.5.40)—to "What I know of thee I bless"—and includes the "stress" that such knowledge of God's holiness and of the speaker's own need for repentance carries "On my being" ("Thee, God, I come from," ll.5-8). The "sir" (a term

[59] Fulweiler 162.

[60] Robert J. Andreach, *Studies in Structure* (New York: Fordham University Press, 1964) 38-39.

[61] Mariani, *A Commentary on the Complete Poems of Gerard Manley Hopkins* 262.

found also in many of Herbert's poems) in "Thou art indeed just, Lord" is echoed here in line 20. Ultimately, Hopkins realizes that he has been hiding from the emotional risks of total commitment to acquiring "Something of thy holiness" (l.8). He confesses that he hid from God—"Once I turned from thee and hid,/Bound on what thou hadst forbid" (ll.9–10)—and now repents of his untoward actions (ll.11–12) in a tone that parallels Herbert's "The Reprisal," where the speaker confesses at the outset that he has "consider'd" God's ways to him and his ways to God, and concludes that "My sins deserve the condemnation" (l.4). Hopkins uses the same childlike innocence and "disentangled state and free" by which Herbert petitions God in "The Reprisal" (l.6) to remind God in "Thee, God, I come from" that "Bad I am, but yet thy child" (l.13). Such purging or "confession" by the speakers in both poems effects a colloquy between themselves and God and yokes together, in metaphysical fashion, the Old Man and the New Man, temporal existence and the "eternal glory" of transcendent realities ("The Reprisal"). Indeed, the Temple upon which Herbert and Hopkins focus is heaven itself. The imperative mood that dominates "Thee, God, I come from," far from positing Hopkins's pietistic doctrinal beliefs, as W.H. Gardner contends, urges "right action. He is dramatizing belief, externalizing and making active an interior bidding through structure and motion of language; he is finding the form that acts out what he wills the words to say.... The use of the imperative encourages the human response that the world calls for; it bids for and would direct attention and action but leaves the reacting will still free."[62]

The verse and prose of Herbert and Hopkins acknowledge that creation is a continuous outpouring of God's being. The unfinished nature of their works is a testimonial to their belief that "God is giving earth her being, and earth in exercising it is pleading with Him both for herself and for the generations that have trod and are treading upon her; she is supporting and brooding over destructive and thriftless man, who should be heir both to the heaven to which earth appeals and to the renewed earth itself."[63] "On terms of such intimacy with his Lord, Hopkins could 'contend' quietly with God, not in combat, but in case at law, laying forth in direct address ('sir') his dryness against the

---

[62] Gardner 262; Motto 87.
[63] Boyle 168.

world's plenteous renewal, and asking very simply for grace to build
some work: 'send my roots rain'" ("Thou art indeed just, Lord,"
1.14).[64]

The speaker in "To thee, God, I come from" ultimately learns that
"like fountain flow/From thy hand out" (ll.2-3) he "lives, and moves,
and has his being," in the scriptural context. Past and future for Her-
bert and Hopkins "flow from and into the Word-made-man and are
summed up in his present, for in his risen person the fullness of time
and eternity now forever exist."[65] Both devotional writers view histo-
ry, not as an endless cycle, but as "a biblical procession as Israel expe-
rienced it, looking back to God's purposes planted in the beginning,
striven for in the present, longed for in the coming deliverer. Time is
directed toward an end which is always present; it is an arrow shooting
at its mark, the inscape of Christ."[66]

Hopkins, surrendering in penitence to the "stress" of God's mercy,
turns mercy now toward humanity—"Man my mate and counterpart"
(1.24)—in an action that redeems the self-concern evident in his earlier
writings. This extension of himself to others, evident in "Thee, God,
I come from," is also a crucial consideration in what many critics
consider his best unfinished work, "On the Portrait of Two Beautiful
Young People" (1887). This poem was written during a visit to Monas-
tereven, a country house in County Kildare, where this family portrait
hung.[67] Hopkins writes to Canon Dixon, in a letter of January 27,
1887, that:

> I was at Christmas and New Year down with some kind people in Co. Kildare
> where I happened to see the portrait of two beautiful young persons, a brother
> and sister, living in the neighbourhood. It so much struck me that I began an
> elegy in Gray's meter, but being back here I cannot go on with it. However
> I must see if I can enclose you a copy of the part done.[68]

By June 18, 1887, he writes to Dixon that he "was down at Mo-
nasterevan lately and managed to see the young lady of the Elegy,

[64] Heuser 93.
[65] Cotter 120.
[66] Cotter 120.
[67] Hunter 110.
[68] Abbott, *The Correspondence of Gerard Manley Hopkins to Richard Watson Dixon* 150.

which however I have had no chance of continuing. She was in the
earthquake on the Riviera and was much frightened."[69] "Hopkins
worked on the elegy between Christmas and January 2, but Dublin
proved 'museless' and he never finished it. What we have, then, are
nine four-line stanzas which Hopkins sent to Bridges, and three stanzas
(and some lines) apparently rejected by Hopkins which exist among his
early draft."[70]

While similar in tone and theme to "The Bugler's First Com-
munion," by its poignant characterization of young people and its hope
that the children bear "burning witness" against "the wild and wanton
work of men" ("On the Portrait of Two Beautiful Young People,"
ll.35,36), this unfinished poem portrays "the selfless self of self, most
strange, most still" (l.27) as it rides down the "tyrant years" (l.2) to
discover its own "landmark, seamark, or soul's star" (l.19).

Peter Milward, S.J., and Raymond V. Schoder, Jr., S.J., in their
Landscape and Inscape: Vision and Inspiration in Hopkins's Poetry
provide a lengthy commentary as well as a plate titled "Portrait of a
brother and sister." They emphasize the significance of this

> bias or bent in the deepest heart of [the Christian disciple], in the inmost 'self
> of self', where paradoxically man is most 'selfless', as most ready to respond
> to the call of another. This response, which is given when 'the heart, being
> hard at bay, is out with it', is either 'No or Yes', either the worst or the best
> word, either rejection or acceptance of the divine invitation. This readiness of
> the heart is expressed in terms of a nautical metaphor, of a ship with her sails
> all trim, 'fast furled and foredrawn' (l.28). So it is not surprising to find the
> same repeated with variations in *The Wreck of the Deutschland* and *The Loss
> of the Eurydice....*[71]

"There is a more distanced wisdom about this later poem," more
detachment and objectivity, than in earlier poems, since Hopkins did
not know the children personally when he saw the portrait.[72] Alison

---

[69] Abbott, *The Correspondence of Gerard Manley Hopkins to Richard Watson Dixon*
152.

[70] Mariani, *A Commentary on the Complete Poems of Gerard Manley Hopkins* 264.

[71] Milward and Schoder, *Landscape and Inscape* 96. This text is a testimonial to the
influence of the visual arts in the life of Hopkins, and exemplifies Donald McChesney's
belief, stated on p. 24 of *A Hopkins Commentary*, that "The artist inscapes his own
perception in a painting, a poem, or a musical composition; these artistic creations
embody the perception of his inscape."

[72] Hunter 11.

G. Sulloway refers to "On the Portrait" as a "professional poem" about the dangers of beauty and talent, and attributes the unresolved nature of the poem to the severe conflicts that Hopkins experienced between the beauties of mind and body.[73] In contradistinction to his earlier poems, "by now it seemed, the more he admired them [the mind and body], the more he feared them."[74] That this elegiac poem treats a hierarchy of values is evident in stanzas four to six where the physical companionship provided by the brother and sister, reminiscent of Milton's description of the ideal love of Adam and Eve in Book IV of *Paradise Lost*, culminates in the speaker's simple yet profound reminder that "There's none but truth can stead you. Christ is truth" (l.20). The scriptural analogue of being weighed in the balance and found wanting is explored further in this poem, as in other of Herbert's and Hopkins's works, now with the enjoinder that man's "will" (l.25) determines the "feast" (l.29) of which he will partake. "In the portrait, the girl leaning, the boy looking beyond, the brother and sister were a forelock of time, a cluster of natural virtues, ripe for the opportunity of good or evil swaying in the scales of choice."[75] The gospel passage of the rich young man who went away sad from Jesus, unable to relinquish his possessions, is also recalled here as Hopkins, like Matthew (19:16–24), emphasizes that only Christ, who is God, can be good, both for the boy himself and for "this sweet maid" who "sways with" him in his affections (ll.21–22).

In an apposite passage, Hopkins writes to Coventry Patmore, in a letter of September 24, 1883: "But why do we find beautiful evil? The explanation is to be sought outside nature; it is old, simple, and the undeniable fact. It comes from wicked will, freedom of choice, abusing the beauty, the good of its nature."[76] The postlapsarian proclivity for chaos and degeneration—"the world's first woe" (l.33)—impels the speaker to a spiritual and philosophic restlessness that paradoxically tosses him in the direction of God.

The self-address in the last quatrain, as in other verse of Hopkins, is in the form of a mild self-rebuke: "What need I strain my heart beyond my ken?" (34). The speaker realizes that the power and wis-

dom of the universe lie outside himself and in the realm of Christ, the
sole possessor of Truth. Like "God's Grandeur," "On the Portrait of
Two Beautiful Young People" critiques humankind's rejection of the
redemption, evidenced in the wanton destruction of nature and the
"havoc-pocked" (1.32) human heart. The oppression which flows from
the original corruption of the world overwhelms the speaker, as it does
the speaker in Herbert's "The Church Militant," stimulating him to
become a "burning witness" "against the wild and wanton work of
men" (ll.35,36). Hopkins "cannot look upon the portrait for long with-
out moral concerns edging insistently into the forefront. Years in the
confessional had made of Hopkins a 'burning witness.'"[77]

In Hopkins's dialectic, creation is never far from destruction nor
growth from decay. Hopkins's works witness to the fact that both time
and material things retain their state of imperfection. He "has just
enough of the mystic's desire for completion, for oneness with the
perfect, to long repeatedly for these times [or things] to transcend time,
fulfilling their shapes and worth."[78] What seems "worst" will become
"the best" (1.31) as the Christian disciple acquires salvation and the
banquet of eternal life.

"The Reprisal" extends the portrait of the Herbert's speaker and
mirrors a writer whose works are "rich in mystical content. [Herbert]
is the poet who has known God and has felt the peace and joy of His
presence and also the pain and agony of His absence in a manner pe-
culiar to the mystics, and he has communicated his experience to us
with the complexity and richness characteristic of a sensitive and sin-
cere artist."[79] The sensitivity, sincerity, and directness that character-
ize his works are readily apparent in "The Reprisal," the final Herbert
poem to be analyzed in this book. In a note to the poem, editor John
N. Wall, Jr., reminds the reader that "'Reprisal' is used in the musical
sense as a return to an earlier theme [that of the preceding poem, 'The
Thanksgiving,' a reinforcement of Herbert's plea for a return to inno-
cence]." "The Reprisal" is titled "The Thanksgiving" in the W Manu-
script. "The shape of the stanzas suggests a roughly cruciform pattern,
underscoring Herbert's devotion to the cross."[80] Mary Ellen Rickey

[77] Mariani, *A Commentary on the Complete Poems of Gerard Manley Hopkins* 267.
[78] W. Johnson, *Gerard Manley Hopkins* 112.
[79] Husain 158.
[80] Wall 150, n.48.

gives an additional significance to the word "reprisal" by defining it as a "retaliation in warfare" and "an extension of the military and musical imagery of its predecessor, 'The Thanksgiving.'"[81] Gene Edward Veith, Jr., reminds the modern reader that "the conflict posited by the Reformation doctrine of sanctification is complex in its psychology. The conscious self will tend to be a function of both 'the inward man' of faith and 'the old man' of sin, so that sanctification will sometimes assume the form of a struggle with the self and sometimes the form of a struggle with God."[82]

The self-reproof evident in "On the Portrait" and previous poems of Hopkins, parallels Herbert's gentle reproof in "The Reprisal": "Though I can do nought/Against thee, in thee I will overcome/The man, who once against thee fought" (ll.14–16). "The man, who once against thee fought" is the Man of the Old Dispensation, the first Adam, who is redeemed "in thee," in Christ, the second Adam. The tone is, from the outset, reflective: "I have consider'd it, and find/There is no dealing with thy mighty passion" (ll.1–2). Herbert's attempts to explain theodicy—the ways of God to the speaker and the ways of the speaker to God—relax in "The Reprisal" into a more delicate and refined harmony of Herbert's art. Although the emotion of the speaker intensifies in the progression of the stanzas, "the conclusion complements the tone of the opening quatrain, just as the assurance of the conclusion explains their tranquility."[83]

The overriding conflict present in the unfinished verse and prose of Herbert and Hopkins in this chapter—what Barbara Leah Harman terms "collapsing" works—is "between self-representation and self-relinquishment, between personal and divine inscription, between the idea of the self as an agent of writing and a vision of him as writing's subject."[84] "The Reprisal" witnesses to the barrenness of language in conveying the nature of the heart of the Christian disciple. "The discovery in the poem's last stanza is a discovery about the failure to be in control of intentions and suggests that the first three stanzas are essentially unconscious work, divorced from insight—not the work of generation, but the work of blind opposition. But narration is really the

---

[81] Rickey 97, 118.
[82] Veith 139.
[83] Grant 74.
[84] Harman 59.

work of opposition because it constructs, in place of the speaker who
has no work, a speaker whose work is warfare [reprisal]."[85] Given
this critical reading of Herbert's work, the reader regards Herbert as
a writer who, rather than taking possession of or claiming *The Temple*,
and thereby assuming the privileges of authorship, disowns and disman-
tles the work of narration. "The last stanza gestures toward a world in
which the narrating speaker himself *becomes the ground* upon which
revision proceeds.... The poems [in *The Temple*] suggest that the
speaker who sings best is a speaker *without* a text, someone who has
given up the fiction that he can generate appropriate discourse on his
own."[86] *The Temple* is a confession that everything, including the
writer's "first fruits," comes from God and, ultimately, belongs to
Him. "Speakers and texts are often, then, about the business of sunder-
ing themselves from each other."[87] The genre of spiritual autobiogra-
phy confirms this detachment and self-abnegation on which the life of
the Christian disciple is centered. Harman concludes that, while the
speaker in "The Reprisal"

> sunders himself from the text in an act of self-relinquishment, he also binds
> himself to the text in an act of self-generation. And while the poem suggests
> that the account before us is a defective one, it also suggests that an alterna-
> tive account is possible—though because the alternative remains to be spoken,
> there is in the poem no final *image* of the regenerate man. In fact the presence
> of a *misconducted* story and the absence of a *corrected counterstory* are, here
> and elsewhere, the features of collapsing poems—which leave the reader with
> the work of revising his own understanding and leave the speaker with the
> work of dismantling and redesigning himself.[88]

Assigning a reading of spiritual autobiography to the works consid-
ered in this book reinforces the intent of the writers to ascribe meaning
and significance, not only to individual works, but also to the relation-
ship of the works with each other. Louis L. Martz confirms this thesis
by stating that "it is the method of the *Temple*, where one poem marks
another, and both make a motion toward a third, which may lie some

---

[85] Harman 61.

[86] Harman 62.

[87] Harman 63.

[88] Harman 63. A postmodern critical approach testifies to the significance and rele-
vance of Herbert and Hopkins. It also substantiates F.R. Leavis's claim that Hopkins is
a major poet in English literature. Leavis, *New Bearings in English Poetry* 119.

ten or twenty leaves away: but the reader strikes a chord, and understands the destiny thus offered."[89]

The world of both the speaker and the reader is unbounded, unconventional, vulnerable to insecure images, and uncomforted by the reversals characteristic of Herbert's "conclusions." In short, an analysis of these select "collapsing poems" of Herbert and Hopkins as spiritual autobiography underscores the essential nature of the genre as an account of the journey of the Christian disciple, not merely of the writers. Herbert and Hopkins are God's co-workers who lay the spiritual and literary foundations on which the reader builds. Self-knowledge is reached by self-immolation through the teaching and discipline of the Church, and an acceptance of God's power, benevolence, and will. Any plans of the Christian disciple that are "against thee fought" ("The Reprisal," 1.16) are misconceived and aborted. A personal confession of "my sins" and "grief's sad conquests" (ll.4,11) to the omnipotent God heightens the purgative, illuminative, and unitive natures of the soul and hastens the time of "perfect freedom" which, for Herbert and Hopkins, lies in subjecting the will to "the will of Jesus my Master."

The "collapsing poems," therefore, support the view set forth in "The Church Militant," namely, that history unfolds *sub specie æternitatis*, under the providential and omniscient eye of God. The tone of these select poems suggests that Christ's suffering and atonement are complete in themselves: there is no further need of rationalizing or justifying God's "mighty passion" ("The Reprisal," 1.2). The speaker's engaging in a colloquy with God and confessing his desire for lost innocence and spiritual freedom is sufficient; for, as St. Paul acknowledged, "in weakness power reaches perfection" (2 Cor. 12:9). As in poems like "The Thanksgiving" and "The Collar," "The Reprisal" contains a "sequence of rhetorical questions, followed by a serene reply, [that constitutes the] staple of the conflict between the soul and God in 'The Church.'"[90] Any attempt by the speaker in either "The Church Militant" or "The Reprisal" to impose his own ideas of the future upon God results in a dramatic conflict that is resolved, at least momentarily, by the speaker's surrendering to God and accepting His will unreservedly.

---

[89] Martz 296.
[90] Stewart, *George Herbert* 135.

A reading of select verse and prose of Herbert and Hopkins as spiritual autobiography "moves the reader toward a moment of self-discovery.... Because the aim of the discourse [in spiritual autobiography] is always the realization of one's dependence on Jesus Christ, the reader's success will be inseparable from an acknowledgement of personal inadequacy, and that, in turn will be preliminary to the larger success awaiting him in a union (effected by grace) with God: 'In thee I will overcome'" ("The Reprisal," 1.15).[91]

This preference for growth and regeneration under the providential eye of God underlies the two poems of Hopkins that conclude this study: "(Ashboughs)" and "Thou art indeed just, Lord." The tender vivacity with which Hopkins sets forth the motion of the trees in "(Ashboughs)" (1885?) recalls the liveliness and precision of his earlier nature poems, which portray both the natural and sacramental character of creation. In "(Ashboughs)," a poem titled by Robert Bridges and ranked by many critics with Hopkins's best works, two alternative endings are presented. "Both Bridges and Gardner have relegated Hopkins' third and final curtal sonnet [the other two being 'Pied Beauty' and 'Peace'] to a section entitled 'Unfinished Poems, Fragments, Light Verse, &c. (1862–89)" because it "is accompanied by an unfinished variant."[92] Gardner maintains that "the only other extant draft of *Ashboughs* is on a separate sheet, so we are probably right in assuming that Hopkins had recovered sufficiently from the gall and heartburn of 'I wake and feel the fell of dark' to return to the nature-poem in the hope of recapturing the mystical vision and pure delight of the poems of 1877."[93]

Hopkins describes the ash, one of his favorite trees, in an early Fragment titled "Richard":

> thinning skywards by degrees,
> With parallel shafts,—as upward-parted ashes,—
> Their highest sprays were drawn as fine as lashes,
>   [(iv), ll.4–6].

The beauty of the ash signifies the desire for union with God and for the inward spiritual grace addressed by Herbert, particularly in "The

---

[91] Fish, *The Living Temple* 47.
[92] Mariani, *A Commentary on the Complete Poems of Gerard Manley Hopkins* 249.
[93] Gardner 348.

Reprisal." Indeed, W.H. Gardner terms "(Ashboughs)" a "nature-parable based on the mystical opening theme of the fragmentary 'Thee, God, I come from.'"[94] "(Ashboughs)" poeticizes a tree whose boughs "break in the sky" (l.3) to provide a sacramental glimpse of heaven which "childs us" (l.11), recalling both edenic and childhood innocence. In depicting creation's desire for God, the poem underscores the biblical analogue: "we know that all creation groans and is in agony even until now.... [A]lthough we have the Spirit as first fruits, we groan inwardly while we await the redemption of our bodies" (Rom. 8:22-23). In the midst of his deepening sense of isolation in Dublin and the penning of his "terrible" sonnets, Hopkins writes the poem-prayer "(Ashboughs)"—an attempt at articulating the "groanings which cannot be expressed in speech" (Rom. 8:26)—and provides a second version beginning with line 7, thereby leaving undecided the "conclusion" of this curtal sonnet. Both the unfinished nature of the poem as well as an analysis as spiritual autobiography are vindicated by William Butler Yeats, whose epigraph to volume 2 (of 8) of his *Collected Works in Verse and Prose* reads:

> The friends that have it I do wrong
> Whenever I remake a song,
> Should know what issue is at stake:
> It is myself that I remake.[95]

The inward groanings and groping for the God of creation and for a refashioning of the writer continue and find justification in one of the final poems of Hopkins, the sonnet "Thou art indeed just, Lord" (1889).

Two letters, in particular, reveal Hopkins's need to create great poems and the misery he endures at his apparent lack of achievement, dual elements he expresses so eloquently in "Thou art indeed just, Lord." In a letter of June 25, 1883, to Canon Dixon, Hopkins writes:

> My time, as I have said before this, is not so closely employed but that some-one else in my place might not do a good deal, but I cannot, and I see no

---

[94] Gardner 351.
[95] Martz 321.

grounded prospect of my ever doing much not only in poetry but in anything at all.[96]

He writes to Alexander William Mowbray Baillie in a letter of February 20, 1887, that:

It is doubtful, so very doubtful, that I shall be able to pursue any study except the needs of the day (and those not enough) at all. I have tried and failed so often and my strength serves me less.[97]

To the end of his life, Hopkins's intensity and passion strive to waken and reconcile his ministerial and poetic vocations, but meet with the "strain" and (w)reckonings of his spirit. In another letter, this one to Robert Bridges, of March 21, 1889, Hopkins expresses his concern that:

The sonnet ['Thou art indeed just, Lord'] will, I am afraid, fade: Miss Cassidy's ink is, I must say, shocking. Observe, it must be read *adagio molto* and with great stress.[98]

This poem, written with ink that itself threatens permanence, intimates a "collapsing poem" in the spirit with which Hopkins regards his writing: as a disappointment, a defeat, and a thwarting (ll.4,7) of his creative abilities. "It is ironic that one of his most enduring poems should be based on the conviction that no work of his would ever endure."[99]

Catherine Phillips notes that "During his last years Gerard Manley Hopkins frequently complained about his inability to complete projects, and his letters show that he started articles and books that remained unfinished."[100] Believing himself unable to finish the projects, Hopkins terms himself "Time's eunuch," unproductive and unable to "breed one work that wakes" (l.13) into a completed state. "If there is a quantitative loss in the creation of only a handful of poems for these

---

[96] Abbott, *The Correspondence of Gerard Manley Hopkins and Richard Watson Dixon* 108-09.
[97] Abbott, *Further Letters of Gerard Manley Hopkins* 275-76.
[98] Abbott, *The Letters of Gerard Manley Hopkins to Robert Bridges* 303.
[99] MacKenzie 204.
[100] Phillips, "The Effects of Incompleteness in Three Hopkins Poems." *Renascence* 42, (Fall 1989-Winter 1990) 1-2; 21.

[Dublin] years, there is toward the end a positive gain in the flowering of a poetic voice with the authentic ring of spiritual humility and acceptance. In the last poems there has been, to paraphrase Hopkins' own words on the nature of grace, an advantage of himself over himself."[101]

The metaphor of the "eunuch" (1.13) highlights Hopkins's private anguish at the paucity of his verse, but also carries a favorable spiritual connotation in its allusion to Matthew 19:21 wherein Christ explains to His disciples the distinction that voluntary and perpetual celibacy holds for the Christian disciple. "If he is 'Time's eunuch,' as Hopkins calls himself, there is good reason for hope because time in its fullness will bring Christ's rain for his 'roots.'"[102]

The image of "roots" is repeated from two of the "terrible" sonnets: "Rare patience roots in these" ("Patience, hard thing," 1.5) and "leave comfort root-room" ("My own heart," 1.11). In "Thou art indeed just, Lord," the speaker acquires roots, but lacks the nurturing rain. Indeed, the final lines of "Thou art indeed just, Lord" "sum up the poem and in part sum up Hopkins's thoughts on the relation between humanity and nature in general, and between himself and God in particular."[103]

In tone, movement, economy of diction, and gravity of thought, "Thou art indeed just, Lord" parallels Herbert's "The Reprisal" and concludes where "The Reprisal" commences: with the conviction that there is no dealing with or comprehending the ways of God to humanity. Both poets humbly submit to the wealth or "[m]ine" found in the "Lord of life" and His spiritual Kingdom.

The Christian themes of theodicy and colloquy underlie this sonnet as the speaker questions the nature of divine justice in the suffering servant paradigm of the prophet Jeremiah. The epigraph and octet are glosses on Jeremiah 12:1:

> You would be in the right, O Lord,
>   if I should dispute with you;
>   even so, I must discuss the case with you.
> Why does the way of the godless prosper,

---

[101] Mariani, *A Commentary on the Complete Poems of Gerard Manley Hopkins* 316.
[102] Mathai 123.
[103] Virginia Ridley Ellis, *Gerard Manley Hopkins and the Language of Mystery* (Columbia and London: University of Missouri Press, 1991) 159.

why live all the treacherous in contentment?
You planted them; they have taken root,
    they keep on growing and bearing fruit.
You are upon their lips,
    but far from their inmost thoughts.

The hortatory mood displayed in the Jeremiah passage parallels the tone, rhetorical questions, natural stress, and colloquy with God in Hopkins's sonnet, and reinforces the demand for a justification of God's ways to "Them" (l.12): both the godless people and fecund "banks and brakes" (l.9) or thickets that seem to flourish. The sonnet also echoes the lament in Book III of *Paradise Lost* wherein Milton reiterates his need for divine assistance and enlightenment:

Thus with the Year
Seasons return, but not to me returns
Day, or the sweet approach of Ev'n or Morn
                (ll.40–42).[104]

In Christ's time—a view also proposed by Herbert in "The Church Militant" and witnessed in the popularity and significance of Hopkins's verse and prose to literature and spirituality—Hopkins embodies the wise person in Jeremiah 17: 7–8:

Blessed is the man who trusts in the Lord,
    whose hope is the Lord.
He is like a tree planted beside the waters
    that stretches out its roots to the stream:
It fears not the heat when it comes,
    its leaves stay green;
In the year of drought it shows no distress,
    but still bears fruit.

To Hopkins's questioning spirit, the "lord of life" continues to "probe the mind and test the heart, to reward [him] according to his ways, according to the merit of his deeds" (Jer. 17:10). The horticultural image used by Jeremiah is rooted in the *schola cordis* tradition and graphically conveys the deception of those who depend upon their own

---

[104] Shawcross, *The Complete Poetry of John Milton*.

resources rather than on the Lord. But the Lord Who reads hearts helps His people to flourish. Hopkins's poetry, like that of Herbert, "presents his spiritual autobiography, or the spiritual biography of any deeply religious [person]. It appeals to the common experience shared by other religious [people], just as the narrative of the Bible—the spiritual biography of a nation and a people—appeals."[105] The biblical injunction—"Let us not grow weary of doing good; if we do not relax our efforts, in due time we shall reap our harvest" (Gal. 6:9)—is realized in Herbert and Hopkins.

The fertility of spirit, the grace to build "one work," the restoration of the balance—all pleaded for in "send my roots rain" (ll.13–14)—are accomplished in the Resurrection that visited Hopkins on June 8, 1889. "The English version of the notice of his death in the official *Register of the English Province* reads, '1889. On the eighth of June, the vigil of Pentecost, weakened by a fever, he rested. May he rest in peace. He had a most subtle mind, which too quickly wore out the fragile strength of his body.'"[106] The fact that his tombstone bears two words repeated in "That Nature is a Heraclitean Fire and of the comfort of the Resurrection"—"Immortal Diamond"—attests to the simplicity, hard-won acceptance, evangelizing, and transcendence of his ministerial vocation, and to the "compression, extraordinary control, the rare cut, and multi-faceted quality" reflected in his poetic vocation.[107]

The highest posthumous honor that can be bestowed on an English poet was conferred on Hopkins in 1976 when he was established in Westminster Abbey's Poets' Corner.[108] On June 8, 1989, in Washington, D.C., at one of four ceremonies memorializing Hopkins's death, there was at the end "a blessing that Hopkins himself had written for a Liverpool sermon in 1880: 'May God's will be done on earth as it is in heaven, a blessing I wish the earth and you.' It was a well-wrought and fitting conclusion, for Hopkins's life and work have themselves blessed the earth and its people. 'Earth is the fairer' for having had Hopkins on it."[109]

---

[105] Olney, *George Herbert and Gerard Manley Hopkins* 114.
[106] R. Martin 415.
[107] Ellsberg 13.
[108] Ellsberg 13.
[109] Feeney, "'Earth is the Fairer': The Centennial of Gerard Manley Hopkins." *America* 161, (Aug. 26-Sept. 2, 1989) 5; 105.

In their poetic and ministerial vocations, Herbert and Hopkins seek and discover a living communion with God, one which the art of spirituality allows them to exercise. This book proposes a comparative analysis of select works of Herbert and Hopkins as spiritual autobiography by demonstrating how this genre, in particular, allows the authors to undergird the Temple of their souls with words and actions befitting the life of Christian discipleship.

"But as I rav'd and grew more fierce and wilde
At every word.
Me thoughts I heard one calling, *Childe*:
And I reply'd, *My Lord*."

Epilogue

AN INTERRELATED STUDY of the meditative verse and prose of George Herbert and Gerard Manley Hopkins as spiritual autobiography illustrates the vagaries and ambiguities encountered by the Christian disciple on the journey to the Eternal City. The reader discovers that the works of these two metaphysical writers are guided by the authors' unique perceptions of both quotidian experiences and the Supreme Being toward Whom they journey. Many times, the journey resembles the threefold method of meditation—purgation, illumination, and union with God—that marks the life of the Christian disciple. Recurrently, the journey is intersected by the cyclic pattern of consolation-desolation. Frequently, the journey to the Eternal Banquet is fraught with questions regarding the ways of God to His people, a dialectical encounter between the Christian disciple and God, and the desire for substantial food for the journey. The three Christian themes of theodicy, colloquy, and nutriment are also developed to explore the unfinished dimension of earthly existence. "Habits of meditation," as Louis L. Martz suggests, "appear to rise in answer to certain basic tendencies of the human mind; such habits do not create these tendencies, but they shape and cultivate, they 'prompt and regulate' these tendencies, developing in gifted minds, in different ages and in different lands, kindred ways of mental action that manifest themselves in the genre of meditative poetry."[1]

An analysis of select poems and prose as spiritual autobiography causes in the reader an individual confrontation with the Logos and the truth of human existence as it is uttered in "current language heightened" by Herbert and Hopkins.[2] If the reader perceives that a spiritually autobiographical reading lends crucial import as well as profound and universal significance to the journey of the soul, then this study is worthy of serious debate and consideration as a work of critical scholarship. If the open mind and listening ear of the reader take exception to the comparative approach used in this book, perhaps a further, more

---

[1] Martz 330.
[2] Abbott, *The Letters of Gerard Manley Hopkins to Robert Bridges* 89.

prophetic, voice is needed to illuminate the journey of Christian disci-
pleship with greater verisimilitude and perspicacity.

In the study of Herbert and Hopkins by James Olney, Number 718
of Herbert's "Outlandish Proverbs" is cited: "Comparisons are odi-
ous." Nevertheless, Olney offers a defense for interrelating the two
writers:

> But comparative analysis is a useful device in reading poetry. We understand
> any poet better by seeing him in relation to another poet who is enough alike
> to give point to the comparison and enough different to define his peculiar
> poetic vision and voice. In this instance we are given a basis of similarity in
> the poets' initial religious assumptions. Behind the instable and transient ap-
> pearances of the world both poets felt the presence of a particular and provi-
> dential order, all-inclusive and unchanging. They had experience of universal
> correspondences giving meaning to observed phenomena and extending beyond
> to the order of their own creative acts, their human response to a feeling of
> divine order. The reaction of either poet is to praise the divine by the use of
> the divine instrument of order.[3]

The success of spiritual autobiography depends, therefore, on the
Christian community of writers and readers, and on their relationship
with God, engagements to which Herbert and Hopkins continually
extend invitations. "Despite the indirection of his art and the fact that
a narrator is always a *persona* and not the 'real' man, the autobiogra-
pher does speak for himself, and he speaks directly to us about our-
selves.... The contemplation of autobiographies can draw us nearer to
ourselves and to one another, can motivate us to 'become what we
are,' both for ourselves and for others, can move us to change."[4]

Like the religion of Christianity to which Herbert and Hopkins sub-
scribe, the verse and prose of the two writers are revelations of the
Divine, rooted in history and representative of the journey of the Chris-
tian disciple. The spiritual progress which both writers address is,
likewise, historical and representative, with the accompanying es-
chatological orientation that marks the journey to God. The verse and
prose of Herbert and Hopkins are essentially true, not because they are
biographical records of the writers' lives, but because they are spiritual
records of the Christian disciple. Indeed, the attitude taken by Herbert

---

[3] Olney, *George Herbert and Gerard Manley Hopkins* 25-26.
[4] Shapiro 454.

and Hopkins toward God is dynamic and changeable, as is their attitude to poetic decorum and style. The complexity of the men does not permit a definitive poetic or ministerial theory.[5] An analysis of their works as accomplishments within a closed literary tradition misrepresents the vision of Divinity and religious consciousness centered in the quotidian experiences that motivate the genuine devotional verse and prose of Herbert and Hopkins.

Protestant theologian Paul Tillich defines religion as "the aspect of depth in the totality of the human spirit."[6] It is this dimension of literature that the genre of spiritual autobiography addresses and authenticates. "Literature, in particular, becomes psychography: it helps render a spiritual biography of the age in which we live and which we shape; it reveals our deeper self in its inner and outer conditions." [7]The genre itself, therefore, is educative, purgative, and rewarding for the reader who engages his or her devotional sensibilities in the journey of faith undertaken by the Christian disciple.

The relatedness and reciprocity which the works of Herbert and Hopkins impel the reader to consider reveal a dimension to human existence that transcends the present and that liberates the soul to a longing for the Absolute Cornerstone, the sole ordering principle of Christian discipleship. "The literature that makes us aware of that 'other world' in which, as Simone Weil says, 'the highest things are achieved,' makes us aware of the religious problem that embraces ultimate concerns and ultimate questions and gives meaning to time. In the relationship between literature and religion we can discover a revelatory critical confluence that becomes a medium for an encounter and, in effect, a conversation with God."[8] Devotional works, then, establish a sense of the Sacred which, ironically, is more apparent in recordings of (w)reckoning and conflict than in works that attempt to reinforce and redefine religious tradition and doctrine.

The intent of this book is to demonstrate how an intertextual analysis of the poetry and prose of George Herbert and Gerard Manley Hopkins as spiritual autobiography is its own best argument. Furthermore, the present study hopes to serve as a "work that wakes" the

---

[5] Daalder 33.

[6] George A. Panichas, "Literature and Religion: A Revelatory Critical Confluence." In *Studies in the Literary Imagination* 1985; Spring; 18 (1), 12.

[7] Panichas, "Literature and Religion: A Revelatory Critical Confluence" 12.

[8] Panichas, "Literature and Religion: A Revelatory Critical Confluence" 15.

reader into the human and religious subtleties, sensibilities, and sacrifices of two "Immortal Diamond[s]" in the metaphysical school of English literature.

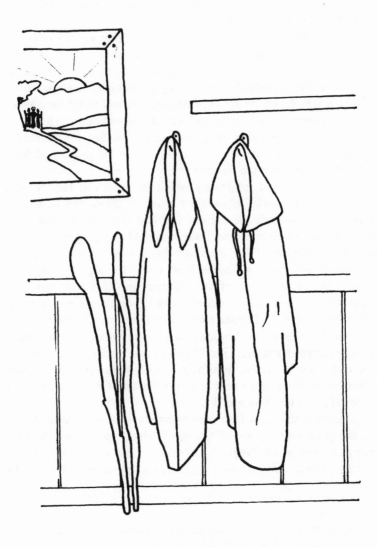

Bibliographies

Herbert Bibliography

Alvarez, A. *The School of Donne*. New York: Pantheon Books, 1961.

Asals, Heather A.R. *Equivocal Predication: George Herbert's Way to God*. Toronto: University of Toronto Press, 1981.

Benet, Diana. *Secretary of Praise: The Poetic Vocation of George Herbert*. Columbia: University of Missouri Press, 1984.

Bennett, Joan. *Five Metaphysical Poets*. London: Cambridge University Press, 1964.

Bloch, Chana. *Spelling the Word: George Herbert and the Bible*. Berkeley: University of California Press, 1985.

Bowers, Fredson. "Herbert's Sequential Imagery: 'The Temper.'" *Modern Philology* 59 (1962): 202–13.

Bush, Douglas. *English Poetry: The Main Currents from Chaucer to the Present*. New York: Oxford University Press, 1952.

Charles, Amy M. *A Life of George Herbert*. New York: Cornell University Press, 1977.

Chute, Marchette. *Two Gentle Men: The Lives of George Herbert and Robert Herrick*. New York: E.P. Dutton and Co., Inc., 1959.

Daalder, Joost. "Herbert's 'Poetic Theory.'" *George Herbert Journal 9* (1985): 17–33.

DiCesare, Mario A. "God's Silence: On Herbert's 'Deniall.'" *George Herbert Journal* 10 (1986–87): 85–102.

Eliot, Charles E., ed. *The Lives of John Donne and George Herbert* by Izaak Walton. New York: P.F. Collier and Sons Corp., 1937.

Eliot, T.S. "George Herbert: Writers and Their Work." In *George Herbert and the Seventeenth-Century Religious Poets*. ed. Mario A. DiCesare. New York: W.W. Norton and Co., Inc., 1978.

Endicott, Annabel M. "The Structure of George Herbert's *Temple*: A Reconsideration." *University of Toronto Quarterly* 34 (1965) 226–37.

Engel III, Wilson F. "Christ in the Winepress: Backgrounds of a Sacred Image." *George Herbert Journal* 3 (1979–80): 45–63.

Festugière, A.J., O.P. *George Herbert: Poète, Saint, Anglican (1593–1633)*. Paris: Librairie Philosophique J.Vrin, 1971.

Fish, Stanley. "Doing Scholarship: The Mystery of *The Temple* Finally Explained." *George Herbert Journal* 1 (1977): 1–9.

_____ *The Living Temple: George Herbert and Catechizing*. Berkeley: University of California Press, 1978.

Gardner, Helen. *Religion and Literature*. New York: Oxford University Press, 1971.

Grant, Patrick. *The Transformation of Sin: Studies in Donne, Herbert, Vaughan, and Traherne*. Montreal and London: McGill-Queen's University Press, 1974.

Greenwood, E.B. "George Herbert's Sonnet 'Prayer': A Stylistic Study." *Essays in Criticism* 15 (1965): 27–45.

_____ "Herbert's 'Prayer (I).'" In *George Herbert and the Seventeenth-Century Religious Poets*. ed. Mario A. DiCesare. New York: W.W. Norton and Co., Inc., 1978.

Halewood, William H. *The Poetry of Grace: Reformation Themes and Structures in English Seventeenth-Century Poetry*. New Haven and London: Yale University Press, 1972.

Hanley, Sara W. "Temples in *The Temple*: George Herbert's Study of the Church." *Studies in English Literature* 8 (1968), 121–35.

Harman, Barbara Leah. *Costly Monuments*. Cambridge: Harvard University Press, 1982.

Huntley, Frank L. "George Herbert and the Image of Violent Containment." *George Herbert Journal* 8 (1984): 17–27.

Husain, Itrat. *The Mystical Elements in the Metaphysical Poets of the Seventeenth Century*. London: Oliver and Boyd, 1948.

Hutchinson, F.E., ed. *The Works of George Herbert*. Berkeley: University of California Press, 1975.

Johnson, Lee Ann. "The Relationship of 'The Church Militant' to *The Temple*." *Studies in Philology* 67 (April 1971), 200–06.

Knights, L.C. *Explorations: Essays in Criticism Mainly on the Literature of the Seventeenth Century*. New York: New York University Press, 1964.

Labriola, Albert C. "Herbert, Crashaw, and the *Schola Cordis* Tradition." *George Herbert Journal* 2 (1978): 13–23.

_____ "The Rock and the Hard Place: Biblical Typology and Herbert's 'The Altar.'" *George Herbert Journal* 10 (1986–87): 61–69.

_____ and John W. Smeltz. *The Bible of the Poor: A Facsimile and Edition of the British Library Blockbook C.9 d.2*. Pittsburgh: Duquesne University Press, 1990.

Leishman, J.B. *The Metaphysical Poets: Donne, Herbert, Vaughan, Traherne*. New York: Russell and Russell, Inc., 1963.

Lewalski, Barbara. *Protestant Poetics and the Seventeenth-Century Religious Lyric*. Princeton: Princeton University Press, 1979.

Malpezzi, Frances M. "Herbert's 'The Thanksgiving' in Context." *Renascence* 34, 1982 (3): 185–96.

Martz, Louis L. *The Poetry of Meditation: A Study in English Religious Literature*. New Haven: Yale University Press, 1962.

McCanles, Michael. *Dialectical Criticism and Renaissance Literature*. Berkeley: University of California Press, 1975.

Meilaender, Marion. "Speakers and Hearers in *The Temple*." *George Herbert Journal* 5 (1981–82): 31–43.

Miller, Edmund. "Drudgerie Divine: The Rhetoric of God and Man in George Herbert." In *Elizabethan and Renaissance Studies*. ed. Dr. James Hogg. Austria: Universität Salzburg, 1979.

Mulder, John. "George Herbert's *The Temple*: Design and Methodology." *Seventeenth-Century News* 31 (1973): 37–45.

Nicolson, Marjorie Hope. *The Breaking of the Circle*. New York: Columbia University Press, 1960.

Nuttall, A.D. *Overheard by God: Fiction and Prayer in Herbert, Milton, Dante and St. John*. London and New York: Methuen and Co. Ltd., 1980.

Pahlka, William H. *Saint Augustine's Meter and George Herbert's Will*. Ohio and London: Kent State University Press, 1987.

Patrides, C.A., ed. *The English Poems of George Herbert*. New Jersey: Rowman and Littlefield, rpt. 1986.

_____ *George Herbert: The Critical Heritage*. London: Rutledge and Kegan Paul, 1984.

Rickey, Mary Ellen. *Utmost Art: Complexity in the Verse of George Herbert*. Kentucky: University of Kentucky Press, 1966.

Riehle, Wolfgang. *The Middle English Mystics*. London: Rutledge and Kegan Paul, 1977.

Roberts, John R., ed. *Essential Articles for the Study of George Herbert's Poetry*. Connecticut: Archon Books, 1979.

Ross, Malcolm Mackenzie. *Poetry and Dogma: The Transfiguration of Eucharistic Symbols in Seventeenth-Century English Poetry*. New York: Octagon Books, 1969.

Schilling, Bernard N. *Dryden and the Conservative Myth: A Reading of Absalom and Achitophel*. New Haven and London: Yale University Press, 1961.

Schipper, Jakob. *A History of English Versification*. Oxford: Clarendon Press, 1910.

Seelig, Sharon Cadman. *The Shadow of Eternity: Belief and Structure in Herbert, Vaughan, and Traherne*. Kentucky: University of Kentucky Press, 1981.

Shafer, Ronald G. *The Poetry of George Herbert and the Epistles of St. Paul: A Study in Thematic and Imagistic Similarities*. Diss. Duquesne University, 1975. Ann Arbor: UMI, 1975. 76-2389.

Shaw, Robert B. *The Call of God: The Theme of Vocation in the Poetry of Donne and Herbert*. England: Cowley Publications, 1981.

Sherwood, Terry G. *Herbert's Prayerful Art*. Toronto: University of Toronto Press, 1989.

Sloane, Mary Cole. *The Visual in Metaphysical Poetry*. New Jersey: Humanities Press Inc., 1981.

Stein, Arnold. *George Herbert's Lyrics*. Baltimore: The Johns Hopkins Press, 1968.

Stewart, Stanley. *George Herbert*. Boston: Twayne Publishers. 1986.

_____ "Time and *The Temple*." *Studies in English Literature* (1966): 97-110.

Strier, Richard. *Love Known: Theology and Experience in George Herbert's Poetry*. Chicago: University of Chicago Press, 1983.

Summers, Joseph H. *George Herbert: His Religion and Art*. New York: Center for Medieval and Early Renaissance Studies, rpt. 1981.

_____ "Herbert's Form." *PMLA* 66 (1951): 1055-72.

Tuve, Rosemond. *Elizabethan and Metaphysical Imagery: Renaissance Poetic and Twentieth-Century Critics*. Chicago: University of Chicago Press, rpt. 1961.

_____ *A Reading of George Herbert*. London: Faber and Faber, 1952.

Veith, Gene Edward, Jr. *Reformation Spirituality: The Religion of George Herbert*. Lewisburg: Bucknell University Press, 1985.

Vendler, Helen. *The Poetry of George Herbert*. Cambridge: Cambridge University Press, 1975.

Walker, John David. "The Architectonics of George Herbert's *The Temple*." *Journal of English Literary History* 29 (1962): 289–305.

Wall, John N., Jr., ed. *George Herbert: The Country Parson, The Temple*. New York: Paulist Press, 1981.

Walton, Izaak. *The Lives of John Donne and George Herbert*. Ed. Charles W. Eliot. New York: P.F. Collier and Sun Corp., 1937.

White, Helen C. *The Metaphysical Poets: A Study in Religious Experience*. New York: The Macmillan Company, 1936.

Willey, Basil. *The Seventeenth-Century Background: Studies in the Thought of the Age in Relation to Poetry and Religion*. New York: Columbia University Press, 1950; rpt. 1967.

Yeasted, Sister Rita Marie, C.D.P. *George Herbert's Poetry and the "Schola Cordis" Tradition*. Diss. Duquesne University, 1981. Ann Arbor: UMI, 1981. 8116845.

Hopkins Bibliography

Abbott, Claude Colleer, ed. *The Correspondence of Gerard Manley Hopkins and Richard Watson Dixon*. London: Oxford University Press, 1955.

_____ *Further Letters of Gerard Manley Hopkins, Including His Correspondence with Coventry Patmore*. London: Oxford University Press, 1956.

_____ *The Letters of Gerard Manley Hopkins to Robert Bridges*. ed. Claude Colleer Abbott. London: Oxford University Press, 1955.

Allsopp, Michael E. and Michael W. Sundermeier. *Gerard Manley Hopkins: New Essays on His Life, Writing, and Place in English Literature*. New York: The Edwin Mellen Press, 1989.

Bender, Todd K. *Gerard Manley Hopkins: The Classical Background and Critical Reception of His Work*. Maryland: Johns Hopkins Press, 1966.

Bergonzi, Bernard. *Gerard Manley Hopkins*. New York: Macmillan Publishing Co., 1977.

Bloom, Harold, ed. *Gerard Manley Hopkins: Modern Critical Views*. New York: Chelsea House Publishers, 1986.

Bowman, Leonard J. "Another Look at Hopkins and Scotus." *Renascence* 29 (1976): 50–55.

Boyd, John D., S.J. "'I Say More': Sacrament and Hopkins's Imaginative Realism." *Renascence* 42, 1989–90 (1–2): 51–64.

Boyle, Robert, S.J. *Metaphor In Hopkins*. North Carolina: University of North Carolina Press, 1961.

Bump, Jerome. *Gerard Manley Hopkins*. Boston: Twayne Publishers, 1982.

_____ "Reader-Centered Criticism and Bibliotherapy: Hopkins and Selving." *Renascence* 42, 1989–90 (1–2): 65–86.

Carson, J. Angela. "The Metaphor of Struggle in 'Carrion Comfort.'" *Philological Quarterly* 49 (1970): 547–57.

Cohen, Edward H. *Works and Criticism of Gerard Manley Hopkins: A Comprehensive Bibliography*. Washington, D.C.: Catholic University of America Press, 1969.

Cotter, James Finn. *Inscape: The Christology and Poetry of Gerard Manley Hopkins*. Pittsburgh: University of Pittsburgh Press, 1972.

Devlin, Christopher, ed. *The Sermons and Devotional Writings of Gerard Manley Hopkins*. London: Oxford University Press, 1959.

Downes, David A. "Beatific Landscape in Hopkins." *Hopkins Quarterly* 1 (1974): 137–61. Continued in *Hopkins Quarterly* 1 (1975): 185–201.

_____ *Gerard Manley Hopkins: A Study of His Ignatian Spirit*. London: Vision Press Ltd., 1960.

_____ *The Great Sacrifice: Studies in Hopkins*. Lonham: University Press of America, Inc., 1983.

Ellis, Virginia Ridley. *Gerard Manley Hopkins and the Language of Mystery*. Columbia and London: University of Missouri Press, 1991.

Ellsberg, Margaret R. *Created to Praise: The Language of Gerard Manley Hopkins*. New York and Oxford: Oxford University Press, 1987.

Evans, Benjamin Ifor. *English Poetry in the Later Nineteenth Century*. London: Methuen and Co., 1966.

Feeney, Joseph J., S.J. "'Earth is the Fairer': The Centennial of Gerard Manley Hopkins." *America* 161, 1989 (5); 102–05.

_____ "The Highgate Hopkins Obituary, with Introduction and Commentary." *Renascence* 42, 1989–90 (1–2): 3–12.

_____ "Hopkins as Teacher: The English Years." In *Gerard Manley Hopkins: New Essays on His Life, Writing, and Place in English Literature*. ed. Michael E. Allsopp and Michael W. Sundermeier. New York: Edwin Mellen Press, 1989.

Fulweiler, Howard W. *Letters from the Darkling Plain: Language and the Grounds of Knowledge in the Poetry of Arnold and Hopkins*. Missouri: University of Missouri Press, 1972.

Gardner, W.H. *Gerard Manley Hopkins: A Study of Poetic Idiosyncrasy in Relation to Poetic Tradition*. London: Martin Secker and Warburg. 1973.

_____ and N.H. MacKenzie, ed. *The Poems of Gerard Manley Hopkins*. New York: Oxford University Press, rpt. 1980.

Harris, Daniel A. *Inspirations Unbidden: The "Terrible Sonnets" of Gerard Manley Hopkins*. California: University of California Press, 1982.

Hartman, Geoffrey H., ed. *Hopkins: A Collection of Critical Essays*. New Jersey: Prentice-Hall, Inc., 1966.

_____ *The Unmediated Vision: An Interpretation of Wordsworth, Hopkins, Rilke and Valéry*. New Haven: Yale University Press, 1954.

Hazo, Samuel John. "An Analysis of 'Inscape' in the Poetry of Gerard Manley Hopkins." Master's Thesis. Duquesne University, 1955.

Hentz, Ann L. "Language in Hopkins' 'Carrion Comfort.'" *Victorian Poetry* 9 (1971): 343–47.

Heuser, Alan. *The Shaping Vision of Gerard Manley Hopkins*. London: Oxford University Press, 1968.

Holloway, Sister Marcella Marie, C.S.J. *The Prosodic Theory of Gerard Manley Hopkins*. Washington, D.C.: Catholic University of America Press, 1964.

House, Humphrey, ed. *The Journals and Papers of Gerard Manley Hopkins*. London: Oxford University Press, 1959.

Hunter, Jim. *Gerard Manley Hopkins*. London: Evans Brothers Ltd., 1966.

Johnson, Wendell Stacy. *Gerard Manley Hopkins: The Poet as Victorian*. New York: Cornell University Press, 1968.

Keating, John E. *The Wreck of the Deutschland: An Essay and Commentary*. Ohio: Kent State University Bulletin, 1963.

Kitchen, Paddy. *Gerard Manley Hopkins*. Massachusetts: West Hanover and Plympton, 1979.

Leavis, F.R. *The Common Pursuit*. London: Chatto and Windus, 1953.

_____ "Metaphysical Isolation." In *Gerard Manley Hopkins*. ed. The Kenyon Critics. New York: New Directions, 1945.

_____ *New Bearings in English Poetry: A Study of the Contemporary Situation*. London: Chatto and Windus, 1950.

Lees, Francis Noël. *Gerard Manley Hopkins*. New York and London: Columbia University Press, 1966.

Leggio, James. "Hopkins and Alchemy." *Renascence* 29, 1977 (2): 115–29.

Litzinger, Boyd. "The Pattern of Ascent in Hopkins." *Victorian Poetry* 2 (1964): 43–47.

Lowell, Robert. "Hopkins' Sanctity." In *Gerard Manley Hopkins*. ed. The Kenyon Critics. New York: New Directions, 1945.

MacKenzie, Norman H. *A Reader's Guide to Gerard Manley Hopkins*. New York: Cornell University Press, 1981.

Mariani, Paul L. *A Commentary on the Complete Poems of Gerard Manley Hopkins*. New York: Cornell University Press, 1970.

_____ "The Consoling, Terrifying Presence of Hopkins." *Renascence* 42, 1989–90 (1–2): 13–20.

_____ "The Dark Night of the Soul." In *Gerard Manley Hopkins*. ed. Harold Bloom. New York: Chelsea House Publishers, 1986. 51–76.

_____ "Hopkins: Towards a Poetics of Unselfconsciousness." *Renascence* 29, 1976 (1): 43–49.

Martin, Philip M. *Mastery and Mercy*. London: Oxford University Press, 1957.

Martin, Robert Bernard. *Gerard Manley Hopkins: A Very Private Life*. New York: G.P. Putnam's Sons, 1991.

McChesney, Donald. *A Hopkins Commentary: An Explanatory Commentary on the Main Poems, 1876–89*. New York: New York University Press, 1968.

McLuhan, Herbert Marshall. "The Analogical Mirrors." In *Gerard Manley Hopkins*. ed. The Kenyon Critics. New York: New Directions, 1945.

McNamee, Maurice B. "The Ignatian Meditation Pattern in the Poetry of Gerard Manley Hopkins." *Hopkins Quarterly* 2, 1975 (1): 21–28.

Miles, Jospehine. "The Sweet and Lovely Language." In *Gerard Manley Hopkins*. ed. the Kenyon Critics. New York: New Directions, 1945.

Milward, Peter, S.J. *A Commentary on the Sonnets of Gerard Manley Hopkins*. Chicago: Loyola University Press, 1969.

_____ "Exclamations in Hopkins's Poetry." *Renascence* 42, 1989–90 (1–2): 111–18.

_____ and Raymond V. Schoder, S.J. *Landscape and Inscape: Vision and Inspiration in Hopkins's Poetry*. London: Paul Elek Ltd., 1975.

_____ and Raymond Schoder, S.J., asst. *Readings of the Wreck*. Chicago: Loyola University Press, 1976.

Mizener, Arthur. "Victorian Hopkins." In *Gerard Manley Hopkins*. ed. The Kenyon Critics. New York: New Directions, 1945.

Motto, Marylou. *"Mined with a Motion": The Poetry of Gerard Manley Hopkins*. New Jersey: Rutgers University Press, 1984.

Newman, John Henry Cardinal. *The Idea of a University*. ed. Martin J. Svaglic. New York: Holt, Rinehart and Winston, 1962.

Nixon, Jude V. "Gerard Manley Hopkins and Henry Parry Liddon: An Unacknowledged Infuence." *Renascence* 42, 1989–90 (1–2): 87–110.

Ong, Walter J., S.J. *Hopkins, The Self, and God*. Toronto: University of Toronto Press, 1986.

Page, Philip. "Unity and Subordination in 'Carrion Comfort.'" *Victorian Poetry* 14 (1976): 25–32.

Peters, W.A.M., S.J. *Gerard Manley Hopkins: A Critical Essay Towards the Understanding of His Poetry*. New York: Johnson Reprint Corp., 1970.

_____ *Gerard Manley Hopkins: A Tribute*. Chicago: Loyola University Press, 1984.

Phillips, Catherine. "The Effects of Incompleteness in Three Hopkins Poems." *Renascence* 42, 1989–90 (1–2): 21–34.

_____, ed. *Gerard Manley Hopkins*. Oxford: Oxford University Press, 1986.

Pick, John. *Gerard Manley Hopkins: Priest and Poet*. New York: Oxford University Press, 1966.

Rader, Louis. "Hopkins' Dark Sonnets: Another New Expression." *Victorian Poetry* 5 (1967): 13–20.

Raine, Kathleen. *Hopkins: Nature and Human Nature*. London: Stanbrook Abbey Press, 1972.

Rathmell, J.C.A. "Hopkins, Ruskin and the *Sidney Psalter*." *London Magazine* 6 (1959): 51–66.

Robinson, John. *In Extremity: A Study of Gerard Manley Hopkins*. Cambridge: Cambridge University Press, 1978.

Schneider, Elisabeth W. *The Dragon in the Gate: Studies in the Poetry of Gerard Manley Hopkins*. Berkeley and Los Angeles: University of California Press, 1968.

Schoder, Raymond, S.J. "Hopkins and Pindar." In *Gerard Manley Hopkins: New Essays on His Life, Writing, and Place in English Literature*. ed. Michael E. Allsopp and Michael W. Sundermeier. New York: Edwin Mellen Press, 1989.

Scott, James F. and Carolyn D., ed. *Gerard Manley Hopkins*. Missouri: B. Herder Book Co., 1970.

Smith, Lyle H., Jr. "Beyond the Romantic Sublime." *Renascence* 34, 1982 (3): 173–84.

Smith, William Stallings. *The Poetry of Gerard Manley Hopkins: A Continuity of the Romantic Tradition*. Diss. Duquesne University, 1985. Ann Arbor: UMI, 1986. 8524586.

Stauffer, Ruth M. "Note on the Genesis of Hopkins' Sonnets of 1885." *Renascence* 22, 1969 (1): 43–48.

Storey, Graham. *Gerard Manley Hopkins*. England: Profile Books, Ltd. 1984.

Sulloway, Alison G. *Gerard Manley Hopkins and the Victorian Temper*. New York: Columbia University Press, 1972.

Villarubia, Malcolm, S.J. "Two Wills Unwound in the 'Terrible' Sonnets." *Renascence* 27, 1975 (2): 71–80.

Walhout, Donald. *Send My Roots Rain: A Study of Religious Experience in the Poetry of Gerard Manley Hopkins*. Athens: Ohio University Press, 1981.

Ward, Bernadette. "Newman's *Grammar of Ascent* and the Poetry of Gerard Manley Hopkins." *Renascence* 43, 1990–91 (1–2): 105–20.

Warren, Austin. "Gerard Manley Hopkins (1844–1889)." In *Gerard Manley Hopkins*. ed. The Kenyon Critics. New York: New Directions, 1945.

_____ "Instress of Inscape." In *Gerard Manley Hopkins*. ed. The Kenyon Critics. New York: New Directions, 1945.

Weyand, Norman, S.J., ed., asst. by Raymond V. Schoder, S.J. *Immortal Diamond: Studies in Gerard Manley Hopkins*. New York: Octagon Books, 1969.

Whitehall, Harold. "Sprung Rhythm." In *Gerard Manley Hopkins*. ed. The Kenyon Critics. New York: New Directions, 1945.

Wolfe, Patricia A. "The Paradox of Self: A Study of Hopkins' Spiritual Confict in the 'Terrible Sonnets.'" *Victorian Poetry* 6 (1968): 85–103.

Young, R.V. "Hopkins, Scotus, and the Predication of Being." *Renascence* 42, 1989–90 (1–2): 35–50.

Herbert and Hopkins Bibliography

Allen-Stainton, Nancy. *Spiritual Autobiography in the Poetry of George Herbert and Gerard Manley Hopkins*. Master's Thesis. Duquesne University, 1982. Ann Arbor: UMI, 1982. 1320135.

Buckley, Vincent. *Poetry and the Sacred*. London: Chatto and Windus, 1968.

Bump, Jerome. "Hopkins, Metalepsis, and the Metaphysicals." *John Donne Journal: Studies in the Age of Donne* 1985 4 (2): 303–29.

DiYanni, Robert. "Herbert and Hopkins: The Poetics of Devotion." In *Like Season'd Timber: New Essays on George Herbert*. New York: Peter Lang Publishing Co.,1987.

Eliot, T.S. "Religion and Literature." In *Essays Ancient and Modern*. New York: Harcourt, Brace and Company. 1936.

Harrison, G.B. *Shakespeare: Major Plays and the Sonnets*. New York: Harcourt, Brace and Co., 1948.

Johnson, Wendell Stacy. "Halfway to a New Land: Herbert, Tennyson, and the Early Hopkins." *Hopkins Quarterly* 10, 1983 (10): 115–24.

Joselyn, Sister M., O.S.B. "Herbert and Hopkins: Two Lyrics." *Renascence* 10, 1958 (4): 192–95.

Kyne, Mary Theresa, S.C. *George Herbert and Gerard Manley Hopkins: Poetry and Prose as Spiritual Autobiography*. Diss. Duquesne University. Ann Arbor: UMI, 1991. 9204470.

Mathai, Varghese. *The Evolution of the Inner Man as Seen in the Writings of Gerard Manley Hopkins and George Herbert*. Diss. Baylor University, 1987. Ann Arbor: UMI, 1987. 4398A.

New American Bible. New York: P.J. Kennedy and Sons, 1970.

Olney, James Leslie. *George Herbert and Gerard Manley Hopkins: A Comparative Study in Two Religious Poets*. Diss. Columbia University, 1964. Ann Arbor UMI, 1964. 64–5550.

Rygiel, Mary Ann. "Hopkins and Herbert: Two Meditative Poets." *Hopkins Quarterly* 10, 1983 (2): 45–54.

Shawcross, John T., ed. *The Complete Poetry of John Milton*. New York: Doubleday and Co., 1971.

Sinclair, John D., tr. *The Divine Comedy of Dante Alighieri, I: Inferno*. New York: Oxford University Press, 1939.

Symes, Gordon. "Hopkins, Herbert, and Contemporary Moods." *Hibbert Journal* 47 (1948–49): 389–94.

T.S. Eliot: The Complete Poems and Plays 1909–1950. San Diego, New York, London: Harcourt Brace Jovanovich, rpt. 1980.

Bibliography on Autobiography and Spiritual Autobiography

Andreach, Robert J. *Studies in Structure: The Stages of the Spiritual Life in Four Modern Authors*. New York: Fordham University Press, 1964.

Bottrall, Margaret. *Every Man a Phoenix: Studies in Seventeenth-Century Autobiography*. London: William Clowes and Sons, Ltd., 1958.

Bougler, James D. *The Calvinist Temper in English Poetry*. The Hague: Mouton Publishers, 1980.

Bruss, Elizabeth W. *Autobiographical Acts: The Changing Situation of a Literary Genre*. Baltimore and London: The Johns Hopkins Press, 1976.

Cockshut, A.O.J. *The Art of Autobiography in Nineteenth and Twentieth Century England*. Connecticut: Yale University Press, 1984.

Cognet, Louis. *Post Reformation Spirituality*. tr. P. Hepburne Scott. New York: Hawthorn Books, 1959.

Garrigou-LaGrange, O.P., Rev. Reginald. *Christian Perfection and Contemplation*. Michigan and London: B. Herder Book Co., 1929.

_____ *The Three Ages of the Interior Life: Prelude of Eternal Life*. Michigan and London: B. Herder Book Co., 1951. Vol. 1 and 2.

Gunn, Janet Varner. *Autobiography: Towards a Poetics of Experience*. Philadelphia: University of Pennsylvania Press, 1982.

Hambrick-Stowe, Charles E. *The Practice of Piety: Puritan Devotional Disciplines in Seventeenth-Century New England.* North Carolina: University of Carolina Press, 1982.

Henderson, Heather. *The Victorian Self: Autobiography and Biblical Narrative.* Ithaca and London: Cornell University Press, 1989.

Hopper, Stanley Romaine, ed. *Spiritual Problems in Contemporary Literature.* New York and London: Harper and Brothers, 1952.

Jones, Cheslyn, Geoffrey Wainwright, and Edward Yarnold, S.J., eds. *The Study of Spirituality.* New York and Oxford: Oxford University Press, 1986.

Kavanaugh, Kieran, O.C.D. and Otilio Rodriguez, O.C.D. tr.*The Collected Works of St. John of the Cross.* Washington,D.C.: Institute of Carmelite Studies Publications, 1979.

Muto, Susan. *John of the Cross for Today: The Ascent.* Indiana: Ave Maria Press, 1991.

Nevins, Albert J., M.M., tr. *Imitation of Christ* by St. Thomas à Kempis. Indiana: Our Sunday Visitor, Inc., 1973.

Olney, James, ed. "Autobiography and the Cultural Moment." In *Autobiography. Essays Theoretical and Critical.* New Jersey: Princeton University Press, 1980.
_____ *Metaphors of Self: The Meaning of Autobiography.* New Jersey: Princeton University Press, 1972.

Osborn, James M. *The Beginnings of Autobiography in England.* Los Angeles: University of California Press, 1959.

Panichas, George A. "Literature and Religion: A Revelatory Critical Confluence." *Studies in the Literary Imagination* 18, 1985 (1): 3–15.
_____, ed. *Mansions of the Spirit: Essays in Religion and Literature.* New York: Hawthorn Books, Inc., 1967.

Pascal, Roy. *Design and Truth in Autobiography.* Cambridge: Harvard University Press, 1960.

Peers, E. Allison, tr.and ed. *Interior Castle: St. Teresa of Avila.* New York: Doubleday and Co., Inc., 1961.

Puhl, Louis J., S.J., tr. *The Spiritual Exercises of St. Ignatius.* Chicago: Loyola University Press, 1952.

Raitt, Jill, ed. *Christian Spirituality: High Middle Ages and Reformation.* New York: Crossroad Publishing Co., 1987. Vol. 2.

Shapiro, Stephen A. "The Dark Continent of Literature: Autobiography." *Comparative Literature Studies* 5 (1968):421–54.

Sharrock, Roger. *John Bunyan.* New York: St. Martin's Press, 1968.

Shaw, Robert B. *The Call of God.* England: Cowley Publications, 1981.

Shea, Daniel B. *Spiritual Autobiography in Early America.* Princeton: Princeton University Press, 1968.

Sheppard, Lancelot. *Spiritual Writers in Modern Times.* New York: Hawthorn Books, Inc., 1967.

Spender, Stephen. "Confession and Autobiography." In *Autobiography: Essays Theoretical and Critical.* ed. James Olney. Princeton: Princeton University Press, 1980.

Starr, George A. *Defoe and Spiritual Autobiography*. Princeton: Princeton University Press, 1965.

Tanquerey, Very Rev. Adolphe, S.S. *The Spiritual Life: A Treatise on Ascetical and Mystical Theology*. tr. Rev. Herman Branderis, S.S. Belgium: Desclée and Co., 1930.

Taylor, Dennis. "Some Strategies of Religious Autobiography." *Renascence* 27, 1974 (1): 40-44.

Weintraub, Karl J. "Autobiography and Historical Consciousness." *Critical Inquiry* 1 (1975): 821-48.

_____ *The Value of the Individual: Self and Circumstance in Autobiography*. Chicago and London: University of Chicago Press, 1978.

Zimmermann, T.C. Price. "Confession and Autobiography in the Early Renaissance." In *Renaissance Studies in Honor of Hans Baron*. ed. Anthony Molko and John A. Tedeschi. Illinois: Northern Illinois University Press, 1971.

Index

P

Pahlka, William H. 63, 78,
192, 193, 223
Palmer, G.H. 187
parables 176
Paradise Lost 19, 36, 46, 57,
110, 113, 174, 204, 213
Parliament of 1624 31
paronomasia 51
parson and poet 144
"The Parson in Sacraments"
154
"The Parson Preaching" 186
"The Parson's Completeness"
186
"The Parson's Dexterity in
Applying of Remedies" 77
"The Parson's Knowledge" 40,
188
"The Parson's Library" 40
"The Parson's State of Life"
80
"The Parson's Surveys" 123
Pascal, Roy 3, 162, 230
Paschal Feast 151, 180
Pater, Walter 8
patience xvi, 54, 80, 92, 121,
135, 138-143, 146, 195, 212
"Patience, hard thing" 92, 121,
135, 138, 140-143, 146, 212
Patmore, Coventry 5, 198,
204, 224
Patrides, C.A. xiii, 9, 16, 17,
26, 32, 50, 51, 153, 154,
162, 176, 195, 223
patristics 10
"Peace" 1, 37, 50, 71, 75, 77,
81, 87, 101, 109, 114, 118,
125, 133, 136, 139-141, 195,
205, 209, 214
"Pearl" 65
"Perirrhanterium" 55

personal confession 208
Peters, W.A.M. (S.J.) 44,
133, 227
Petrarch 3, 4, 117
Petrarchan 45
Phillips, Catherine xiii, 22, 54,
78, 86, 172, 179, 211, 227
Pick, John 9, 47, 93, 104,
147, 148, 197, 227
"Pied Beauty" 41, 44, 45,
47-49, 209
pilgrimage 14, 72, 88, 159
Pindar 67, 68, 227
pitch 78, 85, 114, 115, 118
planctus 168
Playford, John 32, 33
"The Poesy" 5
poetic diction 34, 39, 50, 107
poetic vocation 42, 63, 214,
221
Pope John Paul II 8, 14
"The Possibility of Separating
Ethics from Political Science"
146
post-Romantic 33
praise 6, 23, 24, 26, 27, 29,
32, 38, 39, 41-43, 46, 48-50,
53, 58, 59, 64, 71, 72, 78,
81, 91, 99, 101, 108, 144,
145, 153, 157, 175, 182,
195, 218, 221, 225
prayer 6, 9, 11, 15, 23-25, 31,
36-38, 40, 54, 61, 71, 72,
81, 82, 84, 105, 127, 134,
139, 140, 143, 155, 162,
171, 176, 180, 182, 183,
195, 210, 221, 222
"Prayer (II)" 171
"Prayer before Sermon" 143
"Prayer of Self-Abandonment"
84
pride 27, 100, 111, 115, 128,
130, 140, 169

175, 176, 182, 186, 190-192, 203, 208, 217, 219, 226
soul's conversion
and spiritual autobiography 23
soul's progress 5, 7, 23, 76
sourness and sweetness 166
speaker 20, 22, 27, 29, 30, 32, 33, 35-40, 42-44, 49, 54-61, 68, 70, 71, 72, 74-81, 83, 88, 89, 99, 100, 102, 107, 109, 111, 112-114, 116, 122-130, 133, 134, 136-138, 140-142, 144, 148, 151, 154, 156, 157, 159, 160-167, 170, 171, 173-177, 180, 184-186, 192, 196, 200, 201, 204-208, 212
"Spelt from Sibyl's Leaves" 196
Spender, Stephen 20, 112, 230
Spenser, Edmund 30
spiritual autobiography xi, xii, xiii, xiv, xvii, xix, xx, 1-5, 7, 11, 17, 18, 19-24, 27, 28, 31, 32, 37, 40, 45, 47, 49, 56, 58, 59, 64, 66, 69, 71, 73, 79, 82, 88, 90, 92, 93, 99, 104, 112-114, 118, 120-122, 124, 129, 134, 136, 138, 152, 162, 180-182, 186-188, 193, 197, 207, 208, 210, 213, 214, 217-219, 228-231
and the soul's conversion 23
as a genre that offers no finished product or pattern 181
spiritual dryness 105
Spiritual Exercises xiii, 2, 9, 11-14, 22, 24, 47, 54, 57, 75, 91, 131, 139, 230
spiritual experience

communal 164
individual 164
spiritual life
its flexibility 181
"Spring" 44, 49, 59-61, 73, 97, 111, 183, 219
sprung rhythm 10, 43, 44, 67, 68, 161, 179, 180, 228
SS. Philip and James in Oxford 84
St. Augustine xi, 3, 14, 15, 22, 48, 73, 110, 134
St. Gertrude 84
St. Ignatius Loyola 9, 11, 16, 22, 24, 147, 226, 227, 230
as model for devotional poetry 9
St. Irenaeus 184
St. John Damascene 23, 37
St. John of the Cross 11, 12, 65, 134, 230
St. Paul xi, xiv, 15, 50, 73, 99, 109, 116, 117, 123, 139, 144, 155, 166, 185, 208, 223
St. Paul's epistles
and parallels with Reformation theology 144
St. Peter 86
St. Stanislaus College 114
St. Thomas the Apostle 133
St. Thomas Aquinas 8, 10, 11 14, 179
St. Thomas à Kempis 10, 22, 119, 153, 230
Stein, Arnold 99, 126, 127, 145, 176, 223
Stewart, Stanley 30, 99, 170, 187, 192, 208, 223
"The Storm" 64, 65, 79-81, 85, 86, 89, 91, 129, 148
storm 64, 65, 79-81, 85, 86, 89, 91, 129, 148